UNIVERSITY OF NORTH CAROLINA AT CHAPEL HILL
DEPARTMENT OF ROMANCE LANGUAGES

NORTH CAROLINA STUDIES
IN THE ROMANCE LANGUAGES AND LITERATURES

Founder: URBAN TIGNER HOLMES

Distributed by:

UNIVERSITY OF NORTH CAROLINA PRESS
CHAPEL HILL
North Carolina 27514
U.S.A.

NORTH CAROLINA STUDIES IN THE
ROMANCE LANGUAGES AND LITERATURES

Number 210

PIERRE BOAISTUAU'S *HISTOIRES TRAGIQUES:*
A STUDY OF NARRATIVE FORM AND TRAGIC VISION

Accepted for publication October 4, 1974

Issued Spring, 1979

NCSRLL regrets the delay between acceptance of the book and its publication.

PIERRE BOAISTUAU'S *HISTOIRES TRAGIQUES:*

A STUDY OF NARRATIVE FORM AND TRAGIC VISION

BY

RICHARD A. CARR

CHAPEL HILL

NORTH CAROLINA STUDIES IN THE ROMANCE
LANGUAGES AND LITERATURES
U.N.C. DEPARTMENT OF ROMANCE LANGUAGES
1979

Library of Congress Cataloging in Publication Data

Carr, Richard A
  Pierre Boaistuau's Histoires tragiques.

  (North Carolina studies in the Romance languages and literatures; no. 210)
  Bibliography: p.

  1. Bandello, Matteo, 1485-1561. Novelle. 2. Boaistuau, Pierre, d. 1566 — Criticism and interpretation. I. Title. II. Series.

PQ4606.Z77 1979   843'.3   79-11043
ISBN 0-8078-9210-6

I.S.B.N. 0-8078-9210-6

DEPÓSITO LEGAL: V. 1.356 - 1979   I.S.B.N. 84-499-2750-1
ARTES GRÁFICAS SOLER, S. A. - JÁVEA, 28 - VALENCIA (8) - 1979

TABLE OF CONTENTS

	Page
INTRODUCTION ...	11
PART ONE: BOAISTUAU AND BANDELLO: COMPARISONS AND CONTRASTS ...	29
Chapter I: The Problem of Translation: Liberty or Servitude ...	31
Chapter II: The Tragical and Sentimental Tales ...	48
PART TWO: THE *HISTOIRES TRAGIQUES* AND THE CONVENTIONS OF TRAGEDY ...	79
Chapter I: History ...	81
Chapter II: Character and Characterization ...	92
Chapter III: Theme ...	110
Chapter IV: Style ...	138
PART THREE: PIERRE BOAISTUAU AND THE TRAGIC WORLD OF 1560 ...	163
Chapter I: The *Theatre du monde*: A Prologue ...	165
Chapter II: The Reversal of Order in the *Histoires tragiques* ...	180
Chapter III: The *Histoires prodigieuses*: An Epilogue ...	211
PART FOUR: A TRAGIC WORLD IN SEARCH OF SALVATION ...	219
LIST OF WORKS CITED ...	253

To Diana

INTRODUCTION

In the prologue of the *Heptaméron,* Parlamente suggests to the "compaignye miraculeusement assemblée" at Notre-Dame de Sarrance that the afternoons be spent in the pleasurable exchange of stories in order to "adoulcir l'ennuy" while waiting for the flood waters to recede. It is not surprising that Marguerite de Navarre's ten travelers agree enthusiastically to engage in this favorite Renaissance pastime. Indeed from Marot's anecdotal *épîtres* to the numerous historical and contemporary anecdotes in Montaigne's *Essais,* the sixteenth century cherished the tradition of taletelling, and by means of translation, adaptation, and experiment, developed the short story into a vital artistic form.

Short fictional narrative had of course enjoyed a vigorous development during the preceding centuries. "Dès le moyen âge le conte et la nouvelle ont constitué une des branches les plus vivantes des lettres françaises."[1] Because of such continued favor, medieval France would bequeath to the succeeding age a well-practiced tradition that included the delicate depiction of sentiment in the *lai,* the didactic appeal of the *exemplum,* the popular humor of the *fabliau.* And to crown this rich and varied achievement, the waning Middle Ages produced the first authentic collection of French *nouvelles.*[2] A veritable mine of comic

---

[1] Pierre Jourda, "Préface" to *Conteurs français du XVIᵉ siècle* (Paris: Gallimard, "Bibliothèque de la Pléiade," 1965), p. x.

[2] For a detailed yet succinct discussion of the medieval antecedents of the *nouvelle* and of the various medieval forms of short fictional narrative, see Krystyna Kasprzyk, *Nicolas de Troyes et le genre narratif en France au XVIᵉ siècle* (Varsovie: Editions scientifiques de Pologne, Paris: Klincksieck, 1963), pp. 278-294. While more selective, Janet M. Ferrier offers

situations and character types, the *Cent Nouvelles nouvelles* offered ample material, drawn from the *fabliaux* and the *Facetiae* of Poggio, to be exploited by future *conteurs* such as Nicolas de Troyes, Bonaventure des Périers, and Marguerite de Navarre.

Yet despite his many debts to this collection, the Renaissance teller of tales was not satisfied simply to imitate the deft raillery of this collection nor to repeat the erotic elaborations that had entertained the court of Philippe de Bourgogne. In the hands of its sixteenth-century practitioners, the short story moved beyond the more limited realm of relaxed banter and mere divertissement to become a literary vehicle admirably suited to the examination of a wide range of topics of contemporary interest. No longer was it sufficient merely to scoff at the gullible husband duped by his clever and unscrupulous wife, nor to satirize the priest whose lust belied his clerical garb. A writer such as Marguerite de Navarre begins to probe into a character's motivation and reflects at length upon the implications of his actions. "For Marguerite the situation itself is no longer paramount; she extracts from it, not the piquency of its resolution as did the earlier writers in France, but the light that it can throw upon the characters and the moral standards of the individuals concerned with it." [3] Increasingly preoccupied with the conflict of opposing per-

---

thoughtful insights into the development of the *nouvelle* in her study of the *Forerunners of the French Novel* (Manchester: The Manchester University Press, 1954). Much useful information may be gleaned from Werner Söderhjelm's still valuable study on *La Nouvelle française au XVe siècle* (Paris: Champion, 1910) as well as from Henri Coulet's masterful history of *Le Roman jusqu'à la Révolution* (Paris: Colin, 1967), pp. 19-97. Jens Rasmussen deals in detail with narrative technique and style in his examination of *La Prose narrative française du XVe siècle* (Copenhagen: Munksgaard, 1958); this study will be profitably complemented by Knud Togeby's suggestive article on "La prose française du XVe siècle," *Orbis Litterarum* 14 (1959), 174-183. The finest synthesis to date is Roger Dubuis' admirable study of *Les Cent Nouvelles nouvelles et la tradition de la nouvelle en France au Moyen Age* (Grenoble: Presses Universitaires de Grenoble, 1973).

[3] Ferrier, *op. cit.*, p. 91; *cf.* Gustave Reynier, *Le Roman sentimental avant l'Astrée* (Paris: Colin, 1908): ..."les faits sont donnés; on ne s'interdit pas de les arranger quelque peu, mais, en somme, ils ne sont significatifs qu'à la condition d'être exacts dans leur fond. Le problème est de reconstituer leurs antécédents et de deviner leurs mobiles; on peut se tromper, mais on cherche, et ces essais d'explications, qu'on n'avait pas rencontrés jusque-là dans la nouvelle française, marquent un progrés certain de l'analyse" (p. 132).

sonalities as well as the ethical problems raised by man's actions, the sixteenth-century *conte* and *nouvelle* could not, in short, ignore the thrust of humanism.

The fifteenth-century *conteur* had little appreciation for the humanist inspiration of the works he examined. Although Boccaccio's *Decameron* was available in both French and Italian, its impact remained superficial and, in the case of the *Cent Nouvelles nouvelles*, it contributed little more than the basic framework of the collection.[4] There one finds no imprint "of Boccaccio's elegantly humanistic 'intermediate' style, of his doctrine of love, his service of women, of the human, critical and embracing perspective of the *Decameron*, of the multiplicity of its scenes and its reports of life."[5] His sentimental and tragic tales are scarcely represented.[6] Poggio's *Liber facetiarum* fared little better. Fifteenth-century translations and adaptations reduced the humanist inspiration of the *facétie* to more familiar dimensions: to the *conte gaulois* in the *Cent Nouvelles nouvelles*, and to the moralizing fable and *exemplum* in the translations of Julien Macho and Guillaume Tardif.[7]

The interest of the late medieval *conteur* lay elsewhere. While continuing to compose within traditional forms, he opened his eyes to the world about him and delighted in suggesting a familiar reality:

> There comes into being a level of style which considers the everyday scene of current life worthy of detailed

---

[4] "L'unique allusion au *Décaméron* dans le corps des *Cent nouvelles nouvelles* est une métaphore galante, traduite exactement de la même façon par Laurent [de Premierfait]. Enfin, l'auteur n'emprunte aucun sujet à son célèbre devancier et, en somme, il ne lui doit que l'idée générale du recueil... [celle] de composer un recueil de contes en prose, dans le dessein explicite d'amuser les lecteurs, et de l'organiser à l'aide d'un cadre plus ou moins développé" (Kasprzyk, *op. cit.*, pp. 291 and 288).

[5] Erich Auerbach, *Mimesis*, trans. Willard R. Trask (Princeton: Princeton University Press, 1953), p. 260.

[6] The exceptions, such as the 27th tale, are not due to the inspiration of Boccaccio; the 98th is adapted from the story of Floridan and Eluinde by Nicolas de Clamenges.

[7] See Lionello Sozzi, "Le 'Facezie' di Poggio nel Quattrocento francese," in *Miscellanea di studi e ricerche sul Quattrocento francese*, ed. Franco Simone (Torino: Giappichelli, 1967), pp. 411-516.

and serious portrayal; which at times, reaching upward, attains the realm of tragedy, at times touches the realm of satire and moral didacticism below; which deals much more penetratingly than before with the immediacy of human existence, its physical actualities, its domestic aspects, everyday enjoyments, the harsh decline of life, and its end; and which, in all this, has no fear of harsh effects. [8]

Imposing a mimetic dimension upon the allegorical tradition — a process Helmut Hatzfeld calls "la concrétisation de l'abstrait" [9] — the enthusiasm for realistic detail brought a new level of truth to art, and to the traditional comic situation a new level of ironic commentary. [10]

Yet the extension of this new realism was limited: it suggested many a narrative detail, provided even a setting for the action, but did not touch the characters except in a superficial way. They might be portrayed as contemporaries of the author, but they remained character types without individualization, playing a stylized role in a well-defined series of situations. As Henri Coulet writes with respect to the *Cent Nouvelles nouvelles*: "Ce ne sont que maris trompés, galants morfondus ou heureux, quiproquos entre le mari et l'amant, la femme et la maîtresse, moines et curés paillards, épouses ou veuves lubriques, plaisanteries directes sur le sexe masculin ou féminin." [11]

It is a commonplace of literary history to attribute the distinctively "modern" qualities of French Renaissance fiction to the pervasive influence of the Italian novella and romance:

> L'Italie a apporté les idées et elle a fourni les modèles. A la longue tradition de notre littérature bourgeoise qui ne voit dans l'amour que ses réalités brutales ou ses conséquences comiques, elle oppose une passion ardente, frémissante, dangereuse, ennoblie par l'image tou-

---

[8] Auerbach, *op. cit.*, p. 257.

[9] "La littérature flamboyante au XVe siècle" in *Studi in onore di Carlo Pellegrini* ("Biblioteca di Studi Francese" #2, Società Editrice Internazionale, 1963), p. 90.

[10] Lionello Sozzi, "La Nouvelle française au XVe siècle," *CAIEF* #23 (Paris: Les Belles Lettres, 1971), pp. 80-84.

[11] *Op. cit.*, p. 89.

jours présente de la mort. Aux monotones abstractions de nos poètes de cours féodales, à ces "Amants", à ces "Dames", si impersonnels qu'on jugeait même inutile de leur donner des noms, elle oppose son individualisme intense et profond.[12]

With the Italian models at hand, fictional narrative supposedly progressed from a concentration on situation to an emphasis on human motivation, from the presentation of character types to true characterization. According to this traditional view, Boccaccio played the major role in this revolution. In his works French writers discovered "ce qu'il peut y avoir d'émotion délicate, voluptueuse ou tragique dans de simples histoires du cœur."[13]

It would be foolhardy to minimize the influence of Boccaccio upon the sixteenth-century *conteur*. The zealous admiration for his works in France is an indisputable matter of record.[14] Yet the availability of Laurent de Premierfait's translation of the *Decameron* did not produce a fifteenth-century *Heptaméron*. The question must still be asked: why does the audience of the traditional tale, the audience delighted by the novel manipulation of conventional situations and character types, come to demand a new narrative orientation which emphasizes the role of man, "where the action is brought about by the interplay and conflict of opposing personalities,"[15] and which represents the impassioned individual and suggests the inner torment he experiences? It is not sufficient, as has been the practice since Huet's letter *Sur l'origine des romans*, merely to elaborate upon the ancient and medieval material available to the aspiring writer, to enumerate the translations and editions of Spanish and Italian romances, to insist upon the prominence of women in sixteenth-century literary circles and the increasing refinement of court life. All these conditions are certainly significant, but it is more

---

[12] Reynier, *op. cit.*, p. 15.
[13] *Ibid.*, p. 16.
[14] See Henri Hauvette, "Les plus anciennes traductions françaises de Boccace," *Bulletin italien* VII (1907), 281-313; VIII (1908), 1-17, 189-211, 285-311; IX (1909), 1-26, 193-210, and the important contribution of Lionello Sozzi, "Boccaccio in Francia nel Cinquecento," in *Il Boccaccio nella cultura francese*, ed. Carlo Pellegrini (Firenze: Olschki, 1971), pp. 211-349.
[15] Ferrier, *op. cit.*, p. 5.

to the point to inquire into the Renaissance writer's evaluation and understanding of his literary legacy, to understand the way in which he appreciated the novel or tale he read.

The difference between the literary product of the late Middle Ages and the Renaissance is essentially the result of a change in attitude, an attitude formed by certain tenets of humanism which profoundly affect the Renaissance writer's appreciation of his literary heritage. In a recent study of early French humanism, V.-L. Saulnier examines the *Chevalier délibéré* by Olivier de la Marche (1483), "un long traité poétique sur l'aventure humaine et les accidents de Fortune," and, looking ahead fifty years to Rabelais' *Gargantua*, he suggests the tremendous impact of humanism on the literary and intellectual climate of the sixteenth century.[16] "Vigueur, intrépidité, sveltesse" have replaced the slow ponderous style of the earlier work, heavily laden with allegory. Gone too is that prevailing "odeur de mort, de fin du jour, de dessèchement" by the time Rabelais publishes his "livre d'énergie, de conquête, d'appel à l'effort." Whereas La Marche disconsolately pondered the fate of the warriors of Antiquity as one further proof of the transitory nature of all men, Rabelais looks to the philosophers of Antiquity as his means of achieving that true heroism to be found "dans l'ordre du savoir et de la charité." In the short span of fifty years, humanism had created a hope, "que l'homme se réalise mieux dans sa plénitude," that he might become "peut-être plus heureux, mais surtout meilleur, dans un monde plus beau et plus proche du vrai."[17]

Renaudet called humanism "la conscience de la Renaissance"; for André Chastel, it is a new and vital "tertium regnum" distinct from the spiritual and temporal authorities of the preceding age. "Humanism" is an admittedly troublesome word. Because it is so broad and general a concept, ever changing in emphasis and definition as it is applied to such diverse writers as Rabelais, Ronsard, and Montaigne, to mention but three major figures, the term has been variously qualified in order to define its many

---

[16] "L'humanisme français aux premiers temps du livre," in *L'Humanisme français au début de la Renaissance* (Paris: Vrin, 1973), pp. 17-20.

[17] *Ibid.*, p. 10.

facets with greater precision.[18] However certain attitudes pervade all phases and categories of humanism, foremost of which is a revaluation of man in terms of his inherent dignity and worth.[19] Such a belief, fundamental to the new age, provides a new optic for all serious inquiry. "What is the use," asks Petrarch, "of knowing the nature of quadrupeds, fowls, fishes, and serpents and not knowing or even neglecting man's nature, the purpose for which we are born, and whence and whereto we travel?"[20] As man assumes a greater prominence, as he gains a more privileged position in the world, as he becomes accustomed to considering all things from this renewed and revitalized perspective, gradually "the object of wisdom shifts from divine things, to things divine and human and their causes, then to human things alone."[21] From the knowledge of man to self-knowledge, it was but one logical step, but an essential one in order to regain the full measure of human dignity and to achieve a new heroism. In 1561 Ronsard affirms this canon law of humanism without reservation:

> Le vray commencement pour en vertus acroistre,
> C'est (disoit Apollon) soymesme se cognoistre.
> Celuy qui se cognoist, est seul maistre de soy,
> Et sans avoir Royaume il est vrayement un Roy.[22]

To acquire "parfaicte cognoissance de l'autre monde qui est l'homme," the Renaissance overlooked no source of information.

---

[18] See Helmut Hatzfeld, "Christian, Pagan, and Devout Humanism in Sixteenth-Century France," *MLQ* XII (1951), 337-352.

[19] The theme is certainly not new with the sixteenth century; it had been eloquently developed by the Ancients and during the Middle Ages. But it assumes a new emphasis and vitality during the Renaissance. See Lionello Sozzi, "La 'Dignitas hominis' dans la littérature française de la Renaissance," in *Humanism in France at the end of the Middle Ages and in the early Renaissance*, ed. A. H. T. Levi (Manchester: Manchester University Press and New York: Barnes & Noble, 1970), pp. 176-198.

[20] "On his own Ignorance...", trans Hans Nachod, in *The Renaissance Philosophy of Man*, ed. Cassirer, Kristeller, and Randall (Chicago: The University of Chicago Press, 1948), pp. 58-59.

[21] Eugene F. Rice, *The Renaissance Idea of Wisdom* (Cambridge: Harvard University Press, 1958), pp. 8-9.

[22] "Institution pour l'adolescence du Roy treschrestien Charles neufviesme de ce nom," vv. 85-88 (in *Œuvres complètes*, ed. Laumonier [Paris: Didier, 1946], t. XI, p. 8).

In 1532 Rabelais boldly declared the value of "frequentes anatomies"; less scientific minds examined the historical and moral writings of Antiquity; still others turned to those works in which man's emotions are described, discussed, and analyzed. In what seems to Professor Saulnier a sterile prolongation of "la scolastique courtoise," the early sixteenth century continued to read and imitate the allegories of *Le Roman de la Rose*; in what appears to him as "un didactisme pédantesque," it continued to publish Martial d'Auvergne's *Arrests d'amour* and translated the fifth book of Boccaccio's *Filocolo* containing "Treize elegantes demandes d'amour"; in order to indulge its taste for amorous misfortune, France did not disdain the "abus de l'allégorie, du merveilleux et du chevaleresque" found in the works of Diego de San Pedro, Juan de Flores, and Juan de Segura.[23] In terms of the new humanist anthropocentric focus, these works, abounding in traditional motifs and themes, had nevertheless a significance for the understanding of the human heart.

In 1532 this inquiry into the realm of human sentiment acquired a new vibrancy with the appearance of three translations of Boccaccio's *Elegia di Madonna Fiammetta*. The publication of this "confidence passionnée" that reports "une sucession d'états d'âme finement analysés"[24] marks a turning point in the history of prose fiction in France. The popularity of the chevalric novel begins to wane in favor of the "sentimental novel" as writers such as Marguerite Briet are increasingly drawn to Boccaccio's rhetorical baggage of complaints and confessions, lamentations and accusations in order to inspire lyrically a feeling for the ecstasies and sufferings of love. With each story given an aura or the assurance of authenticity, it becomes another indisputable example of human truth to be added to the increasing body of moral literature.

Like the novel that emerged from the sixteenth century, the short story also responded to humanism. There is a seriousness of purpose underlying the frequently humorous façade of these tale collections, for writers could not escape the stimulation of

---

[23] V.-L. Saulnier, *Maurice Scève* (Paris: Klincksieck, 1948), t. I, pp. 49-51.

[24] Reynier, *op. cit.*, p. 44.

the new intellectual climate. The Breton writer Noël du Fail translated the *Elegantiae* of Lorenzo Valla and letters by Cicero before composing his *Propos rustiques* which itself has passages reminiscent of certain colloquies of Erasmus and is cast in a humanist framework. Writers are fascinated by new ideas and they discuss them with enthusiasm. In composing his *Joyeux Devis*, a collection which parallels so closely the tone and rapid conversational style of the *Cent Nouvelles nouvelles*, Des Périers does not find his inspiration solely in folklore and tradition, but also in those themes revitalized by the humanists.

The short story is one of the arenas in which new ideas could be displayed. Anxious to determine their validity, an author such as Marguerite de Navarre examines them from every angle. Such is the importance of the framework of the *Heptaméron* where ideas and situations are examined by individual temperaments. They are disputed as they stand exposed to the clash of contradictory opinion. They can no longer anticipate a choral sanction. As the theoretical is tested against the experiential, Marguerite de Navarre comes upon a problem that will gain increasing immediacy as the century progresses, for behind the empirical examination of fact which the courtly *devisants* discuss in an effort to define some viable ethic lies the blatant revelation of a single valid truth: the disparity of opinion. No single notion can any longer aspire to the luxury of an absolute; no simple answer can serve as a guide for human action. The Renaissance became aware of the dangerous possibility of varying perspectives and of relative truths.

Nevertheless the problems raised by a new world of secular definition ultimately find a practicable solution for the writers of the first half of the century. Bemused by the diversity of humanity, Des Périers laughs man out of his folly by suggesting the disparity between his "ignorance et présomption, naïveté et arrogance, sincérité et duplicité." [25] Du Fail looks with a more wary eye upon his world of change. However he does not stop at idle reminiscence of a past golden age; ultimately he posits an

---

[25] Lionello Sozzi, *Les Contes de Bonaventure des Périers* (Torino: Giappichelli, 1965), p. 420.

ethic endorsing the joyful fulfillment of man's most creative capacities provided he recognize the necessary limitations of his rational powers. Du Fail's acceptance of the humanist ethic of the golden mean stands as a solid affirmation of his faith in man's ability to guide his life to virtue through the exercise of reason. If Marguerite de Navarre challenges this faith, she does not leave man destitute, but resorts to a more traditional solution fused with a neo-platonic ethic, and proposes the necessity of a constant effort toward the Supreme Good without which man is unable to direct an otherwise meaningless existence. In this case, human drama becomes the story of "ceulx qui cerchent, en ce qu'ilz aiment, quelque perfection, soit beaulté, bonté ou bonne grace; toujours tendans à la vertu." [26] The beauty of a spiritual union with the Divine may seem like an elusive ideal, but it remains at least a vital possibility for those who submit to the worldly code of honor and *honnêteté* and to the dictates of Christian faith.

The various solutions offered during the first half of the century were nevertheless seriously challenged and eventually such ideals were shattered. The proportions of the early Renaissance world became increasingly unmanageable. What had appealed to earlier writers as a comic disparity could no longer avoid tragic proportions. The tale-teller no longer sat down to relate amusing anecdotes in front of a blazing fire; his *joyeux devis* and *baliverneries* could no longer conceal the serious consequences of human action. The predominantly comic and satirical tone deferred to a tragic mood which found its expression in a new form, the *histoire tragique*. And ironically, the first French writer to compose a collection of tales under this significant title, a work which challenged many of the myths and hypotheses posited by the early sixteenth century, was the man

---

[26] *Heptaméron*, "Dix neufviesme nouvelle." In his study of *Marguerite de Navarre's Heptameron: Themes, Language, and Structure* (Durham: Duke University Press, 1973) Marcel Tetel insists upon an essentially bleak and tragic outlook in the work: "[Marguerite] thinks pessimistically of the human condition. Only true faith can save man, but few are eligible, or even have the capacity, to receive the grace of God. Faith and the grace of God then become another unattainable ideal, given the basic weakness of man" (p. 10).

who published the first edition of Marguerite de Navarre's compendium of Renaissance ideals, Pierre Boaistuau, Sieur de Launay.

Despite the fact that he launched the vogue for a short-story form whose popularity would continue well into the seventeenth century, Boaistuau's contemporaries and literary successors felt no compunction about furnishing posterity with only the barest details of his life. Even his publishers, anxious to meet the continual demand for his humanist and fictional works, seem to have registered a singular indifference by recording at least twenty variants of his Breton name. It was not until 1870 that scholarly investigations began to uncover new evidence to supplement the scant biographical notes found in La Croix du Maine. [27]

Of Boaistuau's early years little definite is known. He was born in Nantes about 1520, [28] but there are no clues to his activities preceding his studies at Poitiers in 1543. Shortly thereafter he moved to southern France to study law, first in Avignon and then in Valence. But it was not until his trip to Rome that Boaistuau discovered what would become his lifelong preoccupation. There, untouched by the vestiges of ancient glory in the Eternal City, he spent his time in the company of two doctors who awakened in him an interest in natural science and the wonders of nature. Anxious to further his knowledge, he settled in Paris about 1550 to begin a period of serious scientific inquiry. He conducted a series of botanical experiments and delighted in confirming reports of the wondrous medicinal properties of plants, especially those that provided a welcome cure for melancholy and lust. In addition he boasts of having learned at this time

---

[27] Arthur de La Borderie, "Pierre Boaistuau," *Revue de Bretagne et de Vendée* VII (1870), i: 359-371; ii: 63-75; 111-116. See also Ernest Courbet, "Jeanne d'Albret et l'*Heptaméron*," *Bulletin du Bibliophile et du Bibliothécaire* (1904), 277-290, and Yves Florenne, "Un quêteur de prodiges," *Mercure de France* 342 (1961), 657-688. The following paragraphs on the life of Boaistuau summarize our findings which are presented in the "Introduction" to the critical edition of the *Histoires tragiques* (Paris: Champion, S. T. F. M., 1977).

[28] In his "Notes sur Pierre Boaistuau" (*BHR* XXXVIII [1976], 323-333), Michel Simonin suggests the year 1517, based on the baptismal record of a certain Pierre Bouexcau.

how to make precious stones. From the mysteries of nature he was drawn to the mysteries of man, and in an effort to comprehend them, his empirical mind sought answers in the dissecting room. His curiosity about the wonders of man and nature was further satisfied in 1554 when, as secretary to Jean-Jacques de Cambrai, the French ambassador to the Levant, Boaistuau had the opportunity to travel briefly in Germany, Italy, and possibly Hungary.

After M. de Cambrai was recalled to France, Boaistuau entered the service of François de Clèves, duc de Nevers, to whom he dedicated his *Chelidonius Tigurinus* in 1556. Containing an eloquent apology for monarchy and a portrait of the ideal prince, who is characterized as moderate, learned, pious, just, and fearless in maintaining peace, the *Chelidonius* was well received by Boaistuau's contemporaries, and eleven editions were to appear in the course of the next thirty years.

Encouraged by the success of his first work, Boaistuau decided to devote all of his energy to translating St. Augustine's *De civitate Dei*. This was to be his greatest contribution and one that would guarantee his fame. Although he would never complete his translation nor would any part of it be published, his efforts were not entirely in vain, for in order to get a better grasp of St. Augustine's thought, Boaistuau read widely in the writings of Antiquity, in those of the Church Fathers and even of his contemporaries. From these works he extracted substantial material to support his own view of the paradox of the misery and dignity of man which he published in 1558 as the *Theatre du monde* and the *Bref Discours sur l'excellence et dignité de l'homme*.

In the same year Boaistuau published a third work from which he undoubtedly anticipated further renown, but which brought him only scandal: the first edition of Marguerite de Navarre's short stories, the *Histoires des amans fortunez*. A collection of sixty-seven novellas, which Boaistuau took the liberty to edit, correct, and rephrase, the edition was dedicated to Marguerite de Bourbon, Duchesse de Nevers and niece of Marguerite de Navarre. However Boaistuau mentioned nowhere in the preface the name of the author, and this oversight roused the anger of

Jeanne d'Albret who had the edition suppressed and who immediately commissioned Claude Gruget to prepare a new edition of the tales which appeared in 1559 as the *Heptaméron*. Boaistuau was summarily dismissed by the Duc de Nevers, and, perhaps out of spite, perhaps in deference to his former protector who may have wanted to dissociate himself as much as possible from his tactless secretary, he published a new and slightly revised version of the *Chelidonius* in 1559, dedicated this time to the Abbé de Saint-Sidoine, secretary to the Cardinal de Lorraine.

In spite of the scandal caused by the *Amans fortunez*, Boaistuau lost none of his enthusiasm for the genre of the novella, though he abandoned the hazardous role of editor for the safety and assurance afforded by the title of translator. In 1554 Matteo Bandello, a Dominican friar whom Henri II had named Bishop of Agen, had published in Lucca the first three volumes of his *Novelle*. Posing as a chronicler of his times, Bandello weaves fact with fiction as he presents a vast and detailed fresco of sixteenth-century Italy, "una mistura d'accidenti diversi, diversamente e in diversi luoghi e tempi a diverse persone avvenuti e senza ordine veruno recitati." [29] His versatility as a *conteur* is readily attested by the varied inspiration of his collection, containing tales to inspire laughter as well as fear, wonderment as well as pity. René Pruvost's detailed summary of these volumes suggests the range of his talent and the type of story that appealed to the mid-sixteenth-century audience:

> [Bandello] relates with great gusto the very ingenious tricks resorted to by unworthy priests or monks in order to satisfy the cravings of their fleshly appetite; by adulterous wives or unchaste girls in order to hoodwink their husbands or guardians; by lecherously inclined young men in order to wreak a vengeance, not uncommonly in the worst of bad tastes, against ladies who had resisted them. At other times his tales are tragical and ghastly, and seem to proceed from a radically pessimistic view

---

[29] *Tutte le opere di Matteo Bandello*, ed. *Francesco Flora* (Verona: Mondadori, 1952), t. II, p. 247. Yvonne Rodax develops this point in a lively discussion of "The Kaleidoscopic World of Bandello," *The Real and the Ideal in the Novella of Italy, France, and England* (Chapel Hill: The University of North Carolina Press, 1968), pp. 81-93.

of human character and destiny. Passion knows no bounds, stops at nothing for its gratification, heaps murders upon murders and ruins upon ruins, and love is hardly anything more than a purely physical appetite. The sins against conjugal faithfulness and feminine chastity are most cruelly punished, with a chastisement harder than death. Virtuously inclined young girls escape dishonour only through loss of life. In its conflict with duty, love triumphs only through doing the loved one to death. Indeed, it leads to bloodshed and murder no less than lust, and even when pure and youthful, is debarred by tragic accidents from enjoying the happiness it seems to deserve. But, side by side with these, other novels are of an optimistic, romantic cast. The lustfully inclined are reclaimed from their illicit pursuit by sudden admiration for the virtue, or pity for the hardships, of the ladies whom they have long persecuted. Ladies falsely accused are vindicated, vice is confounded, and virtue emerges triumphant. Lovers reach a secure haven of happiness after being tossed upon the seas of adversity for a long period, all through which they have remained uniformly faithful and constant. Men show themselves disinterested, generous and forgiving, and women courteous, dutiful and loving. [30]

Although John Addington Symonds considers these tales "a school of profligacy," Bandello confesses that his aim was merely to amuse and entertain his reader, and in view of this not unworthy goal, he concedes his rough and unrefined style: ... "ogni istoria," he writes in the prefatory letter to the eleventh tale of the second volume, "ancor che scritta fosse ne la piú rozza e zotica lingua che si sia, sempre diletterá il suo lettore." [31] Boaistuau was one of the first to criticize the avowedly unpolished expression of the *Novelle*. Yet certain of the tales had a dramatic power that appealed to him, and he could not resist offering a revised and refined version to French readers.

Ignoring Bandello's comic inspiration, Boaistuau published early in 1559 six of the tales in a volume entitled *Histoires tra-*

---

[30] *Matteo Bandello and Elizabethan Fiction* (Paris: Champion, 1937), pp. 103-104.
[31] *Tutte le opere, ed. cit.*, t. I, p. 778.

giques.[32] More than a mere translation of the Italian original, Boaistuau allows himself complete freedom with his source, changing details when he feels it is necessary, adding and deleting passages wherever required by his understanding of the story. T. Gwynfor Griffith is amazed that Bandello "so often chose themes which seem to offer opportunity for nothing more than the reporting of some remarkable or singularly scandalous event and which give little scope to his special talents for the description of social scenes or the presentation of psychological detail or the composition of tragic speeches."[33] Boaistuau evidently had the same reaction; yet he was prompt to remedy such shortcomings. It is precisely the "presentation of psychological detail" that interests him, and this is most frequently accomplished by the "composition of tragic speeches" in an elaborate style. Unlike Marguerite de Navarre, Boaistuau had no fear that "la beaulté de la rethoricque feit tort en quelque partye à la verité de l'histoire."[34] In his version of Bandello, human truth is inseparable from lyric and rhetorical expression.

Despite the immediate success of the *Histoires tragiques* — five separate printings in 1559 alone, including a special edition published in October of that year and dedicated to Queen Elizabeth — Boaistuau had no intention of continuing the work and entrusted the completion of the French "translation" of Bandello to François de Belleforest.[35] Boaistuau left the world of fiction to resume his observations of the wonders of nature.

---

[32] Concordance of Boaistuau's *Histoires tragiques* and the tales from Bandello's *Novelle:*

HT I (Edouart et Ælips)	*N* II.37
HT II (Mahomet et Hyrenée)	*N* I.10
HT III (Rhomeo et Julliette)	*N* II.9
HT IV (Le Seigneur du Piedmont)	*N* II.12
HT V (Didaco et Violente)	*N* I.42
HT VI (Mandozze et la Duchesse de Savoie)	*N* II.44

[33] *Bandello's Fiction* (Oxford: Basil Blackwell, 1955), p. 123; see pp. 1-12 for a review of critical scholarship on Bandello's *Novelle*.

[34] *Heptaméron*, "Prologue."

[35] For a detailed discussion of the complex history of the publication of the seven volumes of the *Histoires tragiques*, see Donald Stone, Jr., "Belleforest's Bandello: A Bibliographical Study," *BHR* XXXIV (1972), 489-499.

He had read Conrad Lycosthènes' *Prodigiorum ac ostentorum chronicon* in which he had found an engraving of a seven-headed serpent that the Venetians had supposedly given to François Ier. Although his search for this natural wonder was not rewarded, his rude deception left him undaunted, and this indefatigable "quêteur de prodiges" set out for England, ostensibly to gather further notes for a French version of Lycosthènes' book of marvels. However his itinerary was limited for the most part to London where Boaistuau was well received by the English nobility and even granted an audience with the Queen. In gratitude, Boaistuau sent to her, upon his return to France, the manuscript of his *Histoires prodigieuses,* his final work which was published in 1560. From that moment until the time of his death in 1566, there is no record of Boaistuau's activities. It is likely that he continued working on his translation of St. Augustine, and, during these last years, he began a work which would be completed by Pierre de Cistières and published in 1572, a long and detailed *Histoire des persécutions de l'église chrestienne et catholique.*

During a relatively short career, Boaistuau's interests were wide and varied. For this reason, as early as the seventeenth century, his name would become vulnerable to accusations of superficiality. [36] Nevertheless, despite his fascination with ancient and contemporary writings, with alchemy and the advances of medical science, with the world about him as well as the secrets of nature, he was continually drawn, in good humanist fashion, to that "subject merveilleusement vain, divers et ondoyant que l'homme." His volume of *Histoires tragiques* is his most profound expression of this constant preoccupation. But his subject did not lend itself to the confines of his narrative heritage. Man had

---

[36] In his notes added to La Croix du Maine's article on "Pierre Boaistuau," Bernard de La Monnoye states that Boaistuau "a passé dans son temps pour un beau parleur, avoit quelque lecture, du reste fort superficiel, ne sachant absolument point de Grec, & n'entendant qu'assez médiocrement le Latin" (*Les Bibliothèques françaises,* ed. Rigoley de Juvigny [Paris, 1772], t. II, p. 256). More recently, I. D. McFarlane, in his literary history of *Renaissance France 1470-1589* (London: Ernest Benn Ltd, New York: Barnes and Noble, 1974), qualifies Boaistuau and his prolific collaborator Belleforest as "hack polymaths, Jacks-of-all-trades who did a vast amount of translation, adaptation, and vulgarisation" (p. 252).

gained a prominence which demanded more explicit expression than afforded by the anonymous heroes of earlier tales. Moreover, writing at the critical juncture of the century, when skepticism about any absolute was becoming prevalent, Boaistuau could no longer accept characters simply as illustrative symbols of a series of generalized moral principles. Nor could their actions remain exemplary of preconceived ideas and attitudes.

He had to remold the short story form to his purpose. Boaistuau's study concerns man, but this is a creature who blatantly contradicts his former pretense to nobility. His tales will therefore explore the reasons behind his actions and peer into the workings of his mind. The intricacies of a peripatetic plot which had sustained earlier narratives will be replaced by the complexities of human motivation. He will compose a psychological drama that slowly but methodically examines various responses to the single affliction common to all men: passion. And each inquiry, seen especially in the context of Boaistuau's humanist essays written during the same period (1558-1560), will add a new dimension to an emerging portrait that finally destroys man's heroic image and questions his vaunted potential. These stories do not aim to evoke laugther; they cannot even elicit a wry smile, but only a wince as Boaistuau displays one of nature's most monstrous creations.

PART ONE

BOAISTUAU AND BANDELLO:
COMPARISONS AND CONTRASTS

Chapter I

THE PROBLEM OF TRANSLATION: LIBERTY OR SERVITUDE

> Je ne veulx taire icy la follie d'aulcuns traducteurs: lesquelz au lieu de liberté se submettent à servitude.
>
> —Etienne Dolet, *La Maniere de bien traduire*

In the tradition of the post-Burckhardtian historians of the northern Renaissance, Pietro Toldo claimed in 1895 that the French short story of the sixteenth century was in great part a transalpine importation and a further example of the enormous debt of Renaissance France to Italy.[1] His conclusions provoked an immediate cry of protest that Toldo's study was too selective in its treatment and ignored the varied founts of narrative inspiration, especially that of the oral tradition.[2] While Toldo clearly limits himself to a discussion of "le origini italiane della novella francese," what seems to have incurred Gallic indignation

---

[1] *Contributo allo studio della novella francese del XV e XVI secolo* (Rome: E. Loescher, 1895).

[2] See Gaston Paris, "La nouvelle française aux XVe et XVIe siècles," *Journal des savants* LX (1895), 289-303, 342-361. Students of the French novella have continued to challenge and modify Toldo's thesis. Recently Krystyna Kasprzyk has concluded: "La nouvelle française n'avait pas besoin d'être une importation savante de l'Italie à laquelle elle ne doit au fond que quelques thèmes et l'idée d'organiser d'une certaine manière son propre héritage, suffisamment riche et varié pour lui fournir la matière et, en partie, la forme" (*Nicolas de Troyes et le genre narratif en France au XVIe siècle* [Varsovie: Editions scientifiques de Pologne, Paris: Klincksieck, 1963]), p. 294.

is his repeated insistence upon imitation, as if he were thereby denying the French product any degree of originality.

However the Classical world did not oppose the notions of imitation and originality so rigorously. It was a time when subject matter was the common property of all prospective writers. Racine states openly in the beginning of his preface to *Phèdre:* "Voici encore une tragédie dont le sujet est pris d'Euripide." Writing his "Avertissement" to *Le Cid* in 1648, Corneille follows his quotation from Juan Marina's *Historia d'España* with the statement: "Voilà ce qu'a prêté l'histoire à D. Guillem de Castro, qui a mis ce fameux événement sur le théâtre avant moi." Artistic achievement was measured in terms of the arrangement and expression of the subject regardless of its originality.

The Renaissance was such a time when subject matter was pillaged shamelessly, a fact which is now a commonplace as a result of the efforts of scholarly source-seekers. Indeed it has become fashionable in recent years to minimize the indebtedness of sixteenth-century writers to their literary models in order to emphasize the degree to which their borrowings are incorporated within a new and original vision. And this approach becomes all the more important when dealing with a group of writers who profess no other achievement than the translation of works into their native tongue. Such is the titular pronouncement of Pierre Boaistuau's *Histoires tragiques*: "extraictes des œuvres Italiennes de Bandel, et mises en langue Françoise."

Boaistuau has not traditionally been granted a very illustrious role in the history of the short story, but his name is certainly not unknown. The standard introductory pages of a modern edition of Shakespeare's *Romeo and Juliet* cite his name as the French host with whom the tale rested briefly on its trip from Italy to England.[3] But such favorable recognition of the sig-

---

[3] Ever since Jean-François-Victor Hugo reprinted Boaistuau's version of the Romeo and Juliet story as an appendix to his French translation of the English play (*Œuvres complètes de W. Shakespeare* [Paris: Pagnerre, 1868], t. VII, pp. 425-483), critics have continued to dispute not only Shakespeare's debt to the French tale, but also Boaistuau's debt to the Italian antecedents. Arthur J. Roberts expresses his personal preference for Bandello's version in "The Sources of Romeo and Juliet," *MLN* XVII (1902), 82-87. Henri Hauvette credits Adrien Sévin rather than Boaistuau with

nificant changes introduced by the French translator of Bandello's tale did not save him from the oblivion imposed upon so many writers of the Renaissance by the seventeenth and eighteenth centuries. Although La Croix du Maine praises Boaistuau as an "homme très-docte & des plus éloquens Orateurs de son siècle, & lequel avoit une façon de parler autant douce, coulante, & agréable qu'autre duquel j'aye leu les écrits," [4] the name of this Breton writer remains obscured until the bibliophiles of the nineteenth century begin to examine his works. [5] But it is only in the twentieth century that scholars have begun to reconsider Boaistuau as a teller of tales, the particular aspect about which his contemporaries, and especially La Croix du Maine, spare no praise:

> ...les six premières Histoires tragiques, traduites de l'Italien de Bandel, imprimées à Paris par diverses fois, avec les continuations ou suites de traduction dudit Bandel, par François de Belleforest: mais pour dire ce qui me semble touchant ces deux Auteurs, les six premières dudit Boaistuau sont si excellentes, & traduites si heureu-

---

the creation of the apothecary ("Une variante française de la légende de Roméo et Juliette," *RLC* I [1921], 329-337). Olin H. Moore insists that Boaistuau owes an unacknowledged debt to the version composed by Luigi da Porto ("Le rôle de Boaistuau dans le développement de la légende de Roméo et Juliette," *RLC* IX [1929], 637-643), thereby according to da Porto a proportionately greater influence upon Shakespeare ("Shakespeare's Deviations from Romeus and Juliet," *PMLA* 52 [1937], 68-74), all of which leads Moore to conclude that Boaistuau's originality consists in the addition of a few insignificant details (*The Legend of Romeo and Juliet* [Columbus: Ohio State University Press, 1950], pp. 87-94). The dispute of who copied whom is gamely dealt with by H. B. Charlton, "France as Chaperone of Romeo and Juliet," in *Studies in French Language and Mediaeval Literature presented to Professor Mildred K. Pope* (Manchester: The Manchester University Press, 1939), pp. 43-59. The whole matter has been at least temporarily resolved by Geoffrey Bullough's authoritative study of the *Narrative and Dramatic Sources of Shakespeare*, Vol. I (New York: Columbia University Press, 1966), pp. 269-276.

[4] *Les Bibliothèques françoises de La Croix du Maine et de Du Verdier*, ed. Rigoley de Juvigny (Paris, 1772), t. II, p. 254.

[5] Charles Nodier (*Mélanges tirés d'une petite bibliothèque* [Paris: Crapelet, 1829], pp. 161-168) describes a 1576 edition of the *Histoires prodigieuses* and suggests a possible influence of Boaistuau on La Fontaine's "Paysan du Danube." Arthur de La Borderie constructs a biography of the Breton writer from scattered references in the *Histoires prodigieuses* (see *Introduction*, p. 2, note 27).

> sement, que quand on sort de sa traduction pour entrer en celle dudit Belleforest, le changement est étrange: car cettui-ci avoit rendu son Oeuvre bien poli & limé, pour ne l'avoir précipité à l'impression, & Belleforest avoit fait ses traductions à mesure que l'on imprimoit son Oeuvre, qui est cause que les premières sont plus élabourées que les dernières. [6]

Yet despite the favor accorded to Boaistuau's portion of the *Histoires tragiques,* the initial problem remains: five times La Croix du Maine mentions that we are dealing with a translation.

If this is so, how can Boaistuau be considered to play a justifiable role within the development of the French short story other than introducing a foreign influence? To what extent does he imitate or translate his source? Wherein lies the original expression of the subject? Does his version perceptibly alter the source story so that Boaistuau may be said to have contributed to a developing form? Such questions suggest valid reservations about the importance of Boaistuau's contribution, for we are dealing with a writer whose short stories have received scant attention. Because of the limited corpus of Boaistuau's narrative fiction, critical inquiry has centered more frequently on his humanist essays and compilations such as the *Theatre du monde* and the *Histoires prodigieuses* which reflect his contemporaries' search for a new ethos in a world afflicted with a superfluity of definitions.

In the "Advertissement au lecteur," Boaistuau himself suggests a partial answer to these questions. Obviously drawn to stories of violence, bloodshed, and death, as his selections from Bandello indicate, he was nevertheless so disturbed by the frequent stylistic improprieties that he felt obliged to rewrite the tales entirely:

> Te priant au reste ne trouver mauvais si je ne me suis assubjecty au stile de Bandel, car sa phrase m'a semblé tant rude, ses termes impropres, ses propos tant mal liez et ses sentences tant maigres, que j'ay eu plus cher la refondre tout de neuf et la remettre en nouvelle forme

---

[6] La Croix du Maine, *op. cit.,* p. 255.

que me rendre si superstitieux imitateur, n'ayant seulement pris de luy que le subject de l'histoire, comme tu pourras aisément descouvrir si tu es curieux de conferer mon stile avec le sien. [7]

Denying slavish imitation, Boaistuau takes pride in having recast his source stories completely. [8] Yet such affirmations are always suspect, and all the more so when one considers HT II which follows the original so closely. It will therefore be useful to take Boaistuau's suggestion literally and compare his stories to their source in order to see what specific changes are apparent in the French version of Bandello. [9]

The story of the "seigneur du Piedmont," although not typical of the author's rhetorical style, succinctly illustrates Boaistuau's conception of the short story and his effort to enrich a traditional form with a more probing psychological inquiry, to enlarge the scope of the form beyond the narrower limits of mere anecdotal amusement, and to allow the narrative to serve as its own ex-

---

[7] All quotations from Boaistuau's *Histoires tragiques* are taken from the critical edition by Richard A. Carr (Paris: Champion, S. T. F. M., 1977) and will hereafter be included in the text with the abbreviated reference HT followed by a roman numeral indicating the story in the collection and then a page reference.

[8] Amyot expresses a similar sentiment as the veritable duty of any translator. In his preface "Aux lecteurs des Vies des hommes illustres," he writes: "L'office d'un propre producteur ne gist pas seulement à rendre fidèlement la sentence de son autheur, mais aussi à représenter aucunement et à adombrer la forme du style et la manière de parler d'iceluy" (Cited by D. Thickett, *Estienne Pasquier: Choix de lettres* [Genève: Droz, 1956], p. 121).

[9] Preliminary work based on such a comparison has been done by René Sturel in his admirable study of "Bandello en France," *Bulletin italien* XIII (1913), 210-227, 331-347. Sturel examines three categories of changes in the *Histoires tragiques:* suppressions, in the interest of narrative movement, of superfluous details, historical digressions, and Bandello's personal and moral reflections; changes of detail, many of which are insignificant, such as changing the name of the hero in the fifth tale from Didaco Centiglia to Didaco Ventimiglia; and finally additions, such as letters, speeches, and descriptions, for the analysis of character. In the first part of this study we will examine the effect of Boaistuau's changes on the meaning of the individual tale and the way in which they reflect Boaistuau's conception of narrative art. All references from Bandello are taken from the two-volume edition of his works, *Tutte le opere di Matteo Bandello*, ed. Francesco Flora (Verona: Mondadori, 1952). References are included in the text: a roman numeral indicating the volume, followed by a page number.

pression of an implicit doctrinal attitude rather than standing in a secondary or exemplary relationship to a previously stated ideology. The shortest of the six tales, the fourth insistently refuses any elaboration by lengthy speeches and focuses solely upon the developing plot line. Such a concentrated narrative, devoid of the usual adornment, furnishes the best example in the collection of Boaistuau's manipulation of the skeletal frame of the form.

One major distinction between the French and Italian versions is apparent at the very beginning of the narrative when the protagonist is introduced:

...fu in una parte di Piemonte un nobile e valeroso gentiluomo il cui nome mi taccio... (I, 789)	...il y avoit un grand seigneur vaillant et genereux en quelque contrée du Piedmont, duquel je tairay le nom, tant pour la reverence de ses plus proches parens qui vivent encor' pour le jourd'huy que pour la trop severe justice de laquelle il usa envers sa femme, l'ayant surprinse en faute. (HT IV, 124)

Boaistuau deems it necessary to explain his refusal to name the lord, and both of his explanations are additions to the source text. The first is formulaic, as used frequently in the *Joyeux Devis* and the *Heptaméron,* an excuse for anonymity which obliquely suggests the authenticity of the story in order to lend credence, in this case, to an unusual tale of horror. But the second explanation reveals at the outset the essence of the suspenseful tale as Bandello conceived it. Boaistuau announces his conclusion.[10] However what appears at first glance as a clumsy betrayal illustrates rather his conception of the art of storytelling. Bandello follows the traditional structuring of the tale: a steady development or crescendo up to the conclusion. His

---

[10] In the same way Boaistuau announces the conclusion of HT III in the beginning of the story: ..."il humoit le doux venin amoureux, duquel il fut en fin si bien empoisonné qu'il fina ses jours par une cruelle mort" (68-9). See also HT II, 58, where the murder of Hyrenée is announced.

major interest resides in the description of the terrifying vengeance inflicted by the husband upon his wife. But Boaistuau changes the emphasis completely. His announcement of the conclusion suggests that his purpose is not to progress to a surprise ending that will shock and terrify, but rather to unfold a complex and suspenseful plot to its inevitable conclusion. If he accepts Bandello's conclusion with only slight change, it is merely the necessary means of ending this tale as his source has indicated. But he does not compose a tale of horror for the sake of horror, which is visibly Bandello's narrative intent as underscored by his prefatory moral comments about the dangers incurred by the passion of love.

As suggested by the deletions and additions in the French version, Boaistuau develops instead a powerful drama of human deception. His intention becomes evident early in the narrative with the introduction of the wife. Bandello lavishes description:

> Egli aveva preso per moglie una gentildonna del paese, la quale ben che non fosse la piú bella del mondo, era nondimeno assai appariscente e poteva fra l'altre stare. E in quello che mancava di bellezza ella suppliva con la vivacitá d'ingegno, con bei costumi, con leggiadri modi, con accoglienze gratissime, con la prontezza de le parole e con mille altre belle maniere. Era poi avvista e scaltrita pur assai e quella che vestiva meglio che donna di Piemonte, non tanto in portar ricche vestimenta di che era copiosa e ben fornita, quanto che sapeva troppo ben accomodar ogni abbigliamento ancor che di panno vile fosse stato. (I, 789-790)

Boaistuau, however, disregards the numerous descriptive details of the original:

> Ce seigneur en ce temps espousa une damoiselle de Thurin de moyenne beauté, laquelle il print pour son plaisir, n'ayant egard à la grandeur du lieu dont il estoit issu; et par ce qu'il avoit bien cinquante ans lors qu'il l'espousa, elle s'accoustroit tant modestement qu'elle ressembloit mieux veufve que mariée, et sceut tant bien gagner ce bon homme l'espace d'un an ou deux qu'il se reputoit tresheureux d'avoir trouvé telle alliance. (HT IV, 124)

Sturel maintains that the several details expressed in the Italian original about the woman's character and sumptuous clothing were omitted by Boaistuau out of respect for the necessary condensation of the story to its essential details: "Boaistuau a, suivant son habitude, négligé les détails qui lui paraissent inutiles ou peu vraisemblables."[11] However it is more likely that his basic understanding of the dramatic conflict differs to such an extent that these details are not only useless but meaningless. Since Bandello emphasizes the difference in age between the husband and wife ("Egli era pur vicino ai sessantatré anni e forse gli passava, e la moglie poteva averne circa trentacinque" [I, 790]), this woman of wit and vivaciousness obviously sought in her lover a youthful complement to her own exuberance: "non contenta degli abbracciamenti del marito ed avendone gran carestia, perché il piú del tempo egli stava ove era il duca che il piú de l'anno dimorava in Savoia, gittò gli occhi a dosso ad un giovine vassallo del marito e di lui fieramente s'innamorò" (I, 790). The author clearly places the blame and responsibility for the affair upon the wife. From this point on, with the inclusion of lengthy descriptions on the amorous indulgences of the young couple, Bandello justifies her final punishment.

Boaistuau changes the direction of the story entirely, not to condone the wife's actions, but to insist upon a more purely dramatic development of the action. The initial portrait is radically changed because Boaistuau's heroine is not guilty of the same self-exalting pride of which the fine clothing of her Italian counterpart is the symbolic manifestation. On the contrary she is humble, modest, and unassuming, and quickly gains sympathy by inspiring in her husband a love for the woman whom he had originally "print pour son plaisir." This mutual love does not concern Bandello's more typed cast of characters, but it is a psychological necessity in the French version, since the pathos of the tragic conclusion depends entirely upon this initial bond of affection. Boaistuau carefully assures the logical development of his narrative which is based upon a psychological verisimilitude.

---

[11] Sturel, *op. cit.*, 226.

Boaistuau is constantly preoccupied with the realization that happiness is a fragile state, ever challenged by some kind of contradictory fatality. It is not surprising, therefore, that the two years of contentment enjoyed by the seigneur du Piedmont should culminate in misfortune, that the "seigneur vaillant et genereux" should become a jealous murderer. But the psychological orientation of the French version demands an indication of motivation. Thus whereas Bandello's more capricious heroine immediately falls in love with the young vassal when she sees him for the first time, Boaistuau offers an explanation for this adulterous passion. Both authors emphasize the favor shown the husband in the court, but Boaistuau inserts a single phrase which supplies the necessary logic for the ensuing details of the story:

la piú parte del tempo dimorava in corte, perciò che egli era uomo di gran conseglio e vedere, e il duca faceva non picciola stima di lui. (I, 789)	...la plus part du temps il suyvoit la court *par le commandement du Duc* qui le retenoit tousjours pres de sa personne, usant de son conseil le plus souvent ès affaires grandes. (HT IV, 124)

The Duc, who never appears in either narrative, plays the role of an outside force which ultimately destroys the wife, a type of fatality which reverses the fortune of the characters. "Par le commandement du Duc," that delicate and fragile happiness is destroyed, for "ceste damoiselle, estant servie et honorée en telle grandeur, ennuyée de trop de repos, commença à s'enamourer d'un jeune gentil-homme sien voisin" (HT IV, 125). It is boredom and "l'incommodité de la solitude, specialement pour la continuelle absence de son mary, lequel à peine demeuroit trois moys en tout un an à la maison" (HT IV, 125) which make the wife turn her attention to a man who in the French version no longer occupies a subservient social rank. Moreover, while in Bandello's tale this is a sudden and overwhelming passion, Boaistuau's emphasis is upon the verb *commença*. Thus, whereas the Italian version launches into a long description of this love which is immediately consummated by two people "da troppo amor accecati," Boaistuau concentrates upon the development of this passion within the soul of the unfaithful wife.

If one is to insist upon a more psychologically oriented tale, it is only justifiable to question the rapidity of the change that takes place in the once virtuous woman who seems suddenly to approach Bandello's heroine by her immediate attempts at seducing the young man, "lequel... elle sceut si bien practiquer par regards et autre gestes lascifs qu'il s'en apperceut ayséement" (HT IV, 125). But love in Boaistuau's world is a sudden and blinding passion, and he emphasizes the current mythology when he states that "amour les *aguillonna* si bien..." (HT IV, 125). Her *ennui* was the weakness that allowed love to sting her and render her helpless.

Despite this view of the physiology of love, however, the consummation is delayed by the lover who, "pour le respect de la grandeur [du] mary...ne faisoit ses approches que de loing" (HT IV, 125). He is a type of character for whom Boaistuau has a definite penchant, the gentleman who obeys the social code of courtly love and willingly accepts subservience in honor of his beloved:

> Ce gentil-homme... luy remonstra qu'encor que son amitié eust esté extreme, toutesfois se reputant indigne d'un si haut subject, il avoit tousjours celé son mal, lequel d'autant luy avoit esté plus importable que la crainte le contraignoit de le tenir caché. Toutesfois puis qu'il luy plaisoit de tant s'abbaisser et luy vouloir faire l'honneur de l'accepter pour serviteur, qu'il mettroit peine de recompenser par humilité et humbles services ce que la fortune luy avoit en autres choses denié. (HT IV, 125-126)

A formal code of honor forces this relationship through the necessary preliminaries of "devis," "promenades," and "amytié" until at last "le grand chemin leur estoit ouvert pour conduire leurs entreprinses à leur effect desiré" (HT IV, 126). The necessary change in the lover's social station from a "giovine vassallo" to a "jeune gentilhomme" is immediately apparent. Had the "vassallo" spoken in the above terms, the speech would have been ludicrous. Boaistuau delights in lengthy descriptions of the ideal lover who follows all of the forms of the social code but who cannot quite resist the ultimate pleasures of love. And his characters are therefore of necessity men of high station, exemplary people who nevertheless display human weakness. The note Boaistuau strikes here is one of concern, for the endless discussions of *honneur* are fruitless. Honor is helpless before the strength of passion.

The major changes in the French version of the fourth tale occur in the central portion of the story: the discovery. Bandello's carefully stated suggestions about the nature and character of the husband, "che era uomo grave e da bene," "che niente aveva del geloso," "che era prudentissimo," reduce the story to a tale of vengeance by a *mari trompé*, a traditional theme which moves, however, to a violent instead of a comic conclusion. The husband is construed as a somewhat sympathetic character who is a victim of deception, and although the punishment appears extreme, it is not exacted in a jealous rage incited by an incidental discovery. Bandello relates "il tutto [che] egli faceva per meglio chiarirsi del desonesto amore de la sua donna" (I, 791). One may object to the inconsistency apparent in the portrayal of the husband and the excessive punishment of the wife, but again Bandello's purpose must be underscored. He relishes the final description of the hanging of the lover and the imprisonment of the wife in the room with the putrifying body of the "vassallo." Perhaps he was aware of this incongruity of character and action, and thereby limits the penance of the wife and her maid to six years whereupon, "infermandosi poi gravemente, il marito tutte due le fece cavar fuori e in una camera porre ove in breve la gentildonna morí" (I, 794). The story follows a simple linear structure through the successively rapid stages of crime committed, discovery, and vengeance.

Once again, Boaistuau's interest does not center on the conclusion. Therefore rather than writing merely a tale of vengeance, he creates a drama of deception by developing the husband's role beyond the restrictions of a necessary agent in a tale of horror. Instead of being cast as a prudent and serious character, the seigneur du Piedmont is an "homme acort et experimenté," a perceptive and cunning hero who, after an initial intuition of his wife's infidelity, "se persuada aysément qu'il y avoit quelque anguille sous roche" (HT IV, 127). Accordingly the French tale deals not only with the wife's deception of her husband, but also with the husband's deception of his wife as "tous deux taschoient chacun de son costé de si bien jouer leur rolle que le moins rusé d'eux deux n'eust voulu estre descouvert (HT IV, 127).

The narrative development concentrates upon the various stages of this drama of mutual deception, greatly expanded from the source story and emphasized by the numerous terms suggesting deception, which becomes the leitmotif of the tale:

> ...vivans en ceste *simulation*... (127)
> ...le seigneur (*feignant* un jour d'estre malade)... (128)
> ...il feist response (avec un visage *masqué* de joye)... (129)
> ...et sceut tant bien *dissimuler* son juste courroux... (129)
> ...et à fin de mieux *decevoir* ceste pauvre malheureuse... (130)

In this domestic struggle, the advantage remains with the husband who is aware of the whole truth, but who at the same time ceases to appeal as a sympathetic victim. Boaistuau casts him as shrewd, clever, and conniving, waiting with diabolical joy for the precise moment when he can most profitably thwart his wife's illicit pleasures, and relentlessly plotting his cruel revenge. This new perspective justifies the major image which Boaistuau introduces into the text:

> Et continuerent ces courtoisies si longuement que le seigneur, le voulant prendre au *filé*, l'envoya prier de venir disner avec luy... (127)

> Ceste *pantiere* tendue, ce jeune gentil-homme venoit ordinairement une fois le jour visiter ce seigneur et sa femme. (128)

> ...c'estoit l'heure où fortune ourdissoit petit à petit *la toille* et *le fillé* auquel elle la vouloit enclorre. (129)

The net, or trap, is the husband's sole preoccupation. He is no longer concerned with making certain that his wife is unfaithful, but merely with ascertaining the most propitious moment to assert his vengeful authority. By reinterpreting the role and character of the husband, Boaistuau can readily exploit the dramatic irony inherent in many of the narrative details. In one of the rare moments of direct discourse, the husband baits his victim with an irresistible invitation: "Mon voisin et amy, je suis vieux et melencolique, comme vous cognoissez; parquoy j'ay besoing desormais de me resjoyr. Je vous prie bien fort, venez souvent boyre et manger avec moy, et usez privément des bien de ma maison comme vous feriez des vostres" (128). Later, when pretending to leave on a long trip at the request of the Duc, he entrusts his coffer of treasures to his wife, claiming that "il la luy laissoit pour survenir à ses necessitez" (130). But since the trip is feigned, the coffer is no longer a symbol of trust, but rather an invitation to the wife to compromise herself irrevocably. Likewise, on the day of his departure, the endless caresses are not signs of affection, but rather "c'estoient les faveurs du crocodile qui applaudit quand il veut decevoir" (130).

The distinctions between the two versions are evident: for Bandello the narrative events are all functional and serve to lead to the climax of the story. Boaistuau, on the other hand, prefers to exploit the dramatic possibilities of these events, as further illustrated by a comparison of two major episodes. In the spying scene, Bandello's protagonist first becomes aware of the truth:

> Ora avvene che essendo il marito venuto di Savoia a casa nel principio del mese di luglio, che egli un giorno si mise ad una finestra de la sua camera che guardava sovra un bellissimo giardino che era fuor de la ròcca. La donna col suo amante di poco avanti cena se n'andò nel giardino per lo sportello del soccorso, e quivi sotto un pergolato seco passeggiando, non credendo esser da persona visti, piú volte amorosamente lo basciò, e il giovine due e tre fiate le pose le mani in seno toccandole amorosamente le poppe e esco lascivamente senza rispetto veruno scherzando. Vide il marito da la finestra tutti quegli atti disonesti e fieramente se ne turbò, entrando in còlera grandissima; ma come quello che era prudentissimo, dissimulò lo sdegno che aveva... (I, 791)

Bandello's use of the formulaic "ora avvenne che," frequent in his stories, suggests the discovery to be purely coincidental and the presence of the husband as witness is quickly dismissed in favor of a description of the lovers in the garden.

Boaistuau suggests the same information, but reverses the details in order to change the perspective:

> Arrivé au jardin et acertené de l'indisposition de monsieur, il commença à continuer ses anciennes privautez avec la damoiselle, et la baisa et rebaisa par plusieurs fois, jusques à luy mettre la main au sein et à user d'autres petits preparatifs d'amours qui ne doivent estre permis avec telle privauté qu'au seul mary. Mais ce pendant qu'ils se donnoient là du bon temps, le mary ne dormoit pas, lequel estoit sorty de sa chambre passé à deux heures et estoit monté en la plus haute tour de son chasteau à une petite fenestre treillissée, de laquelle il pouvoit voir tout ce qui se faisoit au circuit de sa maison. Et avisant lors toutes ces caresses, il n'attendoit sinon que le gentil-homme se meist en devoir de passer outre à fin de descharger sa mortelle colere sur tous deux. (HT IV, 128-129)

By feigning illness, the husband has set his trap, and the two victims readily fall into it. But the emphasis is not upon the activity in the garden; Boaistuau stresses rather the tower window, the significant detail that the husband has purposely left his room, the rage which overcomes him. Making the husband the central character of the tale, Boaistuau is concerned with his actions, and these are always calculated, never the result of chance or coincidence.

It is again chance ("ora avvenne") which creates for Bandello the incident that precipitates the climax of the story by allowing the husband to outwit his wife:

> Ora avvenne, del mese di settembre, che il duca di Savoia si ritrovò in Turino e per alcuni affari mandò a chiamar il marito di cotesta donna. Egli alora si pensò esser venuta l'occasione di coglier a l'improviso il gallo e la gallina su l'ova. (I, 792)

But the more artful and insidious mind of Boaistuau's hero creates this opportunity as part of his plan of vengeance:

> Ce seigneur, ne pouvant plus supporter son mal, outré d'une extreme colere, voyant qu'il n'y avoit ordre de les surprendre (estant présent) se delibera de bien tost

> mourir ou d'y pourvoir, et pour mieux executer son vouloir il va contrefaire une lettre du Duc, desguisant son escriture, et la porta secrettement à la poste luy seul, qui n'estoit gueres esloignée de là, et commanda au postillon qu'il la luy apportast le jour sequent au chasteau et feignist que le Duc la luy envoyoit. (HT IV, 129-130)

The major motifs of the tale of deception are all gathered here: "contrefaire," "deguisant," "secrettement," "feignist." And the ruse is astutely designed in every detail by a mind outraged but curiously lucid even in the grips of an overwhelming passion: Boaistuau insists upon this detail by the verb *se delibera*, just as the repetition of the coordinating conjunction suggests the careful devising of each step of his plan. With relentless determination, the betrayed husband carefully and deliberately plots every detail of his revenge.

As this comparison indicates, Boaistuau's debt to his source may be altogether superficial, as is the case in HT I, III, IV, and VI. These tales are not mere translations. Boaistuau accepts the general story line, but beyond that, he allows himself an absolute freedom. As La Fontaine will state a century later with respect to the liberties he has taken in the writing of his *Contes*:

> L'auteur retranche, il amplifie, il change les incidents et les circonstances, quelquefois le principal événement et la suite; enfin ce n'est plus la même chose, c'est proprement une nouvelle nouvelle; et celui qui l'a inventée aurait bien de la peine à reconnaître son propre ouvrage. [12]

Boaistuau would have readily subscribed to this view. Such terms as "imitation" and "translation" must necessarily be qualified when dealing with his stories. On occasion he follows his source devotedly, as in HT II, but more often he boldly introduces changes in the basic plot line of his source, redefines the relationships of characters and even changes their names. By means of this free interplay of imitation and originality, Boaistuau will of course reserve for himself an important footnote in the annals

---

[12] "Préface" to the "Deuxième partie."

of English literature, for his changes in the Romeo and Juliet theme were translated into English and finally adapted by Shakespeare.

Such artistic freedom seems at times to ignore tradition entirely, as suggested by the general presentation of the *Histoires tragiques*. Unlike writers of the preceding generation, Boaistuau makes no attempt to compose a general setting or framework for his six tales. There is no humanist setting for the stories such as Noël du Fail presents in his *Propos rustiques*, nor an elaborate fiction, as in the *Heptaméron*, whereby Marguerite allows her ten *devisants* to gather at Cauterets. The unifying factor of a framework is altogether absent. Several reasons may be suggested. Most practically, Boaistuau recognizes that he is not composing a complete work. He informs his reader in the "Advertissement" that François de Belleforest will continue the translation of the *Novelle*, and he hopes that "il... fera voir le second Tome bien tost en lumiere, traduit de sa main." Nevertheless, given his stylistic and formal preoccupations, it seems unlikely that Boaistuau would purposely overlook a device which had such currency in the first half of the century, especially since he must have been all the more aware of the value of a framework after publishing the *Histoires des amans fortunez*.

However his method of presentation is a natural outgrowth of the general preoccupations to which the short story form had been subjected up to this time. While both Noël du Fail and Marguerite de Navarre insist upon a more conventional framework for their tales, there are marked differences between the two collections. Given his humanist convictions, Du Fail relates the various tales and anecdotes to a defined attitude and outlook. Marguerite de Navarre affects an ethical distance which allows her *devisants* to argue about a particular situation or event in an effort to arrive empirically at a number of acceptable moral attitudes. She realizes the impracticality of imposing an established general truth because of the variability of person and situation. Therefore, in contrast to the *Propos rustiques*, the *Heptaméron* denies the possibility of a single doctrinal attitude by presenting, instead of one point of view, ten. But in one way such a complex elaboration simultaneuosly limits the effectiveness of the device by negating its value as a means of reference. It is reduced to nothing more than a unifying fiction illustrative of the greatest foe of Renaissance order: diversity.

In this respect Boaistuau is quite closely allied to Marguerite de Navarre: he too recognizes the diversity of individual temperaments. In the presentation of his stories, he can either emphasize this diversity by adding to the number of *devisants* who discuss possible solutions, or else dismiss the device entirely and find his representative group in the actuality of his reading public. Boaistuau opts for the latter choice, concentrates his attention completely on the moral dilemma described by the tale itself, and emphasizes its immediacy by making each "bening lecteur" an added member of an increasingly large group of *devisants*.

As a result of Boaistuau's refusal to adopt a contemporary narrative convention, the story itself is removed from a restrictive exemplary relationship to a pronounced ideal or attitude. It begins to exist by and for itself regardless of the particular ideological persuasion of the author whose views, by virtue of the structuring of the tale, remain implicit rather than being stated openly. The author is beginning to disappear from the realm of the narrative. He no longer maintains a directive function such as Des Périers and Noël du Fail assumed by allowing their words to be interspersed in the story. At the same time the reader, in his role of *devisant*, is effectively involved in the situation developed in the tale. He does not sit down to mere entertainment, nor does he await the solutions proposed by the authoritative voice of the author. Art must henceforth assume the task of the reliable narrator.

CHAPTER II

THE TRAGICAL AND SENTIMENTAL TALES

...les fables et histoires
Pleines de morts et de malheurs notoires...

—Héroet, *La Parfaicte Amye*

Describing the great success of Bandello's tales in France, Gustave Reynier suggests that the successive volumes of the *Histoires tragiques* appealed to readers who relished the frequent accounts of bloodshed, violence and death:

> Beaucoup de drames domestiques, intéressant surtout de nobles familles: adultères et homicides, vengeances barbares d'époux outragés, incestes, viols, infanticides. Presque partout du sang répandu, et presque toujours c'est l'amour qui appelle la mort. On tue pour laver son honneur, on tue dans le délire de la jalousie, on frappe en aveugle, et parfois des innocents paient pour les coupables. La passion amoureuse fait mourir de regrets et elle fait mourir de joie.[1]

In examining Boaistuau's volume, however, one finds that the violence upon which Reynier insists is not the predominant aspect of the collection. While it is true that death threatens or occurs in each tale, Boaistuau's interest, as seen in HT IV, is not primarily in the act of brutality itself. Albert-Marie Schmidt offers another definition of the form which, while more

---

[1] *Le Roman sentimental avant L'Astrée* (Paris: Colin, 1908), pp. 162-163.

THE TRAGICAL AND SENTIMENTAL TALES 49

general than Reynier's, fits more specifically the examples selected by Boaistuau: "récits émouvants d'intempérance amoureuse." [2] Boaistuau's stories present six views of love, ranging from a pure and chaste devotion to a raging and jealous passion which seeks vengeance at any cost. The scope of his thematic interest suggests the various effects of passion as it threatens all sense of honor, duty, devotion, and humanity. Such is Boaistuau's experiment, as he allows his reader to consider and to judge love both as an honorable and noble passion and as a "malheureux vice" which "ne cesse de ramper par toutes les plus saines parties du corps humain, jusques à ce qu'il ayt engendré en noz cœurs un tige si puant et infaict que le fruit qui en resort est l'entiere corruption de noz vies et de noz ames" (HT II, 47). Boaistuau is less concerned with those manifestations of cruelty, which he nevertheless depicts graphically, than with the sobering realization that emerges from these descriptions: man's helplessness before passion. At a time when his contemporaries are concerned with the irreconcilable conflict of various ethical theories — the humanist ethic, the courtly ethic, and traditional Christian morality — Boaistuau insists upon the limitations inherent in each of these systems by demonstrating their inadequacy in dealing with the common affliction of every man.

The structure of the individual tales depends mainly upon their proximity either to the pole of violent passion or to that of noble selfless love. Two major groups can thus be discerned. The first, which may be called the "tragical tale," conforms in content most faithfully to Reynier's definition. These stories progress steadily to the final *trait* which, however, is no longer humorous, as in the case of the *Cent Nouvelles nouvelles* and many of Des Périers' stories, but rather violence and bloodshed. The tales in this group (HT II, IV, V) are comparatively short. The plot, devoid of elaborations and complications, follows a linear development, culminating in the final horror of the conclusion.

The tragical tale follows a general tripartite development, even allowing for certain variations in the three sections in

---

[2] "Histoires tragiques," *Nouvelle Revue française* (1961), 486.

HT V. In this instance HT II is the clearest example of the general structure of the tales in this group. The introductory section locates the action temporally and geographically, and introduces the main theme: the destructive force of Mahomet's overwhelming passion. The central portion balances the first as Mustapha tries rationally to dissuade Mahomet from his obsession. The third and final segment relates the brutal murder of Hyrenée. Although the skeletal frame seems rather meagre, Boaistuau admits variations within each part to avoid a simple narration of events and to conceal the linear development of the action from Mahomet the conqueror to Mahomet the conquered.

The first third of the story portrays the gradual deterioration of Mahomet from the fierce warrior "de nature si terrible, cruelle et austere" (HT II, 51), who seized and occupied Constantinople, to the dissolute and indolent sultan who emerges three years later because he "laissoit... escouler sa vie comme effeminé" (51). The swift and complete change is not unusual in Boaistuau's narrative style, for all of his unfortunate heroes, especially those in the tragical tales, are victims of a passion that ravages their whole being with merciless rapidity. They all have a weakness, and Mahomet's is that he is "lascif outre mesure" (50). Boaistuau's emphasis here is not solely upon his lust, but also that this lust is excessive and uncontained. The lack of "mesure" is one of the greatest sins of which his gallery of tragic heroes is guilty, and this tale serves as an example of the dangers incurred by the refusal of moderation. From the lack of "mesure" results a spiritual disorder which eventually destroys the individual. Nevertheless this decline is rapid in this portion of the text, and to make it more credible as well as to emphasize the far-reaching effects of Mahomet's passion and the passage of time which occurs in this initial section — which spans the years from the fall of Constantinople to the battle of Belgrade in 1456 — Boaistuau depicts a gradual and steady deterioration by implication. A parallel development occurs in the political realm with the increasing disorder and confusion in the kingdom once Mahomet "commença à mettre en oubly tout ce qui appartenoit à l'ornement et decoration de son empire" (50). Thus the portrait of a man entirely abandoned to lust is heightened by the description of the disintegration of civil order which begins as murmurs of discontent among his people and grows over a period of three years to treasonous outcries, while the sultan is increasingly "ensevely en ses delices" (51).

Against this portrait of a character devastated by the debilitating effects of a cancerous passion, Boaistuau presents the second and central portion of the tale. He departs from the more traditional development of the tripartite narrative structure, as Des Périers employs it for example, by composing a movement in complete contrast to the first in order to intensify the portrait he has just presented. Changing to a first-person narrative, Boaistuau gives the words to Mustapha, Mahomet's confidant, "un homme genereux," that is, a man of honor who stands therefore in complete contrast to his master. In strict terms of plot development, Mustapha is to point out to Mahomet the error of his ways. But in fact the task is no easy one, and Mustapha must summon forth all of his powers of rhetoric, in which he has fortunately been thoroughly schooled. His speech is a formal discourse and follows closely all the traditional rules for the *inventio*. It will be useful to examine this speech in some detail as an example of the skillful accommodation of oratorical rhetoric to a form that is gradually assuming a new literary and artistic expression as it moves away from the realm of popular entertainment.

The purpose of the various divisions of the *inventio* is to make a proposal logically sound and therefore irrefutable. The whole truth is presented, but rather than stated in an abrupt and direct fashion, it is gradually and subtly insinuated. The introductory section, the *exordium* or *proemium*, engages the attention of the listener and induces a frame of mind such that he will be favorably disposed to the ensuing arguments:

> Je ne doute point, monseigneur, que je ne vous doive sembler par trop presomptueux ou temeraire, vous manifestant si librement les conceptions de mon ame; mais nostre ancienne nourriture, le devoir de ma conscience, avec l'experience que vous avez tousjours eue de ma fidelité, m'ont si bien forcé que, ne pouvant plus commander à moy mesme, j'ay esté contraint (par je ne sçay quel eguillon de vertu) vous manifester les choses que

> le temps et la necessité vous feront trouver bonnes; encore que (peut estre) ayant maintenant les yeux bandez du voile de vostre desordonnée affection, ne les puissiez digerer ou prendre en bonne part. (HT II, 52)

The grave import of the speech is translated by the single complex sentence which comprises the whole introduction and affects a tone of apologetic humility as Mustapha anticipates in self-accusation each possible rebuttal of his master. He accuses himself of presumption; he accuses himself of audacious disrespect for daring to reproach his 'emperor.' But his words carry a double force: apology couches accusation. And in the last present participial phrase, uttered as a type of parenthetical addendum, the apologetic becomes imputative and denunciatory as Mahomet is accused of his crime: allowing a passion to exceed all bounds ("vostre desordonnée affection") and to blind him ("les yeux bandez") to its far-reaching effects upon his realm.

Having ingratiated himself at least superficially with the sultan, Mustapha moves into the second part of his discourse, the *narratio*, which exposes the major facts in a more direct manner. He criticizes the life Mahomet had led for three years. He opens his eyes to the revolt and conspiracy raging throughout the empire. He indicates the cause of this "mutation:" his obsession with Hyrenée has brought about his decline from a former "generosité et grandeur." To conclude this development, Mustapha laments the loss of that nobility which created the empire:

> La gloire de voz ancestres et majeurs, acquise par tant de sang, entretenue par si grande prudence, conservée par si heureux conseil, ne se represente-t-elle point quelque fois devant vous? La memoire de leurs memorables victoires, n'a-t-elle point encore touché le marteau de vostre conscience? La magnanimité et valeur par laquelle ils se sont immortalisez et faict retentir leur nom par tout le monde, est-elle esteincte en vous? Leurs trophées et monumens, gravez par tous les angles de la terre, sont-ils jà effacez du siege de vostre memoire? Mais où est maintenant l'ardent desir qui bouillonnoit en vous dès vostre enfance de rendre l'Italie tributaire et vous faire couronner à Rome Empereur tant d'Orient que d'Occident? Ce n'est pas le chemin d'amplifier vostre empire, ains de le restraindre; ce n'est pas le conserver, mais le diminuer et mettre en proye. (HT II, 53)

THE TRAGICAL AND SENTIMENTAL TALES

By a series of rhetorical questions, Mustapha summarizes in a triple accumulation of participiat phrases the history of the creation of the empire — the sacrifices to acquire it, the prudence and judgment to maintain it — and isolates those qualities of magnanimity and valor which have assured the immortality and fame of the Ottomans as symbolized by the monuments raised to their glory. This is the heritage that Mahomet has repudiated since casting aside his youthful ambitions in order to give himself "en proye à une simple femme." The series of questions are aptly answered in the final antithetical opposition *(amplifier : restraindre, conserver : diminuer)* which stands out in marked contrast by the abruptness and directness of the two statements phrased in the most simple declarative form devoid of the subordinating clauses and phrases which adorned the preceding section. The rapidity of the concluding sentence announces the inevitable fall of Mahomet's imperial power by the denial of his noble heritage.

The long central section, the *argumentatio* or *probatio*, elaborates upon a theme introduced in the *narratio*: the honorable and victorious tradition of Mahomet's ancestry. Here the praise of the sultan's forebears and a descriptive summary of their deeds — a standard *topos* of the panegyric — serve to chastise through a long series of examples which range from the valor and bravery of "Otoman premier tronc de [sa] genereuse famille" down to Amurat (Murad II), the present sultan's father. The following is an extract:

> Passeray-je sous silence les vertueux exploicts de ton ayeul Mahomet, lequel conquesta la Macedonne, fist sentir le trenchant de ses armes jusques à la mer Yonique, sans mettre en compte les admirables expeditions qu'il fist contre les Lydiens et Ciliciens? Mais maintenant je ne puis esveiller la memoire de ton pere Amurat sans douleur, lequel, par l'espace de quarante ans, a faict trembler la mer et la terre sous la fureur de sa main forte, prenant une si cruelle vengeance des Grecs que la memoire des playes en seigne encores à present...
> (HT II, 54)

The initial paralipsis serves to direct attention to the exploits of Mahomet's namesake, who, along with his successor, Mahomet's father and predecessor, are both cast as veritable epic heroes. Not hesitating to exaggerate in order to persuade more effectively, Mustapha employs various devices to build this historical summary in a steady crescendo up to the reign of the present ruler. The use of metonomy ("fist sentir le trenchant de ses armes") and the three conceits ("faire trembler la mer...," "la memoire des playes en seigne...," "la fureur de sa main forte") lend an epic tone to the passage and suggest a heroism which is blatantly contradicted under the rule of the present sultan. The *argumentatio* therefore presents evidence to substantiate the case and to prove it by implication. Following the same progression as the preceding section, of which this is an elaboration, Mustapha eloquently characterizes Mahomet as the very antithesis of the heroic grandeur of his ancestors.

The *refutatio* invalidates any ideas that the opposition might still entertain in defense of his actions. Mustapha suggests again that an indolent life dedicated to sensual pleasure did not build an empire and can now only weaken and destroy it. While the *argumentatio* concentrates on the past, the *refutatio* looks towards the future. By means of hypothetical conjecture, Mustapha foresees the present underground murmurings of discontent gaining momentum and force within the empire as Rome and the Christian monarchs, joined by the Persians and Egyptians, attack the vulnerable sultan. The inevitable conclusion of Mahomet's present course of action can logically be only the utter devastation of his entire kingdom.

The conclusion *(peroratio)* assumes that the adversary is so thoroughly convinced of all of the preceding that he will readily avail himself of the chance to channel his actions in a new direction:

> Reprens doncques desormais, monseigneur, tes esprits, et rapelle la raison, laquelle par si longues années tu as bannye d'avec toy. Esveille-toy de ce profond sommeil, lequel t'a sillé les yeux. Suys, suys la trace de tes majeurs, lesquels ont tousjours mieux aimé une journée d'honneur que cent ans de vie en mespris. Entends au gouvernement de ton empire. Laisse ceste vie effeminée et reprens le sentier de ton ancienne generosité et vertu; et si tu ne peux tout en un coup retrancher ceste ardeur amoureuse qui mine ainsi ton cueur, modere-la peu à

> peu, et donne quelque esperance à ton peuple qui te pense perdu...Ou bien si ceste Grecque te plaist tant, qui t'empesche que tu ne la puisses mener avec toy aux expeditions? pourquoy ne puis-tu jouyr ensemble de sa beauté et de l'exercice des armes?...tu jugeras par effect combien les plaisirs interrompuz sont plus grands que ceux qu'on reçoit à toute heure.... (HT II, 56-57)

All of the motifs and themes are drawn together and summarily stated with the full force of contrast between what is and what should be: Mahomet's blindness ("sillé les yeux") to his heritage ("la trace de tes majeurs"); his indolence ("ceste vie effeminée") which has betrayed his "generosité et vertu." And finally Mustapha suggests the guidelines of an ethic of reason and moderation which have been so long ignored by his master. As if acknowledging his own precepts once he has brought Mahomet to the point of renouncing Hyrenée, Mustapha backs down from his imperious position of demanding strict obedience to either the code of military honor or love, to glory or defeat. To avoid the elimination of one extreme by the imposition of another, he suggests in conclusion a comfortable compromise, neatly summarized in the form of a maxim, whereby Mahomet might regain honor with little sacrifice.

This lengthy monologue is one of two examples in the *Histoires tragiques* of the structural form of the *inventio*. It is indicative of the way in which traditional formalistic devices are skillfully woven into the narrative to enhance the style. Rather than being simply a prolix digression, it is thoroughly integrated within the narrative progression in order to broaden the base of the story by the inclusion of an historical perspective and to give full and elaborate expression to the central dramatic interest of the tale: the heightened psychological tension resulting from the necessity of human choice.

The result of this choice is the subject of the third and final part of the tale. The concluding section, which resumes the rapid third-person narrative and leads directly to the brutal slaying of Hyrenée, illustrates a definite trait of the shorter tragical tales where the central interest is not directed to probing the tormented mind of the protagonist. Mahomet does not surmise and weigh the values and shortcomings of either decision.

Boaistuau suggests that the sultan is briefly victim to "une furieuse bataille en son ame," that the central discourse has dispelled his former blindness and allowed him to recognize that "Mustapha luy avoit dit verité," and further that he still experiences supreme difficulty in trying to dispel "la beauté de la Grecque se representant devant ses yeux" (58). However the decision is quickly made, and without any ponderous effort on the part of Mahomet. The story moves swiftly through a brief series of events to arrive at the inevitable conclusion.

Clearly suspense is not the purpose of the tale. In fact, as he does in HT IV, Boaistuau again eliminates suspense by revealing the conclusion. Once Mahomet has ordered Hyrenée that "elle se aornast de tous les plus riches joyaux et somptueux accoutrements qu'elle eust jamais porté," Boaistuau intercedes to tell the reader that "la pauvrette obeist, ne sçachant point que c'estoit l'appareil de ses funerailles" (58). The irrevocable decision has not only been made but also revealed to the reader. Therefore if suspense were his purpose, the premature disclosure of the conclusion could place the dramatic interest only upon the means of execution. This seems to be the obvious purpose of Bandello's version. The same anticipatory phrase occurs in the Italian original: "non sapendo la miserella che apparecchiava i suoi funerali" (I, 135). But Bandello also adds three concluding sentences to the tale which are absent from the French version:

> Potete adunque vedere che in Maometto non era amore né pietá. Ché se piú non voleva trastullarsi con la greca, non la deveva il barbaro crudele ammazzare. Ma tali sono i costumi turcheschi. E chi volesse le particulari crudeltá da questo Maometto usate narrare, averebbe troppo che fare, essendo innoverabili. (I, 136)

Bandello is interested in presenting a chapter on Turkish customs and in depicting the special cruelty practiced by Mahomet at a time when the Turkish menace was an obsessive reality.

Boaistuau's omission of these final lines is significant, especially in a tale which follows so closely the original version. His purpose is not to relate a suspenseful story nor to present an extract from a catalog of foreign customs. He is concerned specifically with the meaning of the choice Mahomet has made and this he emphasizes in a final historical note:

> Soudain apres, pensant descharger le reste de sa colere, dressa un camp de bien quatre vingts à cent mille hommes, par le secours duquel il penetra toute la Boussine, assiegea Belgrade, où la fortune luy fut tant contraire qu'il fut mis en routte et perdit la memorable bataille contre les Chrestiens... (HT II, 60)

While Boaistuau concludes with an historical truth, it does not have the particularizing and limiting quality of the conclusion in the Italian original. The statement is not a convenient means of ending the story, but suggests rather a final dramatic irony, especially as it is juxtaposed to the boast of Mahomet after the murder of Hyrenée: "Cognoissez maintenant si vostre Empereur sçait commander à ses affections ou non" (59). Mahomet has presumably followed the strategy of his counselor only to be crushed by the Christians.

Initially this defeat appears simply to thwart Mahomet's efforts to recover the past glory of the Ottoman empire. But Boaistuau is not writing a piece of Christian propaganda; he is far more interested in the implications of Mahomet's brutal act, which is provoked by a sentence in Mustapha's *discours*: ..."et si tu ne peux tout en un coup retrancher ceste ardeur amoureuse qui mine ainsi ton cueur, modere-la peu à peu." Recognizing the rhetoric of Mustapha's speech, Mahomet concludes that the *ardeur* of which his slave speaks is a metonymical reference to Hyrenée, and, quite logically, he acts according to the literal sense of the verb *retrancher*. The sentence occurs, however, in the *peroratio* where Mustapha is speaking in a direct and forthright manner. He uses the word *ardeur* in no other sense than "passion," that passion which has enfeebled the sultan, and the verb *retrancher* in the sense of "curtail." His meaning is clear: he urges Mahomet not to cut off Hyrenée's head, but to curb the debilitating passion of love.

Boaistuau's version removes the tale from the restrictive realm of a *fait divers* to insist upon the more generally applicable precepts which it illustrates. Mahomet's choice is not between self-indulgence and military honor, not between lust and continence, but rather between any extreme and moderation. The important verb in Mustapha's appeal is *modere*. Portrayed initially as acting "outre mesure," Mahomet is defeated because he remains true to character.

In comparison with the tripartite tragical tale, the other three stories in Boaistuau's collection (HT I, III, VI) might be called "sentimental tales." Whereas the first group leads ultimately to a cruel act of vengeance, misfortune is generally unwarranted in the sentimental tale and occurs only by the act of a contrary fortune. Thus HT III is qualified as the story of "la piteuse et infortunée mort de deux amants" (62). But the conclusion may also be happy, for Boaistuau portrays not only a destructive and lascivious passion, but also a noble and virtuous love which ultimately overcomes all obstacles to manifest itself fully in all of its purity. No longer does an unrestrained passion direct the action to a catastrophic conclusion by the annihilation of the object of this lust. The sentimental tale gives prominence to the woman as an object of virtue while the lover assumes a more subservient role demanded by his necessary respect for his beloved. Honor assumes heroic proportions and is guarded even at the expense of one's life. While an Edouart may still be victim to an uncontrollable lust (HT I), his love is not consummated until he recognizes and reveres Ælips as a "portraict et exemplaire de chasteté" rather than simply a means of satisfying his desire. The Duchesse de Savoie (HT VI) may pursue the ideal image she has created of Mandozze, but she is duly punished for the very thought of adultery. The sentimental tale does not progress to a catastrophic finale, but rather to the realization of an idyllic vision by means of the successful suppression of base motives. This is a world in which even death assumes a positive value as the only means of uniting an ideal couple (HT III).

In the sentimental tale, Boaistuau abandons the narrative concentration of the tragical tale for a structure and form more compatible with the elaborate rhetorical flourishes that adorn the distinctive thematic developments. A genuine lyric mood pervades the pages of these stories in which lamentations, complaints, and consolations proliferate once a contrary fatality challenges the realization of a perfect happiness. The sentimental tale is therefore comparatively lengthy and the length of the stories necessitates certain variations to maintain interest. Complexity replaces the steady linear development of the tragical tales as the plot becomes circuitous and peripatetic, no longer fitting into the structural pattern of introduction of situation — complication — conclusion. Multiplicity of detail replaces the simplicity of a direct plot progression. The narrative is embellished by lengthy oratorical speeches and lyric complaints in which the characters bemoan the unwarranted misery which fortune inflicts upon mankind. Rather than the compact structure of the tragical tale, the sentimental tale is therefore expansive. The writer seems anxious to break away from the more restrictive function of mere story-telling and to allow himself every freedom for refined and elaborate artistic expression.

The story of Mandozze and the Duchesse de Savoie, the last and longest of the six tales in the collection, most fully illustrates the range of narrative freedom possible in the sentimental tale. As in the case of HT IV, Boaistuau's development of the tale differs considerably from the Italian original, and his distinct treatment of character and theme ultimately justifies the numerous additions he makes to his source.

In his prefatory comments, Bandello underscores the admirable qualities of the passion of love when experienced by the noble soul:

> ...vi narrerò una mirabil istoria che giá da un cavaliero spagnuolo, essendo io altre volte in Ispagna, mi fu narrata; da la quale si comprende quanto poderose sieno le forze de l'amore, quando in cor gentile egli le sue facelle accesse avventa, e senza fine quello arde e dolcemente strugge. (II, 112)

Against a background of the all-powerful strength of passion, Bandello exploits the traditional theme of the painful joy of love. Boaistuau eliminates the lyric antithesis to concentrate solely on the pain caused by a love which is no longer noble, but corrupt:

> Entre toutes les plus griefves passions qui assiegent ordinairement les esprits humains, l'amour a tousjours tenu

> presques le premier lieu, lequel, depuis qu'il s'est une
> fois emparé de quelque subject genereux, il ensuit le
> naturel de l'humeur corrompu de ceux qui ont la fievre,
> qui, prenant son origine au cueur, s'achemine incurable
> par toutes les autres sensibles parties du corps humain.
> (HT VI, 171)

Boaistuau depicts love as a debilitating disease which, as emphasized by the extended military metaphor, perniciously attacks even the noble soul. The exemplary story of grief and suffering begins to move toward the pole of the tragic.

The difference in approach to the story is clearly indicated by the incident of the Duchesse's "illness" and recovery. Bandello employs what is basically a comic device. After the duchessa "suffers" under the influence of Appiano's drugs, which induce a deathly pallor, and after she makes her last confession to the Archbishop of Turin, Appiano hangs an image of San Giacomo above her bed, surrounds the image with linens soaked in wine, sets fire to them, and proclaims a miracle which overwhelms with tearful piety the two maids sleeping in the chamber:

> Le due buone vecchie, veggendo l'imagine dar la benedizione a la duchessa, e quelle pezze di lino che ardevano e facevano un bellissimo splendore dinanzi al santo, e che quel fuoco pareva di varii e bei colori, credettero fermamente quello esser san Giacomo maggiore, fratello di san Giovanni evangelista, e divotamente s'inginocchiarono, piangendo per divozione. (II, 119)

The duchessa's rapid recovery is sufficient testimony to the effective truth of the miracle and her joyful husband is easily duped into allowing her to make a pilgrimage to Spain where she will meet at last the man she loves but whom she has never seen. Bandello is relying on the comic device of the clever duping the gullible and unsuspecting. It is a narrative convenience in order to bring about the encounter of the duchessa and don Giovanni, but wholly in accord with the perspective Bandello offers at the beginning of the tale.

Boaistuau's more serious theme precludes the comic of the miracle and instead exploits pathos to a great extent. Appian's drugs again induce a death-like state from which the Duchesse is saved by antidotes. But during the whole scene, the Duc is most sympathetically portrayed. While his wife is ill, he spends long hours at her bedside bemoaning her imminent death: "le pauvre Duc...ne la voulut abandonner jusques à son resveil, lequel ce pendant ne cessa de prier Dieu pour la santé de sa loyale espouse" (HT VI, 182). The scene portrays the Duc as a tender and affectionate husband, completely devoted to his wife in what he believes to be her final hours. The irony is evident: he still reveres her as a "loyale espouse," but he is no longer the deserving dupe, no longer a character of comedy.

All of the additions in the French version pointedly insinuate the Duchesse's exploitation of her husband's love and faith in a series of scenes that are maudlin in their description. The Duchesse makes every effort to relay graphically the heightened agony of her feigned illness: "Et lors la Duchesse, esveillée comme de quelque pesant sommeil, tournant les yeux en la teste, avec un estrange tremblement de tous ses membres..." (182). And again, the dramatic effect is intensified by developing the Bandello version which relates that "la duchessa, levatasi di letto, si mise innanzi a la figura in ginocchione, pregandola che degnasse guarirla, che le faceva voto d'andar a visitar a piede le sue sante reliquie" (II, 119). Boaistuau "translates" this narrative passage into a "simulée oraison" beginning with an apostrophe to the "Glorieux Apostre" to save her from death.

Another significant distinction in the two versions, the description of the three days the Duchesse spends in the castle of Mandozze, again suggests the divergent interpretations which the two writers give to the tale. In both there is an evocation of the neo-platonic notion of the origin of love — the transmission of love through the eyes, a type of subtle humor which infects the whole body. Bandello calls this an "invisibile ed amoroso veleno" which inflames both the duchessa and don Giovanni. But suddenly he inserts: "Ora, che che se ne fosse cagione, la duchessa, levatasi il quattro giorno a buon'ora, preso congedo da la signora Isabella, si partí con la sua compagnia" (II, 123). Bandello offers no justification for the duchessa's departure, although it is assumed from the ensuing encounter on the road to Compostella that it is a matter of feminine wile which ultimately succeeds in forcing don Giovanni to declare his love and propose that she return after the pilgrimage.

Boaistuau's development of the love intrigue creates an increasingly frustrated heroine. The actions of his characters generally follow a clear logic, and he takes advantage of a sentence in the original tale to clarify the motivation of both characters. On the Duchesse's arrival, Boaistuau tells us that Mandozze "ne fut si grue qu'il ne cogneust incontinent que la Duchesse, en l'aage où elle estoit, n'eust point esté tant liberale de son labeur que faire un tel voyage à pied sans quelque autre respect" (185). But he conceals these suspicions and plays the role of a courteous and gracious host. Immediately any ensuing action is the responsibility of the Duchesse herself, not of Mandozze, as in the Italian story. The Duchesse has accomplished what she had convinced Æmilie she had to do:

> ...adjoustant...qu'elle ne l'aymoit point impudiquement ne pour esperance qu'elle eust de satisfaire à quelque vouloir lascif, mais seulement pour en avoir la veue, laquelle...luy apporteroit tel contentement que son mal prendroit fin. (HT VI, 177)

However "la veue" only incites desire, and while Mandozze is concerned with extending all due hospitality to her, the Duchesse finds no satisfaction:

> La pauvre Duchesse, apres avoir manifesté par gestes et contenances exterieures au seigneur Mandozze quel estoit l'interieur de son cueur, sans en recevoir la satisfaction qu'elle desiroit, delibera, ayant sejourné trois jours en son chasteau, partir le matin au desceu du chevalier pour parfaire son voyage. (HT VI, 187)

Boaistuau insists upon pointing out the Duchesse's guilt as she clearly belies her former pronouncement to Æmilie and ensnares herself increasingly in a web of guilty passion, a passion which ignores that very nobility which she is granted from the beginning of the story. The two versions of the tale have placed the responsibility for this love on different characters. Both are consistent within their own defined terms. Bandello reports the seemingly impossible love of an ideal couple as don Giovanni and the duchessa repeatedly encounter obstacles preventing the realization of their love, while Boaistuau writes the drama of an exemplary woman guilty of adultery. Although there is no consummation of this love, the Duchesse is guilty by virtue of her desire, and it is this guilt that justifies her suffering in the succeeding portions of the tale.³

All of the ensuing action depends upon this distinction of the guilty or responsible character. In Bandello's version, it is don Giovanni who proposes that the duchessa visit him on her return: "Almeno, signora mia, fatemi questa grazia, che al ritorno mi sia concesso come donna reale e come quella che lo vale onorarvi" (II, 124); in the French tale, the plan is more vividly suggested by the Duchesse: ..."je recognois ma faute et vous supplie de l'oublier, à la charge qu'à mon retour de mon voyage de sainct Jacques, je vous en feray telle amende et useray de telle satisfaction en vostre endroit, au lieu mesme où j'ay commis la faute que, demeurant vostre prisonniere pour quelque temps, je ne partiray de voz mains que je n'aye recogneu par une penitence agreable la grandeur de mon peché" (HT VI, 190). It is this difference which makes the timely arrival of the Duc in Compostella not merely an accident of fate, but a dramatic appearance which precipitates a genuine crisis within the soul of the Duchesse. Instead of resulting in Bandello's frustrated don Giovanni, especially since the duca is far from being portrayed as an ideal or even admirable character, the Duchesse is forced to choose between "honneur" and "affection": ..."elle commença à cognoistre que Dieu resistoit à sa lascive volonté, et qu'ayant pris compassion de la bonté du bon Duc son espoux, il n'avoit voulu permettre qu'il eust esté ainsi desloyalement deceu" (HT VI, 192). The Duchesse is a rich character, capable of remorse and repentance as she recognizes "les limites de l'honneur" and vows to forget Mandozze. The duchessa remains a more traditional

---

[3] See the article "Adultery" in the *New Catholic Encyclopedia* (ed. 1967) which states that "though the Decalogue already forbade adulterous desires, Jesus places such desires on the same level with adultery itself." Cf. Matthew 5.28: "But I say unto you, that whosoever looketh on a woman to lust after her hath committed adultery with her already in his heart."

character who, "ancor che in vista si mostrasse allegra, era nondimeno fieramente ne l'animo attristata" (II, 125). She is simply the stock figure suffering from unrequited love.

At this point it will be of value to recall the conclusion of Söderhjelm's oft-quoted definition of the short story: "L'événement raconté aboutit à une catastrophe inattendue ou surprenante...A l'origine tout est concentré dans l'effet de cette pointe... Plus tard, et peu à peu, l'étude psychologique gagne en importance." [4] This distinction is reflected in the two forms of the short story in Boaistuau's collection: the catastrophic conclusion of the tragical tale and the 'psychological study' which is the dominant concern of the sentimental tale. In place of the rapid narrative of the tragical tale, the sentimental tale gives full and detailed expression to a character's feelings and emotional states. In this respect the short story joins a long poetic tradition:

> If the troubadours gave literary form to an erotic fantasy, setting it in the context of a courtly society and giving desire a social goal; if Dante, under the influence of medieval Christianity, sublimated it into a transcendent vision of existence, Petrarch used it to express the drama of his inner life, the drama of a conscience no longer firmly rooted in a transcendent absolute. [5]

This "drama of ... inner life" is the special domain of the sentimental tale; it is in this area that it is richly "psychological."

Bandello's debt to this tradition is evident when he describes the emotional state of don Giovanni after the duchessa's departure:

> Nondimeno egli sofferiva grande ed indicibil pena, e tuttavia gli pareva che le sue fiamme vie piú s'infiammassero e il desio di veder la duchessa ogni momento d'ora piú crescesse, di modo che lo sfortunato amante, ardendo, agghiacciando, sperando e disperando, e piú che mai amando, menava una pessima vita. (II, 126)

---

[4] *La Nouvelle française au XVe siècle* (Paris: Champion, 1910), p. x.
[5] Jules Gelernt, *The World of Many Loves: The Heptaméron of Marguerite de Navarre* (Chapel Hill: The University of North Carolina Press, 1966), p. 38.

The crisis he experiences is set forth in traditional antithetical terms which express the plight of the lover separated from his lady. But Bandello remains descriptive, for he is more concerned, even in his longest stories, with the steady and rapid progression of the narrative. Boaistuau, on the other hand, emphasizes and expands upon these moments of crisis. Rather than merely stating the existence of some inner crisis, he sets these moments apart from the narrative, most often by turning them into direct discourse and allowing the character himelf to describe his own misfortune in dialogue and monologue. In these rhetorical addenda, he tries to delve into the tormented mind which gradually and agonizingly realizes the inevitable effects of passion.

In the beginning of Bandello's tale, after Isabella tells the duchessa that Mandozza is "uno dei piú bei giovini che oggidí si sappia" and "un valeroso e compíto cavaliero" (II, 114), the duchessa falls immediately and hopelessly in love and goes off to relate her plight to her maid:

> Era giá la duchessa alquanto accesa de l'amor del cavaliero per le parole che prima, quando era in carretta, aveva udite, come quella che fuor di modo era desiderosa di vederlo. Sentendo poi di questa maniera sí fermamente a la sorella di lui lodarlo, ella largamente il petto a le fiamme amorose aperse e quelle con tanta affezione abbracciò che tutta divenne fuoco. Né ad altra cosa poteva rivolger l'animo che pensar di continovo come potesse don Giovanni vedere, e tanto in questi pensieri si profondava che bene spesso rimaneva quasi come fuor di sé. (II, 114-115)

With greater subtlety which makes this love — an all-important development in the tale — more credible, Boaistuau emphasizes the agonies of the impassioned and tormented soul of the Duchesse. In one of the more felicitous addenda, we can appreciate the obsessive effect of Ysabeau's words upon the Duchesse, and the successive stages of thought as the obsession becomes a vision, and the vision a torturous reality:

> ...la Duchesse, esguillonnée par les nouveaux propos d'Ysabeau, ayant martel en teste, ne pouvoit dormir, et avoit si bien la beauté de ce chevalier incogneu gravée au plus profond de son cueur que, cuidant clorre les

> yeux, il luy sembloit avis qu'il voletoit incessamment devant elle comme quelque fantosme, de sorte que, pour cognoistre ce qui en estoit, elle l'eust volontiers desiré aupres d'elle. Puis tout soudain, apres une honte et crainte entremeslée d'une pudicité longuement par elle observée, avec la fidelité qu'elle avoit au Duc son espoux se presentant devant elle, ensevelissoient du tout son premier conseil, lequel mouroit et prenoit fin aussi tost presque qu'il estoit né. Et combattue ainsi d'une infinité de divers pensers, passa la nuict jusques à ce que le jour commençant à esclairer avec sa lampe ardente les contraignit de se lever. (HT VI, 175-176)

The introduction of the vision is Boaistuau's means of suggesting more vividly the agony of an overwhelming passion. At the same time he establishes the basis for the central crisis of the story — the Duchesse's guilt resulting from her pondered affection for Mandozze — by describing the torment she inevitably experiences once her sense of duty and obligation to the Duc intrudes upon her newborn dream of love.

For several days the Duchesse struggles helplessly against a love over which she has less and less control:

> Quelques jours apres le departement de l'Espagnole, la Duchesse, pensant amortir ce nouveau feu, l'enflammoit d'avantage, et tant plus l'esperance luy manquoit, tant plus luy croissoit son desir; et apres une infinité de divers pensemens, la victoire demeura du costé de l'amour.... (HT VI, 176)

Traditional antitheses suggest her long anguish; but all struggle is in vain, and, with the rapid *chute* of the past definite *(demeura)*, the Duchesse falls victim to an invincible passion.

Quite obviously the type of addition made by Boaistuau in this portion is due to his more serious interpretation of the source story, and his reordering of the details emphasizes the moral crisis. The Duc, who is an obstacle to this love in the French version, is not even present in the first movement of the Italian story where the duchessa recognizes her love for don Giovanni. The only mention of him is in the introduction of the duchessa as "la moglie del duca de la Savoia." His absence essentially limits the tragic potential of the story. Boaistuau's treatment of the theme of adultery necessitates the inclusion of the husband as a major force and temporary deterrent. Bandello later mentions the husband when the duchessa is pleading with Francesco Appiano and explaining the reason for her love: "Voi sapete molto bene che cosa sia esser femina giovane, delicatamente nodrita, e trovarsi maritata con uomo attempato, che, a parlarvi liberamente, nulla o poco vale nei servigi de le donne" (II, 116). Boaistuau admits no such rationalization for her concession to desire. The Duc is not presented as old and enfeebled; indeed it is he who goes out at the request of the king to protect Turin against the German invaders. Again Bandello is exploiting the theme of an obstacle to the beautiful and desirable union of two superlative characters who are noble and handsome, and therefore ideally suited to each other. And by allowing Appiano to suggest the idea of feigning illness, Bandello relieves the duchessa of the responsibility to a certain extent, since she merely begged the doctor for some remedy for her "focoso disio." But once the Duchesse has resolved her torment in Boaistuau's drama, she has accepted the responsibility for her decision and must suffer accordingly.

The changes necessitated by the theme Boaistuau has chosen to develop do not account for the only addenda within the story. A comparison of the passages in narrative and dialogue in the two versions shows that Boaistuau does not forget the lesson of Boccaccio and uses dialogue and monologue to heighten moments of psychological and emotional tension. These passages are the privileged moments of the story, and although they lengthen the tale considerably, it is evident that Boaistuau's major interest lies in these highly rhetorical passages. A great number of speeches in the Bandello story appear to have been added simply to break the steady narrative flow. These sections are most often transcribed by Boaistuau in simple narrative style. At the same time, the French writer, far more preoccupied with the sequences of emotional crises, almost unfailingly expresses these in direct discourse in order to give greater emphasis to the inner drama.

Relating the trip of Isabella and duchessa to Spain, Bandello writes:

> Ora, quando furono vicini a la cittá dove per l'ordinario don Giovanni dimorava, disse la signora Isabella a la duchessa: —Signora mia, noi siamo vicine a due picciole giornate ad una de le cittá del signor mio fratello. Io con licenza vostra mi spignerò innanzi per far accomodar l'alloggiamento per voi e per la compagnia, e dirò, se vi pare, al signor mio fratello che una signora lombarda, che m'ha fatto in casa sua onore, viene ad albergar meco, e non gli manifesterò altrimenti chi voi siete. (II, 121-122)

For Boaistuau these details are basically insignificant. Ysabeau plays a minor role in both versions of the tale. There is no real need to insist upon the preparations for the Duchesse's visit except perhaps to increase the anticipation of the first meeting of the two central characters. But this was not Bandello's plan, for the encounter of the duchessa and don Giovanni is reported in a rapid passage of narrative. As Mendozza and Isabella ride up to the duchessa's coach, Isabella makes the introduction and immediately, as happened when Eurialus first saw Lucretia, the love which sight alone can inspire burns within don Giovanni's soul:

> Don Giovanni smontato da cavallo venne cortesemente a basciarle le mani, come a gentildonna che in Italia avesse di lui la sorella accarezzata, e quella ringraziando, le disse che ella fosse la ben venuta, offerendole quanto poteva e valeva. E cosí offerendosi e ringraziandosi, parve al cavaliero che quella fosse la piú bella ed aggraziata donna che veduta egli avesse giá mai. Ed in quel poco che insieme ragionarono, avvenne per sorte che gli occhi di amendui vista per vista si scontrarono, di tal maniera che se possibil era accrescer al fuoco da la duchessa nuova ésca, quella vista ve n'accrebbe, e il cavaliero restò sí fieramente da lo splendore di quei dui ardentissimi lumi infiammato, che subito si sentí restar dentro a quelli preso, e in lui non esser parte alcuna che per amore de la bellissima peregrina tutta non ardesse. (II, 122-123)

Boaistuau, on the other hand, reverses the mode of presentation in this section of the tale in order to give greater emphasis to the encounter of the Duchesse and Mandozze. He rapidly summarizes the speech by Isabella since it serves no purpose other than to indicate the arrival of the travelers in Spain: ..."l'Espagnole pria la Duchesse ne trouver mauvais si elle envoyoit quelqu'un de ses gens devant l'advertir de leur venue. Ce que la Duchesse luy accorda" (HT VI, 185). The first meeting of the Duchesse and Mandozze, however, requires greater prominence, since their love is the generating force of the story. Therefore Boaistuau presents the encounter in dialogue form and creates a lyric scene reminiscent of a chivalric romance:

> ...le seigneur Mandozze, apres avoir faict bondir trois ou quatre fois son cheval en l'air avec une grace et dexterité merveilleuse, ayant mis pied à terre, luy baisant la main luy dist: "Madame, je croy que si les chevaliers errans du temps passé, qui ont eternisé leur memoire par une infinité de victoires memorables, eussent eu tant d'heur que de rencontrer souvent entre leurs adventures de telles pelerines, ils eussent volontiers abandonné la lance et le morion pour prendre le bourdon et l'escharpe." Et lors la Duchesse...assaillie d'aise, de joye, de crainte et de honte, pour ne faillir à son devoir luy dist: "Et dea, monsieur, si les chevaliers desquels vous parlez eussent senty quelque heur, ainsi que vous dictes, pour la rencontre de telles pelerines, aussi esperons-nous que le sainct à qui nous sommes vouées, en faveur duquel nous entreprenons ce perilleux voyage, nous en sçache gré, autrement nostre peine seroit du tout perdue, et nostre voyage mal employé." (HT VI, 186)

These initial conversations serve in the French version to characterize Mandozze succinctly. His equine gymnastics suggest his valor as a warrior, while his ease and grace on the horse are complemented by the gallant hyperbole of his words. It is a skillful portrait of the ideal hero depicted by word and action. The style is typical of the conversations so prevalent in these tales. The single extended conditional sentence for both statement and reply and the use of the third person to obscure direct first-person compliments serve to create a distance whereby both speakers may flatter according to the conventions befitting their rank without seeming to implicate themselves by any untoward admission.

The reply of the Duchesse is a clear example of Boaistuau's predilection for the subtleties of the game of love which avoid the overt and relish obliquity. At first sight, the duchessa "restò di modo de la bellezza e leggiadria del cavaliero vinta e sí fieramente accesa, che tutta fuor di sé rapita e nel cavaliero trasformata quasi non sepeva muovere il passo" (II, 122). The Duchesse, however, is not quite so willing to reveal her feelings. She replies to Mandozze in a style which Boaistuau calls "attaincte amoureuse," for the emotions which the Duchesse feels are more complex, given the central theme of the story: the struggle between love and honor. Thus she is assailed not only with joy and happiness, but also with shame and fear. Racked by love and desire, she is nevertheless the sister of the king of England, "autant bien nourrie et bien disante que princesse qui regnast de son temps" (HT VI, 186), and her doubts and hesitations bespeak the nobility of her heritage and training. The experiment is to see which side will be victorious. Again such interiorization of conflict becomes a central motif in Boaistuau's stories.

The sixth tale provides numerous examples of this purposeful transfer of narrative into direct discourse. Instead of the narrative statement relating the duchessa's request to leave Turino and make a pilgrimage to Compostella (II, 121), Boaistuau reports the very words of the Duchesse (HT VI, 184) in order to stress this important moment in the story. Her determination to honor a false vow, a lie fabricated so that she might meet Mandozze, further implicates the Duchesse, makes her guilt readily apparent, and ultimately justifies her suffering to atone for her sin. The final movement of the story, the resolution and union of the protagonists, is similarly expanded in the French version as the numerous speeches by the Duchesse and Mandozze provide a lyric duet to celebrate the happiness they have finally won.

These frequent additions of passages in direct discourse allow Boaistuau to exploit fully the emotional potential of each scene. To this same end he employs another device which will become a standard of the romance: the letter. William G. Crane indicates that letter writing became a veritable art during the Renaissance, an art understood as the application of the rules of oratorical rhetoric as a means of achieving ornateness and amplification.

He cites William Fulwood who, in *The Enimie of Idleness* (1568), defined the letter as "an Oration written, conteining the mynd of the Orator, or wryter, thereby to give to understand to him or them absent, the same that should be declared if they were present." [6] It is logical that these rhetorical embellishments should appeal to Boaistuau who gives three examples in his stories (HT I, V, VI). Like the passages in direct discourse, they relate in detail the emotional torment experienced by the characters. This is another instance in which Bandello prefers direct narrative. While the duchessa is languishing imprisoned in her chambers with the sole company of Giulia, the two women decide that some action is necessary to save the duchessa from her plight:

> Conchiusero poi un giorno tra lor due che non era se non benissimo fatto, che l'Appiano andasse a gran giornate in Ispagna a cercar aita da don Giovanni, con quella meglior via que sapeva, ed assicurarlo che la duchessa era falsamente accusata. Fece la duchessa une lettera di credenza di sua mano a don Giovanni. (II, 131)

In Boaistuau's tale, these few lines are transformed into a lengthy letter. [7]

It is clear that in Boaistuau's hands the sentimental tale, characterized by its numerous events, is considerably expanded by the addition of even more incidents, and given greater elaboration through numerous speeches. These addenda, however, are never superfluous. Each incident is significant to the development of the narrative. Here we discover again a difference with the more rapidly composed tales by Bandello, as is made apparent by the treatment of the prison scene. In the Italian version, don Giovanni disguises himself as a friar in order to enter the cell where the duchessa is being kept prisoner and to learn from her the truth of Pancalieri's accusation. But there is

---

[6] *Wit and Rhetoric in the Renaissance* (Gloucester, Mass.: Peter Smith, 1964), p. 77. According to Gustave Reynier, Æneas Sylvius was one of the first to adopt the letter as a means of expressing sentiment in the novel (*op. cit.*, p. 34).
[7] The style of the letter will be discussed in detail in Part Four.

no motivation for this mascarade nor any apparent reason for his doubt. Mendozza left Spain after reproaching himself for not having gone immediately to the aid of the woman he loves:

> ...don Giovanni a l'infortunio de la duchessa pensando e seco l'amore di quella rammentando, che da Turino fin in Galizia a piedi se n'era venuta solo per amor di lui, giudicò grandemente aver errato a non esser subito corso a liberarla e mettere non che lo stato suo a rischio di perderlo, ma di perder la vita e mille, se tante n'avesse. E non si potendo di questo fallo dar pace, si deliberò... usar ogni sforzo per liberar la misera duchessa. (II, 133)

Yet for some reason, this chivalric resolve falters while he is talking to the friar. As if having second thoughts about the purpose of his trip, don Giovanni admits:

> Io ho assai buona informazione come questa signora a gran torto è stata con falsa accusazione aggravata; ma per meglio chiarirmene, vorrei parlar seco, e sotto colore di confessione intender chiaramente il vero. (II, 135)

His hesitations do lead to the prison scene, but the scene itself becomes highly gratuitous since there is no previous indication of doubt or suspicion on the part of the knight. Boaistuau chooses to retain and expand the prison scene as the second major encounter of the two protagonists, but he carefully provides a justification for its inclusion.

Rather than a traditional hero of completely superlative proportions, a knight who willingly risks his life to save a lady in distress, Boaistuau's Mandozze has been presented throughout as a man of a somewhat skeptical nature. He was sufficiently perspicacious to realize that the motive for the Duchesse's long journey to Spain was certainly not a pilgrimage. And after hearing from Appian about Pancalier's plot, Mandozze "commença à avoir quelque mauvaise opinion de la Duchesse, ne pouvant comprendre en son esprit comme le Comte de Pancalier se fust de tant oublié que de meurtrir son propre nepveu et fils adoptif pour se venger d'une femme" (HT VI, 206).

Such prudence and circumspection likewise explain Mandozze's reaction to Appian's mission when the barber comes to Spain to seek help from the renowned warrior. Mandozze has just suffered a military reversal and taken refuge within a city heavily besieged by the enemy. For Bandello, the incident is one further obstacle separating the two lovers: "Colá dentro adunque fu da' nemici suoi don Giovanni assediato, con poca speranza di poter aver soccorso, di modo che i dui amanti erano ridotti a malissimo partito" (II, 131). But in the French version Mandozze uses his military misfortune as an excuse not to help the Duchesse about whose character he has definite reservations. And Appian's report of his failure to enlist the services of the valiant knight casts the Duchesse into a profound despair as she realizes that the response of her "chevalier ingrat" is divine punishment for her sin, for her "hypocrisie et simulée devotion."

While the Duchesse's suffering has a moral justification — to expiate her sin of adulterous desire — it adds at the same time a dramatic complexity to the relationship of the Duchesse and Mandozze which no longer develops solely from the motif of separation. The element of blindness, misunderstanding, misinterpretation, and confusion gives a dramatic and living depth to the situation of these two characters, especially to the hero who refuses to attach himself blindly to the social code of honor:

> Mandozze luy dist que,...passant par Lyon, on l'avoit averty de l'infortune de la Duchesse, laquelle s'il pensoit estre innocente du crime dont elle estoit accusée, il la vouldroit deffendre jusques à la derniere goutte de son sang. Toutesfois qu'il ne vouldroit hazarder sa vie ny son ame pour defendre le péché d'autruy. (HT VI, 211)

From his concern over the verisimilitude of each event within the tale, Boaistuau is able to justify his inclusion of the prison scene. Because of his portrayal and characterization of Mandozze, he avoids the addition of a gratuitous and psychologically irrelevant incident. His conscious pursuit of verisimilitude directs his choice, interpretation, and exposition of narrative details — a clear example of the artistic advantages of the written form over the lingering oral tradition.

Having justified the prison scene, Boaistuau then exploits as fully as possible this dramatic encounter between Mandozze and the Duchesse. Again a comparison with the source tale is revealing. After don Giovanni introduces himself to the duchessa as a friar who has come to comfort her, Bandello adds: "L'essortò assai don Giovanni a perdonar tutte l'offese che mai ricevute avesse" (II, 136). Bandello quite typically eliminates any elaboration and pushes the episode rapidly to the entrusting of the ring. But a moment of emotional tension deserves its full and elaborate expression in the French tale. It is at this point that Mandozze pronounces a lengthy *consolatio*, offering a religious explanation for the plight of the Duchesse and, by several well-chosen biblical examples, giving her strength to endure her torment.

It is clear that Bandello bows to a more traditional narrative style. The movement of the story is his prime concern, and the complexity of the plot in a tale such as this necessitates abbreviation wherever possible. But Boaistuau sees in these highly rhetorical passages essentially a psychological necessity and can justify them artistically. The elegant phrase and the exploitation of pathos are basic ingredients in a narrative style which is no longer satisfied with the mere relating of events. The art of tale-telling moves away from the situational interest which had sustained earlier tale collections, and emphasizes instead the complexities of human motivation.

The numerous additions give further indication of the freedom which Boaistuau assumes in the role of translator. While he adds numerous passages in direct discourse to his source, the sentimental tale welcomes such liberty as one of its distinctive features. In contrast to the tragical tale, the confrontation of personalities and attitudes is highlighted in the sentimental tale by these sections of dialogue which, however, do not always advance the action of the story, given the fact that they are generally lyric complaints. For this reason, as a compensation perhaps, these passages are set amid a profusion of incidents and events which form the central core of the narrative. Instead of the linear structure of the tragical tale, the sentimental tale is a far more protracted form and its structure is clearly episodic. Incidents and events are more numerous. The "death" scene, the prison scene, the battle between Mandozze and Pancalier all receive a more detailed development than the tragical tale would allow.

The episodic structure is a clear indication of the free and loose form of the sentimental tale in which scenes change constantly, characters are numerous, and complications are the rule. Symptomatic of this freedom is the geographic mobility of the narrative. The setting of the episodes moves between Italy and Spain, ending finally in England. This spacial freedom is balanced by a temporal freedom. The single incident of the tragical tale automatically delimits the time in which the action occurs. But the action of HT VI clearly exceeds the year and a day of the Duchesse's imprisonment with the initial incidents of the story (the Spanish war, Ysabeau's trip to Italy, her encounter with the Duchesse, and finally their trip back to Spain) and the resolution of the tale in the English court.

It is a form that appears to be willfully complex as the writer manipulates the several threads of his story and adds to the complications by such devices as disguises, innumerable separations, and coincidences. And the complications become more evident by the free play of external events, in the guise of fortune, which completely reroute the narrative by reversing a supposedly resolved situation: it is the German invasion in the beginning of the third movement of the tale which accounts for the Duc's absence and allows Pancalier to seek the favor of the Duchesse. The sentimental tale is a form that is becoming more complex as the writer tries to suggest not only a moral lesson, but the very complexity of man himself.

But in a form which permits a loose and free structure, there must nevertheless be some means of containing the numerous incidents. The freedom cannot be rampant lest the story lose all artistic integrity. There must be a means of controlling the events of the tale beyond the delimitations of plot. Boaistuau uses parallelism to tighten the seemingly free structure of the form. The tale progresses with its innumerable incidents, but these parallel earlier events and serve as a commentary and further elucidation of past action. Basically the story contains a limited number of actions which are meaningfully repeated throughout the pages and played one against the other. The Pancalier episode is a significant example.

As the third movement of the story, the Pancalier episode continues to exploit the freedom that the sentimental tale allows by introducing new characters: Pancalier and his nephew, a secondary character who is merely an instrument for the jealous revenge of his uncle. Essentially the tale is getting a new start, for the Duchesse's departure from Spain left the love of the two heroes at an impasse. The intercalation of the Pancalier episode is therefore necessary to allow the two central characters to be reunited. But both versions give a great deal of space to the diabolical machinations of Pancalier and their disastrous results. There must be a further justification for this section.

Despite the freedom of the form, it is a freedom which is under rigid control. While the episode could hardly be called gratuitous, given the ultimate outcome of Pancalier's accusation, it also serves an integral function within the development of the tale by elucidating the particular nature of the Duchesse's adulterous guilt. Pancalier follows, in abbreviated form, the same stages of love for the Duchesse as the Duchesse did for Mandozze. He is presented as an "homme genereux," thus the moral equivalent of the Duchesse. And he too is afflicted by an overwhelming passion at the sight of the Duchesse: ..."la voyant si belle et de si bonne grace, ne peut tant commander à luy mesme qu'il n'en devint amoureux" (HT VI, 193). Her beauty and grace have the same effect on the Count that the valiant and handsome Mandozze had on the Duchesse. Similarly, just as the Duchesse had "manifesté par gestes et contenances exterieures au seigneur Mandozze quel estoit l'interieur de son cueur, sans en recevoir la satisfaction qu'elle desiroit" (HT VI, 187), Pancalier "reitera ses requestes et, eschauffant son stile, la supplia d'avoir pitié de luy" (194), only to be continuously refused and finally threatened by the one he loves. But here the parallel significantly ends. The Duchesse's lascivious passion for Mandozze results in a sincere remorse and repentance as befits the nobility of her character. But Pancalier's actions betray his 'generous' instinct, and, "changeant ceste grande amour en une hayne plus que mortelle, se delibera (quoy qu'il en deust advenir) d'inventer tous les moyens qu'il luy seroit possible pour ruyner du tout la Duchesse" (HT VI, 195). Boaistuau's exposition of the effects of passion on the human soul is enriched by this contrast of Pancalier and the Duchesse. Nobility and honor are not necessarily sufficient defenses against the destructive potential of love.

But Boaistuau is not only a moralist. He is telling a tale and the dramatic interest of the story is a major concern. The parallel of the similar loves of Pancalier and the Duchesse suggests with subtlety the conclusion of the story, it is true; but the irony implicit in this comparison also heightens the dramatic interest of the tale. Whereas the Duchesse is guilty of adultery, she seems to have been absolved of guilt by her new resolve of marital devotion. But once the ruse of Pancalier is successful and he falsely accuses the Duchesse of an adulterous relationship with his nephew, she is imprisoned and subjected to the degradation of public denunciation. However the "divers tourmens" which she experiences for a year and a day until her deliverance are necessary in order to expiate her sin and make her final absolution acceptable.

Nor is this the single example of parallelism in the tale. The Duchesse's trip to Spain disguised as a pilgrim is repeated by Mandozze's trip to Italy disguised as a friar. Just as the Duchesse is imprisoned after her degrading accusation, Mandozze is imprisoned after his military defeat. Ysabeau's pilgrimage to Italy after her vow is repeated by the Duchesse's pilgrimage to Spain after her vow to Saint Jacques. Confessions occur repeatedly on the part of the Duchesse, first to Æmilie, then to her husband, and finally Mandozze. Parallelism is a device which Boaistuau favors in the loose episodic form of the sentimental tale which lacks the concentration and structural tightness of the tragical tale. By the recurrence of motif and situation, Boaistuau ties together the loose threads of the narrative into a more tightly woven fabric, thereby achieving a rich and suggestive narrative unity.

The liberty that Boaistuau allows himself in his version of Bandello's *Novelle* may be nothing more than a petulant reaffirmation of the artistic freedom he demanded a year earlier when he edited the *Histoires des amans fortunez*. With the *His-*

toires tragiques, however, he was not challenged. Freely reworking Bandello's tales, manipulating and modifying his source, changing and adding details, he confers upon the short story a new degree of artistic integrity. Although his collection contains only six stories, they are not all written according to a single narrative pattern. The structure of the individual *histoire tragique* may vary from the terse and concentrated tragical tale to the elaborate and ornamental sentimental tale, a distinction that depends upon the central thematic preoccupation of the story itself. The tragical tale relishes the rapid and dramatic presentation of the destructive effects of passion, while the sentimental tale sings lyrically of the ennobling force of love. In both cases, Boaistuau manipulates his material so as to give an original expression to his source. He accepts the Bandello story only as a guide, and, by avoiding imitative subservience, he asserts his own creative independence.

PART TWO

THE *HISTOIRES TRAGIQUES* AND THE CONVENTIONS OF TRAGEDY

Chapter I

HISTORY

>...les hommes sont faicts de mesme matiere, & mesmement disposez qu'ils estoient anciennement.
>
>—Loys Le Roy, *De la Vicissitude*, liv. XII

As a literary form, the short story had no authoritative pronouncement in which to find established and accepted rules for composition, no poetic to dictate formal and stylistic laws. Writers tended therefore to adapt the conventions of established forms. Des Périers writes a sixteenth-century version of the *Cent Nouvelles nouvelles* which itself finds many a structural precedent in the fabliaux. Noël du Fail builds his fiction around a humanist discourse in the *Propos rustiques*, while Marguerite de Navarre adopts the form and thematic range of Boccaccio's *Decameron*. In composing his *Histoires tragiques*, Boaistuau looks beyond the narrative tradition in his quest for what he calls a "nouvelle forme." In order to give a greater degree of artistic integrity to the Italian tales, he turns to a new source of inspiration: the conventions of tragedy.

As he abandoned Bandello's generic title, Boaistuau was evidently aware of the boldness of his experiment, for he explains in his "Advertissement au lecteur" that he has "intitulé ce livre de tiltre Tragique, encore que (peut estre) il se puisse trouver quelque histoire, laquelle ne respondra en tout à ce qui est requis en la tragedie." Yet even accepting Boaistuau's reservation, it is obvious that he saw in his stories a definite affinity with a dramatic form that was at that time enjoying a renewed interest.

René Sturel writes of Boaistuau's collection that "grâce peut-être à son titre d'*Histoires tragiques,* plusieurs de ses nouvelles servirent de matière à notre tragédie naissante,"[1] citing the *Roméo et Juliette* and *Edouard d'Angleterre* by Come la Gambe (Chasteauvieux) and the *Tragédie d'Elips* by René Flacé, all three of which were unpublished, as possible dramatic adaptations of Boaistuau's HT III, I, and VI. This transposition may have been facilitated or even inspired in large part, however, by the fact that Boaistuau's stories already approximated what his contemporaries considered to be the form of tragedy.[2]

The word *tragédie* appears in French as early as the fourteenth century,[3] but the Middle Ages used it in a formal sense rather than exploring, except in a cursory fashion, the notion of *le tragique,* which does not appear until 1546. The description of those elements comprising a tragedy was maintained by the medieval Latin rhetoricians through the manuscript tradition and ultimately by the publication in the fifteenth century of two works by Latin grammarians of the fourth century: the commentary on Terence by Ælius Donatus and the *Ars grammatica* of Diomedes. The former was especially important since it contained scattered references to the structure and characteristics of the "tragic poem." Known throughout the Middle Ages and printed in 1472, it became an authoritative pronouncement for the Renaissance and provided the basis of the view of tragedy held during the sixteenth century.

According to this tradition, tragedy was defined by four major characteristics: it was to be an historical subject, dealing with noble or royal characters whose actions influence the fortune of their realms, progressing towards a disastrous conclusion

---

[1] "Bandello en France," *Bulletin Italien* XIII (1913), 211; see also Raymond Lebègue, "L'influence des romanciers sur les dramaturges français de la fin du XVIe siècle," *BHR* XVII (1955), 74-79.

[2] The following remarks on tragedy are taken from Lanson, "L'idée de la tragédie en France avant Jodelle," *RHLF* XI (1904), 541-585.

[3] Bloch and Wartburg (*Dictionnaire étymologique de la langue française* [Paris: Presses Universitaires de France, 1964] ascribe its appearance to Oresme at about 1320 in the sense of "discours fatals."

involving horror and bloodshed, and expressed in a grandiose and ornate style. Such was the Renaissance heritage of tragedy, which remained largely theoretical with the persistence of medieval theatrical forms. The perspicacity of these judgments on ancient theatre is unimportant: the doctrine as stated directed understanding and interpretation. The theory was early propagated by such publications as the edition of the theatre of Terence by Jodocus Badius in 1504, which repeats the precepts of Donatus in the introduction and adds, for the sake of precision, that the story describes the fall from good fortune to bad. These ideas were repeated in the successive editions of Terence by Robert Estienne in 1529 and 1542 and by Jean de Roigny in 1552.

The humanists' study and translation of ancient tragedy, the vogue for Italian theatre, and the renewed interest in Aristotle did not provide substantive changes in this description of tragedy, but significantly the sixteenth century emphasized the ethical value of the story itself. Thus in 1537, when Lazare de Baïf published his translation of Sophocles' *Electra*, he offered as his "Diffinition de la Tragédie": ... "une moralité composée des grandes calamitez, meurtres et adversitez survenues aux nobles et excellentz personnaiges," [4] thereby associating the ancient and medieval forms as Sebillet would do in 1548 in his *Art poétique françoys*.[5] In the preface to his edition of *Hecube*, published in 1544, Guillaume Bochetel claims that tragedies were "premièrement inventées pour remonstrer aux roys et grands seigneurs l'incertitude et lubrique instabilité des choses temporelles, afin qu'ils n'ayent de confiance qu'en la seule vertu."[6] To the description of the elements comprising a tragedy as inherited from the medieval tradition, the sixteenth century insisted therefore upon the moral lesson derived from these tales of horror to complete its definition of tragedy.

All that was needed was some indication of the explicit structure of tragedy. There were two possibilities: Donatus had

---

[4] Bernard Weinberg, *Critical Prefaces of the French Renaissance* (Evanston: Northwestern University Press, 1950), p. 73.

[5] See ed. Félix Gaiffe (Paris: Droz, 1932), pp. 161-162.

[6] Quoted by Lanson, *op. cit.*, 574.

insisted upon a tripratite composition, while Seneca, Aristotle, and Horace recommended a five-act structure.

In adapting these various characteristics of tragedy, a favorite Renaissance form turned to a new inspiration, exploited it, and in turn served as a source for the creation of tragic drama. But we are still dealing with narrative prose, and it is therefore necessary to examine the way Boaistuau accommodates these prescriptions to the short story form.

The first rule of tragedy — namely that it deal with an historical subject — was easily accommodated within a form that had long insisted upon the authenticity of the most improbable plots. Boaistuau does not ignore this traditional device of fictional narrative, and assures his reader that each tale in his collection has an authoritative source:

> ...je puis acertener une fois pour toutes que je n'insereray aucune histoire fabuleuse en tout cest œuvre de laquelle je ne face foy par annales et chroniques, ou par commune approbation de ceux qui l'ont veu, ou par autoritez de quelque fameux historiographe Italien ou Latin. (HT III, 61)

Fable is dismissed in favor of a story which has historical or actual truth. And in each tale Boaistuau carefully gives some indication of its authenticity.

The first two stories are clearly of an historical nature, given the central characters. Nevertheless, following his preliminary remarks to HT I, Boaistuau cites the name of a sixteenth-century historian to give an added note of credibility to his tale of intemperance:

> Polidore Vergile, faisant mention en ses histoires Latines des Roys d'Angleterre, escrit qu'Edouart second espousa Ysabelle, fille de Philippe le Bel, Roy de France, de laquelle il eut Edouard troisiesme, qui est celuy duquel est faicte mention en nostre histoire. (HT I, 10)

Similarly the second tale begins with an historical note, of which Boaistuau's contemporaries more than likely had little need:

> Celuy duquel je veux descrire l'histoire est Mahomet, non le faulx prophete, mais le bisayeul de Soliman Otoman, Empereur des Turcs qui regne de ce temps. C'est luy qui, avec le vitupere et eternelle infamie de tous les princes Chrestiens de son temps, print Constantinople et ravit l'empire d'Orient des mains de Constantin, Empereur Chrestien, l'an de grace mil quatre cens cinquante et trois. (HT II, 49)

The last two stories in the collection are supposed to have been recorded by contemporaries of the incidents. HT V concludes with mention of the death of Violente:

> Et fut executée en la presence du Duc de Calabre, fils du Roy Federic d'Arragon, qui estoit en ce temps là Vice-Roy et mourut depuis à Torcy en France, lequel incontinent apres feit enregistrer l'histoire avec les autres choses memorables avenues de son temps à Valence; duquel j'ay voulu faire mention, parce que l'autheur Italien descrit que l'esclave Janique fut deffaicte avec sa maistresse, mais Paludanus, Espagnol de nation, qui regnoit de ce temps, lequel a escrit l'histoire en Latin fort elegant, acertene nomméement qu'elle ne fut jamais apprehendée. Ce que j'ay ensuyvi comme le plus probable. (HT V, 167)

Similarly, HT VI, so Boaistuau states in his introduction to the tale, has a more faithful source than the Italian tale by Bandello:

> Valentinus Barruchius, natif de Tollette en Espagne, a faict un gros Tome Latin, escrit purement et en bons termes, de nostre presente histoire; duquel j'ay voulu faire mention, parce que je l'ay ensuyvi plus volontiers que les autheurs Italiens qui l'ont semblablement escrite. (HT VI, 169)

To authenticate the two remaining tales, Boaistuau assures his reader that those involved in the story or related to the characters were alive at the time of composition. The story of Rhomeo and Julliette is cast as an "histoire non moins admirable que veritable" (HT III, 62) set amid the beautiful environs of Verona:

> Ce que j'ay voulu rechercher un peu de plus loing d'autant que l'histoire tres-veritable que je veux deduire cy apres en depend, et en est encores pour le jourd'huy la memoire si recente à Veronne qu'à peine en sont essuyez les yeux de ceux qui ont veu ce piteux spectacle. (HT III, 64)

And finally, the actuality of HT IV is used as an excuse for the anonymity of the characters: ..."il y avoit un grand seigneur vaillant et genereux en quelque contrée du Piedmont, duquel je tairay le nom, tant pour la reverence de ses plus proches parens qui vivent encor' pour le jourd'hui..." (HT IV, 124).

With all three groups presented as *histoires*, it appears nevertheless that Boaistuau made a distinction between the types of stories in his collection. The first group might be called historical tales, the second, chronicle tales, and the last, *nouvelles*. It may be noted, moreover, that the author composes a tragical tale and a sentimental tale in each category. But all six supposedly have a foundation in truth. The problem remains, however, about the extent to which Boaistuau considered these sources he mentions, since he is presenting an edition of Bandello's *Novelle*, and since the claim of authenticity is a traditional narrative *topos*.[7]

The citing of sources is entirely consistent with the Renaissance penchant for authoritative assertion. Just as Montaigne "supports" his developing ethic by quoting ancient and contemporary sources, any pronouncement seems to have required some reassuring testimony. In the realm of narrative, such a practice had a further importance. The assertion of the truth of a tale frequently serves as a formulaic introduction by means of which the reader or listener is persuaded that the author is a reliable narrator and that he is avoiding, as does Boaistuau, the "histoire fabuleuse" in favor of factual truth. In the case of the *Histoires tragiques,* the ploy goes no further. René Sturel searched diligently for the Spanish chroniclers mentioned in HT V and HT VI, but without success; there is indeed no evidence that

---

[7] *Cf.* Boccaccio, *Decameron,* IX.5: ..."il partirsi dalla verità delle cose state nel novellare è gran diminuire di diletto negli 'ntendenti."

Boaistuau sought anything more from the sources he mentions than to give the impression "qu'il avait soigneusement contrôlé le témoignage de Bandello." [8] Boaistuau bows to a narrative convention in order to lend credence to the plot of the tale and to give it an aura of historical authenticity.

In this respect, the historical and chronicle tales are related to the traditional *exemplum*. Both forms function in much the same manner. Historical examples of human weakness were powerful tools in the hands of the Renaissance moralist who readily accepted the notion that "history teaches by example." [9] The humanists capitalized upon the belief that the present does not differ vastly from the past. Similar motivations call forth similar responses. The historical subject therefore had its intrinsic value. It is in this sense that Boaistuau composes his historical and chronicle tales. The assertion of historical truth does not imply the writing of history mimetically; it suggests rather that the writer is dismissing the "histoire fabuleuse" in favor of indisputable evidence which will confirm his own observations and convictions. The author thereby becomes an authoritative narrator of a tale which relates a general and applicable moral truth.

It was in this same spirit that one of the most popular books of moral instruction, Plutarch's *Lives*, was written. "Its subject is real, a 'historical' personage, but its substance is highly fictionalized in the interest of emotion and moral instruction; to move and to teach is its object." [10] Indeed the chronicle and historical

---

[8] *Op. cit.*, 216-217.

[9] Felix Gilbert, "The Renaissance Interest in History," in *Art, Science, and History in the Renaissance*, ed. Charles Singleton (Baltimore: The Johns Hopkins University Press, 1967), p. 375. See also p. 377: "Imitation was not only a question of literary form, of organization, and choice of subject matter. It was predicated on the assumption that the events of the past can be treated in the same way as those of the present because the factors which determined the actions and thoughts of men in the past are identical with those which determine them in the present. If the humanists were receptive to any general theory of history, it was the cyclical theory of the ancients, which postulated that history was repetitive and that everything that had happened would happen again."

[10] Scholes and Kellogg, *The Nature of Narrative* (New York: Oxford University Press, 1966), p. 66.

tales closely approach the concept of the 'life' as Plutarch defines it, several of which had already appeared in translation in France during the 1530's and 1540's:

> ...je n'userai d'autre prologue que de prier les lecteurs qu'ils ne me reprennent point, si je n'expose point le tout amplement et par le menu, mais sommairement en abrégeant beaucoup de choses, mêmement en leurs principaux actes et faits plus mémorables; car il faut qu'ils se souviennent que je n'ai pas appris à écrire des histoires, mais des vies seulement; et les plus hauts et les plus glorieux exploits ne sont pas toujours ceux qui montrent mieux le vice ou la vertu de l'homme; mais bien souvent une légère chose, une parole ou un jeu, mettent plus clairement en évidence le naturel de personnes, que ne font pas des défaites où il sera demeuré dix mille hommes morts, ni les grosses batailles, ni les prises des villes par siège ni par assaut. Tout ainsi donc comme les peintres qui portraient au vif recherchent les ressemblances seulement ou principalement en la face et aux traits du visage, sur lesquels se voit comme une image empreinte des mœurs et du naturel des hommes, sans guères se soucier des autres parties du corps, aussi nous doit-on concéder que nous allions principalement recherchant les signes de l'âme, et par iceux formant un portrait au naturel de la vie et des mœurs d'un chacun, en laissant aux historiens à écrire les guerres, les batailles et autres telles grandeurs. [11]

This passage could well serve as a preamble to the historical and chronicle tales, for while they deal with characters such as a Mahomet and an Edouart, Boaistuau is not concerned with presenting a history of their reign. He concentrates on the fatal weakness in the nature of each, a trait which may be historically insignificant, but which nevertheless reveals the soul of the protagonist, "les signes de l'âme." The result is a portrait of the hero without his heroic garb, the "naturel des hommes," a portrait which meaningfully warns the common run of humanity that even the great are prey to the same passions as they.

---

[11] Plutarch, "Vie d'Alexandre-le-Grand," trad. Amyot (Paris: Gallimard, "Bibliothèque de la Pléiade," 1959), t. II, p. 323; quoted in part by Scholes and Kellogg, *op. cit.*, p. 65.

Boaistuau announces in HT I that against the lascivious desires of Edouart, Ælips appears as a "portraict et exemplaire de chasteté" (9). For each tale the same formula could be applied: Mahomet is a "portraict et exemplaire" of incontinence; the Duchesse of adulterous desire; Didaco of self-indulgent and egotistical lust.

The parallel with the humanist method of presenting history is therefore immediately apparent:

> Their procedure in writing history was the following: they would pick out an event, an action, or a historical figure, and they would present their subject so that it became immediately relevant to the present. They were not averse to stylizing and embellishing the event or the person about whom they were writing, for their intention was to make the lessons which history taught as clear as possible. Their historical accounts were kept on a consciously high, generalizing, and idealizing level. The humanists were not concerned with the individually unique features of an event or personality. A man was described and judged according to the traditional scheme of cardinal virtues and vices. [12]

The historical and chronicle tales adapt the contemporary notion of history to the popularized form of the exemplary life or portrait and thereby begin to assume their definitive form.

Clearly HT III and HT IV do not fit into this historical framework. To distinguish them from the historical and chronicle tales, we have labeled these tales *nouvelles* in the etymological sense of the word. [13] The authenticity *topos* for HT III and HT

---

[12] Felix Gilbert, *op. cit.*, pp. 377-378.

[13] In his article, "La genèse de la nouvelle en France au Moyen Age" (*CAIEF* n° 18 [1966], 9-19), Roger Dubuis disputes the traditional view that the form of the novella was an Italian importation by virtue of its appearance in 1462 in the title of the *Cent Nouvelles nouvelles*. He maintains that the influence of Boccaccio's *Decameron* was not really profound until the 1545 translation, while the sense of the "nouvelle" was etymologically present in France from the earlier Middle Ages with the meaning of "ce qui est neuf, nouveau." With the noun existed the verb *noveller* (*noveler, nouveller*), used in the sense of speading news, and which later assumed the meaning of telling or narrating. On this basis the author defines *nouvelle* in the fifteenth-century context as "un récit assez bref qui présente dans sa matière ou dans sa manière un caractère de nouveauté" (p. 12).

IV suggests that the events in these stories occurred during the life of the author's contemporaries who are related to the characters in the tales. The author is therefore telling something that is new or newsworthy.

The living witness is sufficient testimony to the truth of the events narrated, and he can confirm the episodes of the story with the same authority as the historian or chronicler. This fiction allows for the two *nouvelles* the same degree of authenticity as the historical or chronicle tales. But it apparently denies the basic value of historical truth as demanded by the theory of tragedy. The very vagueness and anonymity of the central character in HT IV — "un grand seigneur... en quelque contrée du Piedmont" — removes the tale from the realm of exemplary action to that of a mere *fait divers*. However Boaistuau uses the *nouvelle* as a complement to the historical tale to prove the actuality of his central thesis. If history is of value because of its inevitable identity with the present, the *nouvelle* illustrates the patterned recurrence of what history teaches by example. It forcefully persuades that the extreme situations of a Mahomet or a Didaco have their counterparts readily available in the contemporary world. The *nouvelles* thereby contribute to the ultimate moral purpose of the collection by serving as meaningful examples of the ravages of passion and the eternal weakness of man who submits to its dictates.

The three types of *histoires* all present some form of historical "truth." They take place in a past that is temporally (the historical and chronicle tales) or spatially (the *nouvelles*) defined. "The gradual abandonment of ritual requires a gradual turning either to other elements of daily sensory experience or to the facts of history as a new basis in actuality for esthetic imitation."[14] The scene is peopled not by gods, or superhumans, or allegorical figures, but by men who dramatically display human weakness. We are not concerned with Mahomet the

---

[14] Scholes and Kellogg, *op. cit.*, p. 136. We are indebted to this work, especially chapters IV and V, for the theoretical background of the following discussion on character and characterization.

insuperable conqueror, but with Mahomet the conquered, who, in a very human way, exhibits human failings. Myth is displaced by reality — the authoritatively recorded or observed fact — in order to give fitting expression to the central preoccupation of tragedy: *fragilitas humanarum rerum.*

Chapter II

CHARACTER AND CHARACTERIZATION

> ...vous vouldriez doncques faire d'un amoureux ung meurdrier?
> —*Heptaméron*, I.4

Although the subjects of the six tales are historical in accordance with the theory of tragedy, a basic problem nevertheless becomes evident. If the characters are to be exemplary humans, they are, despite their claim to high social rank or their affiliation with royalty, so closely allied to the moral truths their actions illustrate that we are presented with a gallery of types if not, in certain instances, with allegorical representations of vices and virtues in historical or contemporary dress. The tragic climate demands a humanizing of the exemplary status of characters who thereby become sufficiently representational or mimetic that their words and deeds have a meaningful relationship to actuality. Tragic theory calls for noble or royal characters whose actions influence the fortune of their realms. Within that microcosmic setting, the exemplary character, whether through human failings or blindness, is subject to the same misfortune as the rest of humanity, though the catastrophic effects of his actions are greatly increased given his position of authority.

It is this "human" quality which at first appears to be lacking in Boaistuau's stories. His characters seem nothing more than illustrative symbols of predetermined ideas. In each story, they are introduced by a simple narrative statement relating those physical and moral traits upon which the ensuing action depends.

CHARACTER AND CHARACTERIZATION 93

If HT III is to illustrate the "parfaicte amitié" of an ideal couple, Boaistuau provides no more information than is necessary to allow his characters to fulfill this exemplary role. Thus Rhomeo is presented as "aagé de vingt à vingt et un ans, le plus beau et mieux accomply gentilhomme qui fust en toute la jeunesse de Veronne" (HT III, 64). Julliette has the same youth, beauty, and nobility as Rhomeo. She too comes from a noble family and is "une fille... d'une extreme beauté" (HT III, 68). The characterization is wholly traditional. The ideal couple is sketched in the same superlative terms as its predecessors in the medieval romance. Ideal physical traits and high social station bespeak the moral absolutes which the characters illustrate. Julliette sighs significantly that Rhomeo is the "exemplaire de toute vertu et gentillesse" (HT III, 80). In this story which has had the greatest fortune with posterity, these three phrases are the only indications of the character and nature of the two lovers. Any elaboration is unnecessary, for given such qualities, their actions will be comprehensible.

The pattern is formulaic. As the daughter of the king of England, one is assured of the nobility of the Duchesse who, moreover, "avoit le bruit d'estre la plus belle femme de toutes les parties Occidentales" (HT VI, 172). And her adulterous desires are perhaps somewhat more understable once it is learned that "le chevalier Mandozze estoit bien l'un des plus beaux chevaliers qui se trouvassent en son temps en toutes les Espagnes" (HT VI, 173).

While HT III and HT VI describe the obstacles preventing the union of the ideal couple, HT I and HT II vary the formula by dramatizing the confrontation of morally admirable and reprehensible characters. Hyrenée differs from Julliette and the Duchesse only in nationality: she is "une vierge Grecque de si rare et excellente beauté qu'elle attiroit les yeux d'un chacun à l'admirer et contempler comme quelque chose miraculeuse" (HT II, 49). But Mahomet is "jeune et lascif outre mesure" (HT II, 50), "de nature... terrible, cruelle et austere" (51), thereby explaining his debilitating passion as well as his brutal execution of Hyrenée. HT I comes closest to the purely allegorical. Edouart is not even described in physical terms. There is simply a moral portrait of a general nature included in the introductory passage. The king is the embodiment of lust, and, as the tale progresses, lust confronts chastity in the person of Ælips, another in Boaistuau's collection of superlatively beautiful women. No effort is made in either tale to suggest any nuance of character by elaborating upon the basic moral attributes. Vice encounters virtue. The results are predictable as virtue rises triumphant in the sentimental tale and vice has its destructive repercussions in the tragical tale.

The fourth and fifth stories refine this technique of direct characterization by a more subtle interplay of stated and unmentioned traits. The anonymous hero of HT IV has the briefest presentation of any of the characters in the collection. He is simply "un grand seigneur vaillant et genereux" (124). Yet his nobility and magnanimity are tried and challenged throughout the story and gradually degenerate into a jealous and vengeful wrath. Similarly Didaco is cast, like Mandozze, as a *chevalier*, "renommé de tous pour le plus liberal et courtois gentil-homme de la cité" (HT V, 139), but his weakness ultimately proves fatal: "dressant l'amour à toutes les femmes indifferemment sans qu'il eust l'une plus affectée que l'autre" (140). His passion for Violente, "une jeune fille de moyen aage, mais de beauté fort exquise" (140), testifies to the limited extent to which one can put faith in external traits of character, and provides the collection with one of its most fascinating portraits.

Unlike the previous descriptions, the portrait of Violente is well developed and presented as the information gathered as a result of Didaco's inquiry into the background and nature of the latest object of his passion:

> Et apres avoir curieusement recherché tout son origine, il trouva par le rapport de plusieurs qu'elle estoit fille d'un orfevre decedé depuis quelques années,...qu'elle estoit reputée tant chaste et spirituelle qu'il ne se trouvoit encores aucun qui eust eu le bruit d'avoir faict breche à son honneur,...et que c'estoit peu de la beauté exterieure, qui apparoissoit en elle, eu regard aux graces qui se manifestoient en sa parole, car combien qu'elle eust esté nourrie en sa maison bourgeoise, il y avoit peu de damoiselles et dames en la ville qui la peussent esgaler en vertu et gentillesse. (HT V, 140)

The longest of all character descriptions, this passage emphasizes the two aspects which are important to the development of the action: Violente's social station and her beauty, honor, and chastity. But the violation of her honor provokes a reaction which Didaco had little reason to anticipate from appearances alone.

The protagonists are surrounded by numerous type characters, secondary characters who, in an even less "real" way, provide the necessary elements for forwarding the plot or elucidating a situation. Such a plot accessory is Mahomet's counselor Mustapha, "un homme genereux," therefore worthy of the sultan's attention, and "libre en parole" (HT II, 51), thereby justifying his long tirade. Similarly Æmilie, "qui avoit le bruit d'estre l'une des plus subtiles et accortes damoiselles de Turin (HT VI, 177), can fittingly suggest to the Duchesse an involved plan whereby she can at last meet Mandozze. But unless such characters have a direct bearing on the plot, they are simply accepted as part of the narrative equipment. Thus confidants, servants, and spiritual advisors require mere identification as "vieilles," "serviteurs," or "beaupere religieux."

Two important exceptions are Pancalier, whose description is necessary to indicate, as a parallel to the Duchesse de Savoie, the dangers incurred by passion, and Frere Laurens, who is versed not only in matters pertaining to the Holy Scriptures, but also in philosophy and the occult. A lengthy description (HT III, 76) establishes his reputation in Verona, his friendship with Rhomeo, and his knowledge of magic, all of which are essential to the ensuing complications of the story.

Little effort is initially expended on the characters in these tales. They are all essentially types ranging only slightly from moral abstractions in human form who act out their roles to illustrate ethical ideas to versions of historical characters and accepted social types. Such is Boaistuau's heritage from Bandello's *Novelle*, where plot is of primary interest. If not almost allegorical figures, they are presented as "illustrative symbols for consciously stipulated and controlled ideas;"[1] and since they

---

[1] Scholes and Kellogg, *The Nature of Narrative*, p. 137. Donald Stone arrives at essentially the same conclusion in his study of sixteenth-century French fiction: ..."portraying the human animal meant showing and stating

are to act in a generally given fashion, elaboration is unnecessary, nor is any indication of a complex inner life essential to the basic moral purpose.

This brevity is understandable in the tragical tale which, by its very structure, refuses elaboration. But in the sentimental tales, where Boaistuau insists upon justifying the motivations of his characters, where an elementary psychology is apparent, the technique would be self-defeating. Therefore he makes a definite effort to avoid the creation of intellectual abstractions, and adopts certain techniques and devices by means of which characters begin to evolve from the traditional type cast. This is a problem which all narrative artists of the Renaissance faced; yet dependent upon the purpose of the tale collection, its importance increased or diminished accordingly. Des Périers' essentially comic province admits the character type since the goal of the tale is most often situational and, as in the tradition of the fabliau, the frequent imbroglio demands only the skillful manipulation of events by the narrator. Noël du Fail and Marguerite de Navarre similarly present types, often working in the realm of the comic, but the seriousness of their ultimate narrative purpose is assured by the presence of the representational authority of the narrator. In the *Propos rustiques*, he is the wise humanist, while in the *Heptaméron*, the *devisants* assure the authenticity of each story.

Although dismissing the convention of the framework, Boaistuau compensates for the loss of this representational authority by including a second type of authenticity *topos* which emphasizes the historical moment or the geographic setting of the action. After the moral portrait of the central character in HT I, Boaistuau adds the following historical note:

---

the simple generalities that summarized human existence. Man's inner world belonged to, was determined by the familiar symbols that spoke such generalities. The tales about him were in the main not constructed, conceived, or written to convey any illusion of psychological reality but rather a one-to-one relationship between event (or emotion) and the apothegm it exemplified" (*From Tales to Truths* [Frankfurt am Main: Vittorio Klostermann, 1973], p. 54).

> Il y a eu un Roy d'Angleterre, nommé Edouart, qui espousa la fille du Comte de Henaut en premieres nopces, de laquelle il eut des enfans, l'aisné desquels s'appeloit aussi Edouart, prince de Galles fort renommé, lequel pres de Poictiers subjuga les François, print le Roy Jean, l'envoya prisonnier en Angleterre. C'est Edouart, pere du Prince de Galles,...avoit encores continuelle guerre avec les Escossois ses voisins... (HT I, 11-12)

The statement is intended to project the reader back to the fourteenth century to the reign of Edward III and the beginnings of the Hundred Years' War, to recall the early English victories over Jean II, and the battles leading to the conquest of Scotland. And while these details are not essential to an understanding of Edouart's passion for Ælips, they do allow him to begin to shed his allegorical garb and to assume a definite representational function within the tale.

The same result is achieved in HT II where Mustapha, in the *argumentatio* of his long discourse to the sultan, recalls Mahomet's ancestry and summarily reviews the formation of the Ottoman empire. And the ideal chevalier of HT VI likewise receives the stamp of historical authenticity, for "ceux qui ont leu les anciennes annales et croniques d'Espagne ont peu voir en plusieurs lieux l'occasion de la cruelle inimitié qui a regné l'espace de plus de quarante ans entre les Mandozzes et de Tolledo" (HT VI, 171).

In the other three tales, whose characters are insignificant historically, Boaistuau describes in detail the setting of the story. In HT V the action is set in Valencia, a city reputed to be "bien peuplée de dames et damoiselles accortes et gentilles qui sçavent... bien appaster les jeunes hommes et passer leur temps de leurs follies" (139). HT IV contains a lengthy description of the rustic retreats in Piedmont, while HT III opens with an enthusiastic appreciation of Verona, a city that is "incomparable,

> tant à cause du fleuve navigable nommé Adisse, qui passe quasi par le milieu de la ville et au moyen duquel se faict une grosse traficque en Alemaigne, comme en semblable pour le regard des fertiles montagnes et vallées delectables qui l'environnent, avec un grand nombre de tresclaires et vives fontaines qui servent pour

l'aise et commodité du lieu, sans deduire par le menu plusieurs autres singularitez, quatre ponts et une infinité d'autres venerables antiquitez qui se manifestent de jour à autre à ceux qui sont curieux de les contempler. (HT III, 62-63)

The historical and geographic indications add a mimetic dimension to the tales. Although the characters are initially presented as standard types, they begin to veer toward the representational by an association with specific time and space. The more mythic tales (HT III, IV, V) which deal with recognizable social types are set in a familiar reality. The reality which surrounded the character in the *fabliaux* and the traditional comic tale is here adapted to disengage the characters from a purely illustrative role. The movement is similar in the case of HT I, II, and VI. As in tragedy, where there is an integration of legendary elements to form a background to the play, the historical "truth" of these tales provides a backdrop of actuality against which the noble or royal character moves and acts. An Edouart becomes more than merely an allegory of lust by virtue of his historical truth. With all of his major characters, therefore, Boaistuau creates a tension by humanizing to a certain degree the otherwise purely allegorical, exemplary, and heroic types. The technique is certainly not new, but it was an essential ingredient for Boaistuau in order to enhance his specific view of the tragic.

And yet such accommodation does not create a character in the modern sense of the word, characters who visibly struggle with inner conflicts. "The most essential element in characterization is this inward life. The less we have, the more other narrative elements such as plot, commentary, description, allusion, and rhetoric must contribute to the work." [2] But Boaistuau is aware of the value of such internalization, and while he does not explore new means of presenting the thoughts of his characters, he does adapt techniques from the traditions of tragedy and the romance to allow the reader some perceptive awareness

---

[2] Scholes and Kellogg, *op. cit.*, p. 171.

CHARACTER AND CHARACTERIZATION

of the living reality of those conflicts with which his exemplary heroes struggle.

Significantly the tragical tales are not greatly concerned with this problem. Cast within the confines of a traditional narrative mold, these stories center all attention upon plot and reject elaboration in order to move swiftly to the conclusion of horror. The few indications of internal struggle are merely brief factual statements indicating the presence of a conflict but which remains unexplored. Once Mustapha has forcefully spoken to the sultan, we are told that Mahomet "sentoit une furieuse bataille en son ame" and that he was "agité de diverses tempestes" (HT II, 58). But in the tragical tale, his ruminations are virtually unimportant. What is essential is the result of his pondering. Quite typically the element of plot takes precedence over mental probing.

HT V elaborates slightly upon this type of cursory indication by enumerating the various emotions which grip the mind of Didaco after he reads Violente's letter:

> ...et ayant bien pesé le contenu d'icelle, il fut incontinent surpris de grand sursault, car haine et pitié, amour et desdaing...commencerent à se debattre et contrarier en son cueur; puis ayant quelque peu pensé à son affaire, il luy dist.... (HT V, 157)

The text jumps from the verb "commencerent" to the conclusion which Didaco announces to Janique. No effort is made to penetrate the mind of the hero. His decision alone is of importance.

Equally brief, though more subtle, are the associative references to external or civil disorders which mirror the internal confusion of the central character. The technique occurs only in the historical tales and is a clear derivative of tragic theory whereby the actions of royal characters influence the fortune of their realms. Mahomet's inordinate love for Hyrenée blinds him to his imperial obligations and results in sedition and rebellion. Boaistuau indicates the parallelism by a conspicuous repetition: "Pendant ce desordre, le vulgaire commença tacitement à murmurer, tant de la confusion et desordre de l'Empire..." (HT II, 50). Similarly, because of his excessive love, Edouart ignores "les armes et l'administration de la justice" with the result that the affairs of state are "reduites à... piteux estat"

(HT I, 37), reflecting the emotional state of the king tormented by despair. Although oblique, this technique provides a more detailed expression of the psychological state of the character than the mere statement of the existence of such a state.

All of the stories use another device long honored in the narrative tradition: the external sign. The sudden change of facial color suggests that the character is dealing with thoughts of momentous significance or else is gripped by strong emotion. Once Mahomet has been eloquently reprimanded by his counselor, "une soudaine mutation de couleur donnoit asseuré tesmoignage des diverses agitations de son ame" (HT II, 57). Most frequently it is the blush which serves as an emotional confession of that which verbal and social conventions forbid. Even the daughter of the king of England cannot prevent some visible reaction to Ysabeau's ideal portrait of Mandozze: "La Duchesse... respondit avecques une petite honte qui embellissoit la couleur de son teinct" (HT VI, 174). Rhomeo's inability to reply to Julliette is quickly explained once the blush betrays his love: ..."elle... apperceut par sa mutation de couleur que le deffault procedoit d'une trop vehemente amour" (HT III, 70). Despite her pride and sense of honor, Ælips cannot fail to react to the gallant flattery of Edouart: "La Comtesse, un peu honteuse et esmeue de se sentir louée si avantageusement d'un si grand seigneur, commença à embellir et rehaulser d'un teinct de rose la blancheur d'albastre de son visage" (HT I, 14).

The pallid complexion, synonymous with suffering, succinctly describes the torment experienced by Julliette during Rhomeo's absence: ..."la miserable Julliette ne sceut donner si bonnes trefves à son deuil que par la mauvaise couleur de son visage on ne descouvrit aisément l'interieur de sa passion" (HT III, 92). And the sudden paling of Ælips is the visible sign of her displeasure at the king's extravagant attentions and assures him once more that her sense of honor remains an insuperable obstacle:

> Et s'il advenoit que quelque fois le Roy la caressast plus que son devoir ne requeroit, soudain on eust veu une couleur ternie en son visage qui declaroit le peu de plaisir qu'elle prenoit en ses caresses, et commençoit à

> apparoistre en son visage un rayon de rigueur qui rendoit un asseuré tesmoignage au Roy qu'il se travailloit en vain. (HT I, 20-21)

Although the external sign declares the thoughts and feelings of the character, although it is indicative of mood and emotion, it has its limitations in the extent to which it allows a penetration of the mind, limitations which the Duchesse discovers during her first visit with Mandozze:

> La pauvre Duchesse, apres avoir manifesté par gestes et contenances exterieures au seigneur Mandozze quel estoit l'interieur de son cueur, sans en recevoir la satisfaction qu'elle desiroit, delibera, ayant sejourné trois jours en son chasteau, partir le matin au desceu du chevalier pour parfaire son voyage. (HT VI, 187)

A more eloquent and direct elaboration of thought is necessary, especially in the sentimental tale which concentrates upon the emotional crises of love resulting from the challenge of moral dictates or of external forces seeking to prevent its consummation. For the sentimental tale is less concerned with plot as an end in itself than with its direct relationship to characters and with their reactions to a specific situation. Therefore Boaistuau's attention is inevitably drawn to methods of representing thought and portraying internal conflict in detail unsuitable to the structure and form of the tragical tale whose demands are satisfied by mere statement.

The first category of techniques is the most elementary and indeed traditional: an analytical description within the narrative. When Julliette tells Frere Laurens that her father, unaware of her marriage to Rhomeo, has promised her hand to Comte Paris, the friar retires to his chambers to ponder the problem and find some solution:

> ...il commença à projetter diverses choses en son esprit, se sentant ores sollicité en sa conscience de souffrir qu'elle espousast le Comte Paris, sçachant que par son moyen elle en avoit espousé un autre; ores faisant son entreprinse difficile et encores plus perilleuse à l'execution, d'autant qu'il se commettoit à la misericorde d'une jeune simple damoiselle peu acorte, et que si elle de-

> failloit en quelque chose, tout leur faict seroit divulgué, luy diffamé, et Rhomeo son espoux puny. Neantmoins apres avoir esté agité d'une infinité de divers pensemens, fut en fin vaincu de pitié, et avisa qu'il aimoit mieux hazarder son honneur que de souffrir l'adultere de Paris avec Julliette. (HT III, 98)

The first clause is the type of statement used in the tragical tales to relate the existence of internal debate. But the sentimental tale elaborates upon the purely factual statement and suggests the careful weighing of alternatives, as indicated by the use of the correlatives *ores... ores.* Finally a conclusion is reached as the friar decides on the lesser of two negative choices, and resolves to chance an involved scheme based on his knowledge òf magic and drugs rather than risk allowing Julliette to commit a mortal sin. The situation has a precise parallel in HT I where Ælips must also make a decision: her honor or the welfare of her family. As in the case of the friar's choice, both courses appear ominous. This standard motif of tragedy prevails in the sentimental tale, and the tragic choice confers upon these characters a living and representational quality which removes them from pure moral concepts and types. For Ælips becomes more than an embodiment of chastity, Frere Laurens more than a wise counselor because of this effort to penetrate their minds and suggest their thoughts. They confront a situation from which there can apparently come no happy issue and, by explicit use of rational faculties, make a difficult but necessary decision.

Boaistuau adopts a variation of the descriptive statement when probing the tormented mind. Love, or the obstacles which hinder love, produce anguish, and anguish is depicted by visions. The Duchesse's obsession with the image of Mandozze, "gravée au plus profond de son cueur," is so powerful that each time she closes her eyes, "il luy sembloit avis qu'il voletoit incessamment devant elle comme quelque fantosme" (HT VI, 175). Afraid to swallow Frere Laurens' drug, lest Rhomeo not be at her side when she awakens, Julliette is haunted by a nightmarish vision:

> ...son imagination fut si forte qu'il luy sembloit avis qu'elle voyoit quelque spectre ou fantosme de son cousin Thibault en la mesme sort qu'elle l'avoit veu blessé

et sanglant; et apprehendant qu'elle devoit vive estre ensepvelie à son costé, avec tant de corps morts et d'ossements desnuez de chair, son tendre corps et delicat se print à frissonner de peur et ses blonds cheveux à herisser tellement que, pressée de frayeur, une sueur froide commença à perser son cuir et arrouser tous ses membres, de sorte qu'il luy sembloit avis qu'elle avoit desja une infinité de morts autour d'elle qui la tirailloient de tous costez et la mettoient en pieces. (HT III, 104)

In this single example of the fantastic in the *Histoires tragiques*, as distinct from the horror of the tragical tales, Boaistuau presents a veritable *danse macabre* which vividly describes a young girl in the grips of terror. The vision offers a graphic analysis of the anguish experienced by the suffering heroine. And this example is unusual in the collection which generally avoids the visual. The descriptive analysis, moreover, departs from the regular use of narrative in the sentimental tale. If, as suggested by the structure of HT VI, the passages of direct discourse are the major interest of the writer, narrative is generally reserved for the eventual interludes bringing about a new confrontation of characters. But where Boaistuau probes the thoughts of his characters, he is adapting narrative to a descriptive function which is rare in these tales, except for the initial portraits and occasional developments of setting used to authenticate the *nouvelles*.

The other methods of probing the inner life of the characters are adapted from theatrical convention as well as from the psychological romance in the tradition of Boccaccio. In theatre, where character is revealed principally by speech, the spoken word may be presented in dialogue or by means of soliloquy. The *Histoires tragiques* accommodates both of these techniques of character revelation.

We have seen that the sentimental tale, both expansive and rhetorical, employs dialogue in order to heighten moments of emotional stress. Indeed these numerous passages of dialogue distinguish the sentimental tale from the tragical tale not only in form and structure, but also in narrative concern which is no longer concentrated solely upon plot, but begins to assume a genuine interest in the characters themselves. And once emotion reaches a point of intensity, dialogue is used again, this time as a suitable vehicle for a fuller description of personally experienced anguish. Boaistuau calls these speeches *discours,* for they delve into the mind of the speaker and present a truthful account of his inner feelings. When Edouart has concluded his admission of love to Ælips' father, the Comte is ready to sacrifice even his own life for the king, so great is his pity once he has "entendu ce piteux *discours,* fidele tesmoing de son interieure passion" (HT I, 25). This is the second sense of *discours* as defined by Cotgrave: "a survey, perusall, examination, pondering of things in the mind." Clearly the *discours* is a valuable technique for depicting the internal struggle of a character, and the words assume their meaningful authenticity by being uttered by the character himself who is hiding no relevant fact.[3]

Since formulaic speech and external signs of emotion had no effect in furthering the relationship of the Duchesse and Mandozze, the chevalier turns finally to the *discours* in order to express more directly his personal sentiments. Overtaking the Duchesse's coach on the road to Compostella, after her sudden departure from his chateau, he admits more openly the words the Duchesse had long been waiting to hear:

> ...je sens maintenant, depuis vostre venue en ce pays, une si cruelle bataille et furieux assaut en mon cueur que, n'y pouvant plus resister, je me sens vaincu et captivé de telle sorte que je ne scay à qui me plaindre, sinon à vous qui estes le motif du mal...Et pour me reduire à ma derniere fin, vous estes partie ce jourd'huy de ma maison sans me dagner voir, ny complaire d'un seul à-Dieu, ce qui renflamme tellement ma passion que je meurs mille fois le jour; vous suppliant pour l'advenir me traicter plus humainement, ou vous verrez en moy ce qui vous deplairoit en vos ennemis, qui ne peut estre moins qu'une trescruelle mort. (HT VI, 188-189)[4]

---

[3] Boaistuau also uses *discours* in the general sense of "story" or "narrative:" ..."l'amour qu'il portoit à sa premiere damoiselle demeura vaincu par ce nouveau feu, lequel print tel accroissement et vigueur qu'il ne se peust oncques esteindre que par la seule mort, comme vous pourrez entendre par l'un des plus estranges *discours* que l'homme mortel sçauroit imaginer" (HT III, 68).

[4] This passage is selected for its brevity. Generally these confessional *discours* are far more lengthy and detailed, as in HT I, 23-25, or HT V,

The *discours* assumes the form of a confession to either a main or secondary character who acts as a reliable witness as the central figure confides an elaborate and truthful "tesmoignage de son cueur." Like all the passages in direct discourse, it is ornate and rhetorical, thus appearing to mask directness. But while rhetoric often seems to compromise psychology in favor of esthetics, its does not preclude the psychological, and it is precisely for this reason that the confessional *discours* assumes its value for the progression of the emotional plot. Moreover the metaphorical language is a necessary means of expression for the characters in these tales. Cast as an ideal chevalier, Mandozze understandably speaks of his passionate yearning and suffering in hyperbolical and metaphorical terms.

The use of the *discours* permits a more detailed and explicit expression of personal emotion than can be suggested by mere narrative descriptions, and serves to remove the omniscient narrator from a totally directive role in the tale. The characters in the sentimental tale are no longer conceived strictly in terms of plot. They begin to assume a more authentic existence independent of the interpretive observations of the author. The tension between the mythic and the representational may still be present, but it is at least partially resolved by a free interplay between the two poles. The mythic dictates words, actions, and style which the character obeys in an exemplary fashion. The noble character speaks and acts in a manner befitting his rank. But the *discours* reveals the representational side of these characters who, even at the height of suffering, remain lucid and rational, capable of analyzing with classical precision the passion of which they are victim and the reasons for their suffering.

Whereas the *discours* is similar to dialogue insofar as it suggests the relating of information to another person, the disappearance of the listener changes the nature of these personal confessions to an interior monologue. It is again an adaptation of the dramatic tradition and is analogous to the soliloquy, the dramatic form of monologue. While the soliloquy may be a device

141-143, which contains a series of *discours* by both Violente and Didaco. However these two tales exploit the form of the discours to present a false confession. Allusion is made to these speeches in Part Three, Chapter II.

for relaying ideological messages, it is frequently "an interior debate" and is used as a "vehicle for self-expression and subjective utterance." [5] Boccaccio had, of course, bequeathed to the Renaissance precious examples of this device in such a work as the *Fiammetta,* and his influence is apparent in the *Histoires tragiques* where the interior monologue becomes the characteristic element of the sentimental tale.

Boaistuau labels these passages variously as *complaintes* and *lamentations,* although the terms appear to be more or less synonymous and differ only in degree (Cotgrave defines a lamentation as a "pitiful complaint"). These speeches are monologues in the basic sense of the word: they are presented as passages of direct discourse, spoken by a single person who is alone and who laments his unfortunate state. They are also defined textually as *deliberations,* which insist upon the rational pondering of the character, the reasoning of the solitary mind presented directly to the reader. Interior monologue is the general term used here to cover all of these categories. [6]

The most striking example of the interior monologue occurs in HT III once Julliette is "avertie tant de la mort de son cousin Thibault que du bannissement de son mary." Entering her room, she "faisoit retentir l'air par une infinité de cruelles plainctes et miserables lamentations" (85). Her double grief imposes a dual structure upon the monologue. In the first section, she condemns Rhomeo for killing Thibault:

> Ah Rhomeo, Rhomeo! quand au commencement j'euz accoinctance de vous et que je prestois l'oreille à voz fardées promesses confirmées par tant de juremens, je n'eusse jamais creu qu'au lieu de continuer nostre amitié

---

[5] Henry W. Well, "Monologue," in *Encyclopedia of Poetry and Poetics* (Princeton: Princeton University Press, 1965).

[6] Kellogg and Scholes point out that during the Renaissance, monologues tend to be rhetorical devices in the romance and psychological in the realistic narratives. Significant for our purpose is the effort to reconcile this distinct separation: "One of the first European writers to struggle with this problem was Boccaccio, who... did much to liberate the interior monologue from its traditional employment as a set piece to be indulged in primarily to render the pangs of awakening love or the inward debate of a conflict between desire and duty" (*op. cit.,* p. 189).

> et d'appaiser les miens, vous eussiez cherché l'occasion de la rompre par un acte si lasche et vituperable que vostre renommée en demeurera à jamais interessée et moy (miserable que je suis) sans consort et espoux. (HT III, 86)

Boaistuau is partial to the single complex sentence which most often serves either as a means to suggest the rapid succession of events in narrative passages or as a rhetorical device of elaboration in direct discourse. Here it is used to project Julliette's disillusioned grief. The sentence contains as much self-criticism as accusation, as the apparent love ("amitié," the leitmotif of the tale) seems shattered by a cowardly act. And the monologue is all the more poignant since it is an apostrophe addressed to the absent Rhomeo.

But her deep love for Rhomeo readily contains this initial response to family allegiance, and Julliette is overcome with self-reproach:

> Ah, langue meurtriere de l'honneur d'autruy! comme oses-tu offenser celuy auquel ses propres ennemis donnent louenge? Comment rejectes-tu le blasme sur Rhomeo, duquel chacun approuve l'innocence? Où sera desormais son refuge, puis que celle qui deust estre l'unique propugnacle et asseuré rampart de ses malheurs le poursuit et diffame? Reçoy, reçoy doncques, Rhomeo, la satisfaction de mon ingratitude par le sacrifice que je te feray de ma propre vie.... (HT III, 86-87)

The series of rhetorical questions are self-accusations, and although Julliette is prone to elaboration through Latinisms and emphatic repetitions, the rhetoric stresses her grief. The whole passage assumes the rhetorical form of the *disputatio*, "the reasoning of a matter within the self," and illustrates the purposeful assimilation of the traditional complaint in order to portray the heroine in a more meaningful tragic posture.

The interior monologue occurs at a critical point in HT I after Edouart has been subjected to the Comte's long discourse admonishing him for his willful disdain of all sense of honor and for submitting instead to the dictates of a powerful lust. Moved by the counselor's rhetoric, Edouart considers the value of the Comte's words:

> O miserable, retranche ceste practique amoureuse; comment es-tu si despourveu de sens, de penser à celle que tu deusses avoir en telle reverence que ta propre sœur, pour les services que toy et les tiens avez receuz du bon homme de Comte son pere? Ouvre les yeux de ton entendement et te recognois toy mesmes; donne lieu à la raison et reforme tes impudiques et desordonnez appetits; resiste vivement à ceste lascive volonté qui te tient assiegé sans te laisser transporter ou decevoir à ce tyran amour. (HT I, 31)

Reviewing all the arguments which the Comte made at such great length, Edouart ponders their unquestionable validity and tries to summon the strength of reason to repress his lascivious desires. But reason is not sufficiently strong to combat the power of passion, and it is passion which inspires his words in the counter-argument and which ultimately proves decisive:

> Je sens en mon ame la coulpe de mon peché et recognois mon tort, mais que feray-je? veu ceste meurtriere beauté qui me force et maistrise si bien que je n'y puis resister. Facent doncques fortune et l'amour comme ils entendent. Ælips sera mienne, en advienne ce qu'il en pourra avenir. Le vice est-il notable à un Roy, d'aimer la fille de son vassal? Suis-je le premier à qui tel inconvenient est survenu? (HT I, 32)

Edouart's reasonings not only describe dramatically the torment and conflict which he recognizes as the result of his love for the Comtesse; his final rationalizations, dictated by a misguided reason, prepare for his threats of dishonor to the Comte and his family should Ælips remain unwilling to yield to his love. The passage is no mere rhetorical embellishment: it gives the impetus to the second half of the story by illuminating the helpless state of the king who is willing to go to any extreme to satisfy his lust.

Like the *discours*, the interior monologue emphasizes characterization through a presentation of thought and the thought process rather than subjecting a character's ideas and motives directly to the examination of the author's critical mind. As the short story assumes a greater interest in motivation and personal emotion rather than trying to please simply through the intricacies of plot, the interior monologue becomes a valuable device for penetrating the complex mind of the more intense and complicated hero. Sentiment and emotional reaction are not to be dictated by social treatises, cannot be adequately formulated by ethical codes. The *Histoires tragiques* invalidates their pronouncements. Reality destroys the mythic purity and reliability of the knight, the king, the adoring husband, and characters are forced to make desperate decisions. Or else it belies the ideal to such an extent that the individual can only try to reason independently through an emotional crisis that is new because it departs so radically from the ideal. In every instance the ethical and esthetic ideals are insufficient by themselves, and, with confidence in these ideals either challenged or destroyed, the literary figure is forced into a more representational role. Although this adaptation is not made in the *Histoires tragiques* by any narrative innovations, what is significant is the recognition of this fact and the effect that it has on the portrayal of character.

CHAPTER III

THEME

> ...Fortune ne recongnoist point de superieur auquel d'elle et de ses sors on puisse appeller.
> —Rabelais, III.12

According to the third recommendation of tragic theory, the action should progress to a disastrous conclusion involving horror and bloodshed. The distinctions between the tragical and sentimental tales indicate that the former alone adheres to this specific prescription. The conclusions of HT II, IV, and V relate the horrifying vengeance exacted by Mahomet, the Seigneur du Piedmont, and Violente. These stories fall within a category which was to have increasing popularity during the latter half of the sixteenth century: the tale or tragedy of revenge.

"Revenge is a kind of wild justice," writes Francis Bacon, and if one can put any faith in the chroniclers of the sixteenth century, it was a kind of justice that was altogether prevalent. Little wonder that such a motif finds some degree of expression in each of Boaistuau's tales. Elliott Forsyth maintains that the notion of revenge was part of the medieval heritage of the Renaissance,[1]

---

[1] *La Tragédie française de Jodelle à Corneille: le thème de la vengeance* (Paris: Nizet, 1962). Forsyth's study divides the theme of vengeance into various categories — personal, collective, divine — and examines the sources of these attitudes — social, religious, ancient, and foreign — with specific reference to their importance to dramatic expression in the sixteenth and seventeenth centuries. We have limited our commentary to the years preceding 1560 in order to suggest those attitudes prevailing in France at the

for while administrative justice was concerned, during the earlier period, with crimes against the state, it considered individual offenses a private matter beyond its authority, and these were left to the efforts of the victim and his family. The Middle Ages accepted private vengeance therefore as a legitimate right "pourvu qu'elle s'exerce ouvertement et sans trahison"; especially in the avenging of personal honor, it held that "la vengeance privée est un moyen de défense normal et légitime." [2]

During the first half of the sixteenth century, a definite effort was made to dismiss this medieval custom in favor of a more formal justice. Private revenge was forbidden. But judicial theory was unable to curb entirely this natural proclivity of the enraged and the impassioned. A far more effective argument was presented by the defenders of the Christian attitude who insisted that "la vengeance de Dieu s'exerce contre les malfaiteurs individuellement, et pendant leur vie terrestre, en les frappant comme ils ont frappé leurs victimes." [3] The Gospels not only forbid private vengeance but underscore the reality of divine punishment.

Yet the "eye for an eye" prescription of the Old Testament appeared as a blatant contradiction. Theorists needed to rationalize this idea into a single principle, which became the general Christian view of the time, a definite compromise of the judicial and Christian attitudes:

> Dieu défend l'exercice de toute vengeance humaine issue d'une rancune personnelle; il permet aux hommes, pourtant, d'intenter des poursuites judiciaires, et il permet aux magistrats d'infliger une peine judiciaire, même la peine de mort, pour le bien public, car en punissant le

---

time of the composition of the *Histoires tragiques*. It is interesting to note, however, the similarity between certain tales and those *faits divers* quoted by Forsyth from such chroniclers and *mémorialistes* as De Thou, Pierre de l'Estoille, and Henri Estienne.

[2] *Ibid.*, p. 29.

[3] *Ibid.*, p. 44. Again the insistence upon a single attitude is misleading. Forsyth cites Brantôme *(Grands Capitaines français)* and his scorn for the Christian attitude of 'turning the other cheek' as one which destroys all sense of honor and nobility (p. 38). The Christian belief, however, is the final ethical stance assumed by Boaistuau and serves as an answer to his own sense of the tragic. This will be discussed in Part Four.

> malfaiteur le magistrat exerce, en quelque sorte, la vengeance de Dieu.[4]

Exercising God's justice on earth, the magistrate becomes a judicial counterpart of the priest. It is this function which explains the conclusion of HT V, for although Violente has committed murder because she had "perdu son ancienne reputation par le moyen de Didaco," the judges and magistrates of Valencia are less moved than is the populace by her tale of "infortune," and they do not hesitate to pronounce their harsh sentence:

> Et fut Violente par la plus commune opinion de ceux qui assisterent au conseil condamnée à estre decapitée, non seulement parce que ce n'estoit à elle de punir la faute du chevalier, mais pour la trop excessive cruauté de laquelle elle avoit usé envers le corps mort. (HT V, 167)

The fact that her act of vengeance is censured does not suggest the impossibility of avenging one's honor, but rather that the act itself, and especially the mutilation of Didaco's body, exceeded the limits of individual responsibility. However certain Renaissance moralists went so far as to state that personal honor was lost once it was defended by the act of revenge, since "the honour that is wonne by her, hath an ill ground... Honour is a thinge too noble of it selfe, to depend of a superfluous humour, so base and vilanous, as the desire of vengeance is."[5]

Nevertheless Violente is condemned, and not only because her act of revenge was a judicial and not an individual matter, but also because it was excessive. The atrocities of the brutal slaying are given in lurid detail as the author depicts the transformation of a "simple damoiselle" into a veritable monster of vengeful fury, the same transformation that is present in the portraits of Mahomet and the Seigneur du Piedmont. If Boaistuau associates his tales with the form of tragedy, it is clear that the

---

[4] *Ibid.*, p. 74.
[5] John Eliot, *Discourses of Warre and Single Combat* [1591], cited by Fredson Bowers, *Elizabethan Revenge Tragedy* (Princeton: Princeton University Press, 1940), p. 14.

tragical tale is composed thematically in the tradition of the theatre of horror.

When Du Bellay recommends the revival of comedy and tragedy in France, he does not elaborate upon the composition of these plays, but merely tells the aspiring dramatist: ..."tu scais ou tu en doibs trouver les archetypes." [6] For the Pléiade true theatre existed with the Ancients. And while medieval forms persisted, the discoveries of the humanists and the current theories of imitation could not go unheeded. During the years of groping for a modern expression of an old form, French playwrights went to the school of the Ancients and discovered "les trois dramaturges qui ont servi de modèles...: Sénèque, Euripide et Sophocles." [7] In their works they found many an example of horror and revenge that so strongly appealed to the Renaissance as a definitive notion of tragedy itself.

But of the Ancients, Seneca "became the rule of art for the early French tragedians." [8] By 1561 there were thirteen complete editions of his works as against four of the Greek tragedians. [9] Traditional arguments maintain that humanist interest in ancient theatre encountered no true linguistic barrier with Seneca such as the Greek tragedies presented, especially in their transmission in manuscript. But it is also true that Seneca's theatre presented topics which were of engaging interest to the sixteenth-century

---

[6] Du Bellay, *Deffense & Illustration de la langue françoyse*, ed. Chamard (Paris: Didier, 1961), p. 126.

[7] Raymond Lebègue, *La Tragédie française de la Renaissance* (Bruxelles: Office de Publicité, 1954), p. 16.

[8] John W. Cunliffe, "Early French Tragedy," *JCL* I (1903), 312.

[9] *Ibid.*, 301; for a detailed discussion of the interest in Greek plays during the period of 1530 to 1550, see René Sturel, "Essai sur les traductions du théâtre grec en français avant 1550," *RHL* XX (1913), 269-296, 637-666. Despite the number of translations during this period, however, Raymond Lebègue maintains that "l'influence de la tragédie grecque n'a été sensible que sur ceux de nos dramaturges qui étaient de bons hellénistes: Buchanon, Théodore de Bèze.... En général, nos dramaturges ne demandaient au théâtre grec qu'un appoint, un complément de ce que leur fournissait leur principal modèle: Sénèque" (*op. cit.*, pp. 10, 18-19). Of course Seneca was not unread during the Middle Ages, but the tragedies were known mainly through collections of *sententiae* (see Manlio Pastore-Stocchi, "Un chapitre d'histoire littéraire aux XIVe et XVe siècles, Seneca Poeta Tragicus," in *Les Tragédies de Sénèque et le théâtre de la Renaissance*, ed. Jean Jacquot [Paris: C. N. R. S., 1964], pp. 11-36).

reader,[10] as well as gripping examples of the third prescription of tragedy with its portraits of avengers and the realistic descriptions of the atrocity of their crimes:

> Horrors are piled on horrors, with the cruelty of the scenes augmented by the keen delight Seneca takes in the realistic descriptions of bloody actions and physical torture. Pity is felt, however, not only for the innocent but even for the guilty in the midst of the torments of their retribution or of their remorse.... The physical is often used to enforce this pity, just as it had originally been employed to raise the horror.[11]

While such plays offer immediate thematic parallels with the tragical tales, there are other similarities which add a Senecan tone to such tales as HT II, IV, and V. First there appears a definite structural similarity between these stories and a revenge play such as the *Medea*. Often criticized for being simplistic since the heroine is committed to her act of revenge from the very beginning, the play has been viewed negatively as a mere excuse to lead to the horror of the conclusion which has been announced from the start. But as Bowers insists, basing his argument upon a structural analysis of the *Thyestes*, the revenge plays are precisely "the dramatization of a revenge... with the catastrophe... kept in mind from the start and led up to with little or no faltering in the course of the action."[12] They follow a linear structure which we have noted in the tragical tales where the story deals with the relentless progression to that horrible act likewise announced in the beginning.[13]

---

[10] See Raymond Lebègue, "Préface" to *Les Tragédies de Sénèque et le théâtre de la Renaissance (ed. cit.)*, pp. ix-x: "Les personnages de Sénèque discutaient des idées qui, au XVIe siècle, retrouvaient une valeur d'actualité: clémence ou sévérité, bonheur d'une vie modeste et campagnarde, malheurs subits des Grands. La violence meurtrière des passions, l'atrocité des crimes qui sont commis dans *Médée* et *Thyeste*, les récits affreusement réalistes des morts violentes ou de la mutilation d'Œdipe, les spectacles macabres, loin de rebuter le public moderne, lui plaisaient: les convulsions politiques du temps, les guerres qui ensanglantaient la France, les Pays-Bas, l'Allemagne, lui faisaient rechercher les émotions fortes."

[11] Bowers, *op. cit.*, p. 43.

[12] *Ibid.*, p. 47.

[13] This parallelism can obviously not be pursued to its ultimate conclusion, for there is a determinism present in Senecan theatre that is foreign to the

This structural reservation about Seneca's theatre is associated with the major criticism that his characters are not sufficiently nuanced, that they do not evolve as do their Greek counterparts. It is undoubtedly for this reason that the Hellenist H. D. F. Kitto speaks of "l'effroyable Sénèque" as a poor choice by English Renaissance dramatists.[14] In a perceptive article Pierre Grimal offers an answer to such criticism, and his views suggest a further parallel with Boaistuau's tales. He maintains that Seneca is not presenting characters who have to make a "tragic choice" which results in disaster. This choice has been made for them by legend. Moreover, as legendary characters, they had come to represent certain philosophical positions and ethical attitudes: Achilles was the symbol of the man who would sacrifice everything for glory, while an Agamemnon was equated with ambition. Myth and legend, given dramatic form by the Greeks and continuing into Seneca's time, had solidified these heroic characters so that Seneca appropriated a traditional and characterized cast and subjected it to a close moral examination:

> ...les vieilles légendes du cycle troyen ou celles que les tragiques avaient popularisées étaient devenues comme un univers où l'expérience morale s'exerçait à propos de situations traditionnelles et de caractères préalablement définis. Dans ces conditions, les tragédies de Sénèque peuvent, elles aussi, apparaître comme des *exempla* qui ont moins pour but d'analyser des caractères que de présenter, grâce à des situations pour ainsi dire "expérimentales," des états de crise où l'âme humaine se révèle dans sa vérité.[15]

Histoires tragiques even in the historical tales, since Boaistuau is not concerned with the presentation of historical incident but rather with a fiction presented as historical truth. For Seneca history or legend determines his plot which is summarily recalled by the very name of his characters. The outcome has been decided in advance, and the characters merely fulfill a destiny that has been marked out for them. This determinism accounts for the oppressive bleakness which hangs heavily over Seneca's plays.

[14] "Le déclin de la tragédie à Athènes et en Angleterre," in *Le Théâtre tragique*, ed. Jean Jacquot (Paris: C. N. R. S., 1962), p. 68.

[15] Pierre Grimal, "Les tragédies de Sénèque," in *Les Tragédies de Sénèque et le théâtre de la Renaissance* (ed. cit.), p. 6.

Grimal's apology might well serve as Boaistuau's, for he too appropriated a characterized cast, historical figures and men of high social rank who are supposed to act in a manner befitting their station. But the situations to which they are exposed reveal a truth that no amount of moral drapings can conceal. They surrender their mythic disguise to give vent to their vindictive passions. Didaco's murder and mutilation by Violente make her a worthy successor to Seneca's wrathful heroines, and Boaistuau cannot avoid comparing her to her mythic archetype. Once Violente has realized her "marriage" was nothing more than defilement, since it was mere deception, she entices Didaco to the same room in which the pleasures of their wedding night took place, and the bed of love becomes the setting for death. Having tied Didaco securely to the bed,

> ne tarda gueres Violente qu'elle ne se saisist de l'un de ces grands cousteaux et, s'estant doulcement eslevée, elle tastoit avecques la main le lieu le plus propre pour luy faire un fourreau de la chair de son ennemy. Et toute saisie d'ire, de rage et de furie, enflammée comme une Medée, luy darda la pointe de telle force contre la gorge qu'elle perça de part en part. (HT V, 162)

Another "dix ou douze coups" are still unable to assuage Violente's thirst for revenge. The frenzy of her hatred produces the most detailed scene of horror in the *Histoires tragiques*:

> Et lors ne pouvant encores repaistre son cueur felon ny esteindre l'eschauffé courroux qui bouillonnoit en son cueur, elle luy tira les yeux avec la poincte du cousteau hors de la teste...Puis...continuant sa rage, elle s'attaqua à la langue, et l'ayant avec ses mains sanglantes tirée hors de sa bouche,...elle feist avec le cousteau une violente ouverture à l'estomach; et lançant ses cruelles mains dessus le cueur du chevalier, l'arracha de son lieu...Puis acharnée sur ce corps mort, comme un lyon affamé sur sa proye, il n'y eut presque partie à laquelle elle ne donnast quelque atteincte...Puis...Janique...print avecques Violente le corps du chevalier, et le precipiterent par l'une des fenestres de la chambre en bas sur le pavé, avec toutes ses parties. (HT V, 162-163)

The tragical tale relishes such examples of violence and bloodshed, such portraits of characters who surrender to the most brutal instincts of destructive passion, such examples of a love which is in a moment transformed into a vengeful hatred. There is, however, one story in the collection which presents a moral problem. In HT II Mahomet is defeated and killed by the Christians after his brutal slaying of Hyrenée; in HT V, Violente is decapitated for the extremity of her revenge. But in HT IV, the seigneur seems to escape all punishment after condemning his wife to the agony of spending the rest of her days locked in the room with the putrifying corpse of her lover whom she was forced to hang. No conclusion is offered in the text to indicate any punishment inflicted upon the husband who is Boaistuau's most successful portrait of the passionate criminal. This is all the more peculiar since there are explicit ethical comments made in the prefatory notices of even those stories which end happily.

However the fourth tale conforms more completely than the others to the spirit and meaning of the tragic in Seneca's theatre. In a sensitive appreciation of Senecan tragedy, Ronald Tobin suggests that there is a distinction to be made between the horror of the catastrophe and the sense of the tragic. "The tragic torment in Seneca ... is ... born of that anguish whose source lies in the knowledge that one's personal conception and esteem of self has been destroyed." [16] In the *Medea*, Jason's marriage to Creusa stings Medea's pride and awakens her craving for revenge after suffering such blatant ingratitude. The "attack on her pride and conception of self" serves as the motivation for her actions throughout the play and precipitates the catastrophe.

There is a similar development in HT IV. The jealous vengeance of the seigneur is incited by the same act of ingratitude. In his final words to his wife, he alludes to her apparent disdain for all that he had offered her:

> Femme mal-heureuse entre les mal-heureuses, puis que tu n'as eu egard au rang d'honneur auquel fortune t'avoit

---

[16] Ronald Tobin, "Tragedy and Catastrophe in Seneca's Theatre," *The Classical Journal* 62 (1966), 70; see also Professor Tobin's study on *Racine and Seneca* (Chapel Hill: University of North Carolina Press, 1971), pp. 41 ff.

> appellée, ayant esté (par mon moyen) faicte de simple damoiselle grande dame, et que tu as preferé l'acointance lascive d'un mien subject à ma chaste amytié, aussi veux-je que tu luy faces desormais continuelle compagnie sans que tu partes jour de ta vie d'aupres de luy, tant que son corps putrifié ait donné fin à la tienne. (HT IV, 134)

An injured pride unleashes the seigneur's jealous wrath. The realization of his wife's infidelity not only transforms his love into a vengeful hatred; it also destroys his nobility as a *seigneur*. Presented initially as "vaillant et genereux," it is precisely this *générosité* which he surrenders as he patiently plots his revenge. Significantly he remains anonymous throughout the tale. The only way of referring to him is by his title, so that his social rank is constantly repeated as are, thereby, his assumed traits of character. But his final words reveal that his "conception of self" has been destroyed since his passion and revenge belie those very qualities that he should represent. The retribution is the literal destruction of the *seigneur*; the tragedy lies in his realization of this truth.

This distinction between the catastrophe and the tragic also applies to the other tragical tales. Mustapha reveals to the sultan Mahomet's loss of the conception of self in much the same way that it is made apparent to Violente when she learns the truth about her marriage to Didaco. This revelation unleashes in both characters a frenzied wrath which knows no truer expression than the destruction of the supposed cause of their deception. For this reason the revenge tales approximate the Senecan conception of the revenge tragedy more closely than the revenge plays of Euripides, the other tragedian who had such favor during the Renaissance and who likewise presents gripping portraits of characters caught up in the fury of vengeance.

Indeed as the "bitch of Cynossema" announces proudly to her victim: "I rejoice in my revenge," [17] she strikes a pose of

---

[17] Euripides, *Hecuba*, trans. W. Arrowsmith (Chicago: The University of Chicago Press, 1956), vs. 1258. All subsequent references are to this edition and are included in the text. Of all Greek plays, the *Hecuba* had unusually good fortune during the sixteenth century: Erasmus translated the play

which Violente and the Seigneur are reminiscent. But Hecuba's "savage, ruthless hate" (1119) which accomplishes its "hideous, inhuman crime" (1125) is based ultimately, even in its extremity, upon a higher notion of justice. As she pleads with Agamemnon for help, Hecuba is referring to a higher universal order:

> But the gods are strong, and over them
> there stands some absolute, some moral order
> or principle of law more final still.
> Upon this moral law the world depends;
> through it the gods exist; by it we live,
> defining good and evil. (799-803)

This notion of a transcendent moral order or *Moira* is the central problem with which Euripides is dealing as he ponders the extent to which such retributive justice as Hecuba's may continue.

The tragical tales are not concerned with this ultimate sense of justice. They are more immediate, less philosophical and metaphysical. The vengeance never exceeds the personal. Such a limitation ethically necessitates the intrusion of the magistrates at the end of HT V to pronounce sentence on Violente's act of revenge. The action is of this world and is related to a personal and exemplary ethic rather than to a higher transcendent power. Violente cannot, like Hecuba, persuade the magistrates that she acted in accordance with a higher moral law. While a play such as the *Hecuba* therefore gives a further instance of the extremes of brutality of which man is capable, this appeal to the sixteenth century was more likely overshadowed by the recurrence of such themes as the fall of the great, the ephemeral nature of power, the vanity of worldly pleasures, and the ravages of war, themes which found such favor with the humanists.

---

into Latin in 1506; Bochetel into French in 1544; and Bandello himself presented his Italian version to the Queen of Navarre in 1539. Of the translations of Greek theatre during the first half of the sixteenth century, Lanson claims that their value to the developing theory of tragedy was to confirm the notion that "la tragédie représente l'instabilité de la grandeur et de la félicité humaine [et] qu'elle veut des spectacles cruels et pitoyables" (*Esquisse d'une histoire de la tragédie française* [Paris: Champion, 1954], p. 9). The final inhumanity to which the former queen of Troy is reduced is a fitting expression of these two preoccupations.

There is another theme in the *Hecuba,* however, which recurs in Seneca's theatre and continues to be developed throughout the Middle Ages and the Renaissance. With a background of skepticism bathing Euripidean theatre, a skepticism over the ultimate order of the universe in the face of a prevailing indifference on the part of the gods whose justice seems so haphazard, the Euripidean hero can only suggest that their authority is superseded by a force far more powerful, far more terrible. He needs to believe in an ultimate order which gives meaning not only to the world he lives in, but also to himself and his own acts. However a mysterious and inexplicable force constantly challenges this belief, a force beyond the range of his understanding and therefore all the more fearful.

"How strange in their reversals are our lives" (846), the Chorus sympathetically observes. And how fearful is human life when subjected to the uncontrollable and unforeseeable dictates of the mysterious, the unpredictable, the imperceptible. But the mind craves some kind of comprehension of the unknown, if only to affix a label to identify a force which is beyond understanding despite its recurrence in human affairs. Luck, chance, fortune, fate, sometimes synonymous, sometimes distinguished in an effort to probe more deeply into the mystery, these are the names indicated by the despairing as ultimately responsible for mutability and change:

> ...do we, holding that the gods exist,
> deceive ourselves with unsubstantial dreams
> and lies, while random careless chance and change
> alone control the world? (489-492)

Talthybius' query resounds and echoes through centuries of similar doubts; the strength of this "random chance" may increase or diminish, but it is impossible even for the Renaissance rationalists to dismiss it entirely.[18]

---

[18] Even a pragmatic empiricist such as Machiavelli concedes the prominence of Fortune and portrays it in the *Discourses* as an unassailable force (II.29), equating it with God. The equation does not offer him any doctrinal problems since he is merely enumerating the opponents of free will. But in orthodox terms, the alliance was unholy and resulted in necessary rational-

In Seneca's heavy and oppressive tragic climate, chance is both a willful and capricious fate. Determined to act as the final leveler, Fortune lashes out at the proud and the highly placed:[19]

> ...as does Fortune roll on the headlong fate of kings... (*Agam.*, 72)
>
> Never did Fortune give larger proof on how frail ground stand the proud. (*Troades*, 4)

Yet there seems to be no discernible meaning to her acts:

> O Fortune, jealous of the brave, in allotting thy favors how unjust thou art unto the good! (*Herc. fur.*, 524)
>
> ...which fickle Fortune disturbs with changeful lot... (*Medea*, 287)
>
> On doubtful wings flies the inconstant hour, nor does swift Fortune pledge loyalty to any. (*Hipp.*, 1141)
>
> O Fortune, who dost bestow the throne's high boon with mocking hand.... (*Agam.*, 58)

Except for a more bleak pessimism, the Euripidean conclusion is repeated in Seneca's *Hippolytus*. Observing the nature of this capricious force, one can only conclude that "Fate without order rules the affairs of men, scatters her gifts with unseeing hand, fostering the worse" (978).

---

izations and accommodations similar to those the medieval theologians had to propose. Fortune, chance, fate, destiny, providence needed to be assigned to an acceptable position. According to Hiram Haydn (*The Counter-Renaissance* [New York: Charles Scribner's Sons, 1950]), the Christian humanists maintained that "Christianity brought chance under law, thus freeing nature from fortune," while the neo-Stoics "even welcomed Fate into the fold. For they found the Stoic idea of man enduring and thus overcoming the buffetings of Fate irresistible." On the other hand while "Calvin might (and did) deny emphatically that predestination had anything to do with Stoic Fate, some of the humanists might (and did) explain that Fate was just the expression which the benighted ancients used for God's Providence" (p. 436).

[19] All quotations from Seneca's plays are taken from the two-volume Loeb edition of *Seneca's Tragedies*, trans. F. J. Miller (Cambridge: Harvard University Press, London: William Heinemann, 1917). References are included in the text.

The prevalence of Fortune in Seneca's theatre prompts Pierre Grimal to observe:

> Tout, dans le tragique de Sénèque, ne se réduit pas à l'opposition entre *furor* et *bona mens*. On pourrait aussi bien soutenir que ces tragédies sont une méditation sur l'idée de Fortune: il est des destins exceptionnels, et des êtres qui sont capables d'y faire face, d'autres qui se laissent engloutir par la tempête. [20]

Therefore Seneca's tragedies and Euripides' *Hecuba* more than likely appealed to the Renaissance reader not only because of the numerous examples of horror and bloodshed, but also because they treat a theme which appears constantly in sixteenth-century theatre as well as in historical and moral discourses. [21]

The theme of Fortune is of central importance to the *Histoires tragiques*. Invocations to Fortune are more than a stylized or poetic complaint; evocations of Fortune more than a narrative *topos*. The word occurs frequently in Boaistuau's tales, but predominantly in the sentimental tales. [22] To the same extent that the theme of vengeance is the basic element of the tragical tale, the theme of Fortune is one of the major motifs in the sentimental tale. Although the textual references contain a few contradictions, they do in general provide a coherent description of the active role played by Fortune in the six stories The contextual

---

[20] "Les tragédies de Sénèque," p. 5.

[21] It is hardly necessary to insist upon the fact that we are not dealing with a single influence, that of the theatrical tradition alone, since Fortune is dealt with in the moral essays and letters of the Ancients. Moreover the preoccupation with Fortune continued throughout the Middle Ages during which time the Church was unable to theorize it out of existence (see Howard R. Patch, *The Goddess Fortuna in Medieval Literature* [Cambridge: Harvard University Press, 1927]). The Middle Ages preserved the pagan figure and passed it on to the Renaissance which found in this personification of chance a meaningful explanation of contemporary problems. In a time defined by movement and change, in a period when political fortune was fragile and temporary, Fortune was a fitting answer for these recurrent patterns of variability and inconstancy.

[22] The following tabulation refers to the number of specific evocations of Fortune in the six tales:

Tragical tales:	II: 2	IV: 5	V: 4
Sentimental tales:	I: 11	III: 21	VI: 21

meanings of "fortune" vary considerably and reflect all of the translations offered by Cotgrave: "hap, chance, luck, lot, hazard, adventure, destinie, fatall necessitie."

Whether or not Fortune is considered as pure chance, it becomes ultimately a power which can exert control over human life and direct man's affairs:

> Le Duc...se rencontrant (de fortune) à quelque escarmouche, fut tué. (HT VI, 223)
>
> ...ou que vous souffrez que je vous accompagne la part où la fortune vous guidera. (HT III, 90)
>
> ...frere Laurens...le retint en quelque lieu secret du couvent jusques à ce que la fortune en eust autrement ordonné. (HT III, 84)
>
> ...mais fortune luy en appresta une plus prompte occasion qu'il ne pensoit. (HT VI, 224)

One metaphor suggests that Fortune's power and control are indistinguishable from the complete determinism of the Fates: "C'estoit l'heure où fortune ourdissoit petit à petit la toille et le fillé auquel elle la vouloit enclorre" (HT IV, 129).

Such a role makes Fortune the equivalent of fate or destiny, while, in an implied hierarchy, Boaistuau distinguishes it from the other two external determining powers: "Car puisque Dieu le veult, la nature le permet, et ma triste fortune le consent, je m'y achemine de bon cueur, sçachant que la sepulture n'est autre chose qu'un fort rempart" (HT VI, 202-203). Boaistuau's traditional ethic necessarily makes Nature and Fortune secondary forces existing beneath God. He also retains in this instance the distinction that was current in the Middle Ages, whereby Nature provides properties of the body and the soul while Fortune is concerned with mundane and temporal goods such as dignities, riches, and prosperity.[23] To this extent Fortune is a positive force. It has the power to better man's lot:

> Monseigneur, combien que je n'aye jamais esperé de me voir eslevée en si hault degré d'honneur, comme maintenant la fortune me range... (HT I, 45)

---

[23] Patch, *op. cit.*, pp. 63-66.

> ...j'en suis assez abondamment pourveu pour maintenir moy et les miens, non comme ambicieux ou taché de convoitise, mais comme bien voulu de la fortune. (HT I, 31)

> ...puis que tu n'as eu egard au rang d'honneur auquel fortune t'avoit appellée... (HT IV, 134)

In this context, Fortune is generally associated with love. Guiding the paths of the lovers, it gives the opportunity for their love to flourish:

> ...mais quelle bonne fortune vous conduict icy maintenant? (HT I, 41)

> Le Roy, averty de la venue de la Comtesse, pensa que fortune luy avoit ouvert le chemin pour bien conduire son entreprise à son effet desiré. (HT I, 20)

> ...ainsi qu'ils cherchoient tous deux les moyens de parler ensemble, fortune leur en appresta une prompte occasion. (HT III, 69)

> Rhomeo s'accoustra des plus sumptueux habits qu'il eust, et guidé par la bonne fortune, se sentant approcher du lieu où son cueur prenoit vie,...il franchit agilement la muraille du jardin. (HT III, 80)

But Fortune is capricious. If it can unite lovers, it can turn upon them just as easily. Envious of their happiness, it inflicts pain and suffering. The greatest number of references deals with Fortune as a malicious force. Fortune is inconsistent and contrary:

> Quelques jours apres le Roy Edouart l'envoya en Flandres en la compagnie du Comte de Suffort, où la fortune leur fut tant contraire qu'ils furent tous deux prins prisonniers par les François et menez au Louvre à Paris. (HT I, 12)

> ...mais maintenant, mes destinées tournées au contraire... (HT VI, 176)

> ...et assiegea Belgrade, où la fortune luy fut tant contraire qu'il fut mis en routte.... (HT II, 60)

> Mais ainsi qu'ils se preparoient pour se donner du bon temps...fortune ce pendant estoit en embusche, qui rompit si bien le fil de leurs entreprinses que l'issue ne fut pas telle qu'ils avoient esperé. (HT VI, 190)

The suffering that Fortune's treachery inflicts upon the protagonists gives ample opportunity for extended lamentations and complaints on the wretchedness of the human lot. Apostrophes abound as Fortune is qualified by such epithets as "malheureuse," "estrange" ('harsh,' 'rude'), "cruelle." The victim becomes the "infortuné:"

> Ah! fortune ennemie de mon heur... (HT V, 150)
>
> Ah miserable que je suys et delaissée de toute bonne fortune! (HT V, 150)
>
> ...puis que ma triste fortune m'a icy amenée comme l'aigneau innocent au sacrifice... (HT I, 42)
>
> Et pour la compassion d'un si estrange fortune... (HT III, 119)
>
> ...vous preniez desormais pitié et compassion de mon estrange et cruelle fortune... (HT VI, 203)
>
> ...et au triste spectacle où la malheureuse fortune m'a maintenant reduict... (HT III, 114)
>
> Infortuné et miserable que je suis. (HT I, 24)

Iconography depicts Fortune and her wheel, symbolic of her inconstancy and of the change of man's estate, turning from prosperity and happiness to despair and misery according to Fortune's capricious moods. Boaistuau's two evocations of this image adequately summarize all of the preceding motifs:

> Et continuerent ainsi quelque moys ou deux leurs aises avec un contentement incroyable, jusques à tant que la fortune (envieuse de leur prosperité) tourna sa roue pour les faire trebucher en un tel abisme qu'ils luy payerent l'usure de leurs plaisirs passez par une trescruelle et trespitoyable mort... (HT III, 82)
>
> M'amie, je n'ay pas maintenant deliberé de vous deduire la diversité des accidens estranges de l'inconstante et

> fragile fortune, laquelle esleve l'homme en un moment au plus hault degré de sa roue, et toutesfois en moins d'un cil d'œil elle le rabaisse et deprime si bien qu'elle luy appreste plus de miseres en un jour que de faveur en cent ans. (HT III, 89)

Herein lies the affective pathos of the sentimental tale: the continuous movement and change from the heights of happiness to the depths of misery according to the whim of some external retributive force which seems to relish inflicting agony and pain upon a weak and powerless man. He, on the other hand, has few resources at his disposal to combat this unpredictable power, and is generally grateful that Fortune has at least been willing for him to experience happiness, which is at least some small compensation for his actual or impending suffering:

> Mais maintenant que je vous tiens entre mes bras, facent desormais la mort et la fortune comme ils entendront, car je me tiens plus que satisfaicte de tous mes ennuys passez par la seule faveur de vostre presence. (HT III, 80)

> Or face donc fortune desormais comme elle entendra, car quelque ennuy qu'elle me puisse jamais apprester, je me confesseray par la seule grace qu'elle m'a faicte ce jourd'huy luy estre eternellement redevable. (HT VI, 227-228)

In the narrative context of the *Histoires tragiques*, the inconstant and changeable character of Fortune effects the reversals which are so frequent, especially in the sentimental tales. For this reason, they might be called "tragedies of Fortune" while the tragical tales are more appropriately described as "tragedies of vengeance." The play of Fortune is manifested generally by external events which often appear gratuitous. But in the sentimental tale they are the causes effecting the meeting, reunion, or separation of the major characters who become victims of change and are thereby forced to struggle helplessly against the tide of events.

Three such external incidents in HT VI ultimately affect, and to a great extent control, the lives of the protagonists. The war between the two Spanish families in the beginning of the tale gives the impetus to the whole story, since it is in the face of apparent defeat that Ysabeau makes her vow to go to Rome. Her trip precipitates the first two movements of the drama. Upon learning of the German invasion, the Duc leaves his affairs in the hands of Pancalier, thereby giving him the opportunity to express to the Duchesse his overwhelming passion, which gives the impetus to the third and fourth movements of the tale. Finally the death of the Duc at the hands of the German invaders results in the Duchesse's brother recalling her to England so that she might remarry. It is here that she encounters Mandozze who has been sent as head of the Spanish delegation to arrange the details of the proposed marriage between the crown prince of Spain and the daughter of the king of England.

HT III is the clearest example of the tragedy of Fortune since it presents a love which is pure and therefore free of any moral condemnation. Edouart is guilty of uncontrollable lust and the Duchesse of adulterous desire, but Rhomeo and Julliette are representative of a pure love, a "parfaicte amitié," and their tragedy occurs not through personal responsibility but because of an external fatality envious of their happiness. It is ironic that in the three sentimental tales, the one example of a positive and morally unreprehensible love should alone end with misfortune and death.

The story is structured according to the implied role of a beneficial Fortune, favorable to love, and a destructive Fortune which contradicts happiness. And typical of the sentimental tale, the changing mood of this capricious force, as the wheel turns from high to low, is signaled by parallel narrative incidents which play the part of external events influencing the lives of the protagonists. In this instance it is the quarrel between the Montesches and the Capellets, described initially to set the scene for the insurmountable obstacle which the perfect love of the most perfect couple must face. Rhomeo experiences the full range of Fortune's power, for he encounters Julliette at the Capellet's masked ball, and it was "fortune" which "l'avoit adressé en lieu si perilleux" (72). In the beginning Fortune favors this young idyllic couple and allows their marriage and the consummation of their love. But the faith and optimism of their youth counted too heavily on Fortune's blessing. Their union was secret in order to bypass the obstacle of their families' quarrel, and the marriage was to reconcile the two families, although remaining undivulged "jusques à ce que la fortune leur eust appresté seure occasion de manifester sans crainte leur mariage à tout le monde" (82). The irony is blatant, for Fortune does comply with their desire: the reconciliation is effected, but not before it takes its payment for the happiness it bestowed.

As the wheel turns "pour les faire trebucher en un... abisme" (82), the other face of Fortune is evidenced by the public manifestation of family enmity during the street-fight scene. This parallel incident begins the second movement of the story which contrasts antithetically with the first. An external incident, during which Rhomeo kills Thibault in self-defense, results in his banishment from Verona. Julliette's only consolation is her nurse's observation that "la fortune le vous eslongne pour un temps" (88). However Fortune is not to be so easily outwitted. Rhomeo's refusal to allow Julliette to follow him in the errant life imposed upon him by his banishment is an effort to overcome misfortune by reason, to "obeïr à la raison" (91) rather than yield to the temptations of their hearts. But reason is powerless, as a series of events betray its limited validity in the unstable world under Fortune's guidance. Julliette's grief over their separation leads to her father's plan to marry her to Comte Paris in the hope that Julliette's visible unhappiness might be dispelled. The threat of adultery forces Julliette to put herself in the hands of Frere Laurens, whose risky plan seems to be the only salvation possible. This solution is frustrated by another external event, the quarantine at the Mantuan monastery where Frere Anselme is detained and thereby unable to deliver the letter to Rhomeo. And at length two final external events cause the final tragedy. The report of Julliette's "death" reaches Rhomeo, who is determined to die beside her; and Julliette is left to her own desperate resources once she awakens and discovers the body of Rhomeo, because Frere Laurens and Pierre, believing they hear the civil authorities approaching, leave Julliette alone in the tomb.

Boaistuau's experiment is to pit a pure and selfless love against the ravages of Fortune, or, as he indicates in his prefatory remarks, "une si rare et parfaicte amitié" against "la varieté des accidents estranges" (61). The odds are against the lovers who grope helplessly in their unhappiness and move steadily closer to their *tragedie*, the descriptive term which occurs twice in the story. Rhomeo's letter to his father recounts the tangle of misfortune culminating in his death, and the contents are viewed as a pitiful summary of "sa triste tragedie" (109). When Frere Laurens is about to relate the whole story to the magistrates, he observes that "le discours de ceste piteuse tragedie" (116) will move them to temper justice with pity. This *tragedie*, a series of unhappy events leading to an unwarranted death, is Boaistuau's most perfect example of the adverse power of a malicious and jealous fatality.

But such conclusions raise the inevitable moral problem of the death scene. If the tale is the drama of a confrontation with Fortune or fate, the ideal lovers do nevertheless resort to suicide in their final despair. Their thwarted efforts to establish their happiness in a permanent fashion appear to lead to no other solution. In the search for possible explanations, we may turn again to Seneca in whose plays Fortune is an implacable fatality which has imposed its will even before the tragedy begins. Throughout the plays, the characters are tested, they react to their pleasure and pain, and from these reactions and observations come suggestions on how to deal with an all-powerful fatality:

> Ungoverned power no one can long retain; controlled, it lasts; and the higher Fortune has raised and exalted the might of man, the more does it become him to be modest in prosperity, to tremble at shifting circumstance, and to fear the gods when they are overkind. That greatness can in a moment be overthrown.... (*Troades*, 259ff)

Several attitudes are implicit in this statement about the variability of things human. There must be a courageous recognition of Fortune's power so that one is ready and prepared to deal with the inevitable reversals. A fatalism is complemented by a stoic acceptance that reversal is imminent, happiness is temporary. Seneca's endorsement of moderation comes from a recognition that change will temper present prosperity. Once it has disappeared, another recommendation is made: "Let none be over-confident when fortune smiles; let none despair of better things when fortune fails" (*Thyestes*, 618). The patient endurance of misfortune is an ironic faith in Fortune's caprice, for the wheel will inevitably turn again.

But Seneca's stoic formulae are complemented by more positive suggestions. "'Tis death alone saves innocence from fortune," he suggests in the *Œdipus* (934). Death is inevitable, and it is moreover a liberation from the torment inflicted by fate. Death is a refuge from the overwhelming unhappiness in life, and in the extremes of misfortune it is often the only recourse.[24] It is only one small step to the escape offered by suicide, for which there is an eloquent apology in the *Agamemnon*:

> All bonds will he break through, who dares scorn the fickle gods, who on the face of dark Acheron, on fearful Styx can look, unfearful, and is bold enough to put an end to life. A match for kings, a match for the high gods will he be. Oh how wretched 'tis to know not how to die! (605-610)

Such an open defiance of Fortune allows man to regain heroic proportions and to outwit Fate.

Fredson Bowers suggests that there is a definite hierarchy in these various responses, that "Seneca sympathizes with suicide when it saves honor or gives an escape from a life too full of pain; yet he feels it more courageous to combat misfortune than to succumb without a struggle."[25] Whichever stands as more prominent and desirable, and this changes according to the play, Seneca did bequeath several answers to posterity on how to deal with this intemperate force: a wise moderation, a courageous acceptance of the inevitable, death as a liberation.

The first two attitudes were easily assimilated within a Christian framework. However Seneca's final recommendation of suicide was a blatant contradiction of Church doctrine and totally

---

[24] See Grimal, "Les tragédies de Sénèque," p. 10: "La mort que tous ces héros appellent n'est pas un moyen d'échapper au malheur; ce n'est pas un repos, c'est le seul recours qui leur reste, une fois qu'ils ont découvert la fatalité de leur être. Et la mort acquiert, par elle-même, la valeur d'une rédemption, indépendamment de toute vie future."

[25] *Elizabethan Revenge Tragedy*, p. 42.

incompatible with Christian belief. Yet, as Raymond Lebègue points out, the theme of suicide had great currency in France during the Renaissance:

> Au XVIe siècle, les moralistes et les compilateurs, à l'envi, citent avec admiration les suicides de Lucrèce, de Caton d'Utique, de Brutus, de la femme de Pétus, etc. Les auteurs tragiques mettent à la scène, ou plutôt en récit, ceux des personnages que leur fournissent l'histoire ou le théâtre de l'Antiquité: de la Cléopâtre de Jodelle à la Sophonisbe de Montchrestien, en passant par le Saül de Jean de La Taille.... Tous ces suicides de héros et aussi de personnages secondaires ensanglantaient la "catastrophe" et excitaient la crainte et la pitié. [26]

However the mere prevalence of the theme does not condone suicide. Professor Lebègue continues by suggesting that writers of the sixteenth century accepted those ideas of Seneca's which offered no problem with Christianity, and, as for the rest, "ils ont essayé de surmonter ou de contourner les obstacles." [27] His example, drawn from Garnier's *Cornélie*, is Cicéron's indictment of suicide since God's gift of soul and life is His alone to take away.

But we look in vain in HT III for some such positive indictment of the ending. Elsewhere in the *Histoires tragiques*, Boaistuau suggests means of combatting Fortune which echo Seneca's first solutions, those which insist upon an awareness of Fortune's possible disfavor:

---

[26] "Christianisme et libertinage chez les imitateurs de Sénèque en France," in *Les Tragédies de Sénèque et le théâtre de la Renaissance (ed. cit.)*, p. 90.

[27] *Ibid.*, p. 94. For a detailed discussion of the ambivalent attitude towards suicide in the sixteenth century, see Albert Bayet, *Le Suicide et la morale* (Paris: Félix Alcan, 1922), pp. 520-558. According to Bayet, it is precisely in the novels, plays, and stoic treatises of the period that suicide emerges as a heroic virtue, especially for the noble and well-born: ..."les gens du monde reconnaissent que 'le saint christianisme' interdit le suicide. Mais quand le motif en est noble, ils s'empressent d'ajouter qu'il n'y a rien de plus brave et de plus généreux" (p. 539). Whereas suicide remained more a heroic ideal than a social reality, the eloquence of the apologists provoked the stern reproval of the Council of Trent.

> ...lesquels prendroient les armes contre toy si la fortune te tournoit le doz... (HT II, 55-56)

> ...je vous prie, s'il advient que la fortune me soit contraire, apres ma mort manifester en public qui je suis. (HT VI, 216)

A modicum of human effort:

> ...il mettroit peine de recompenser par humilité et humbles services ce que la fortune luy avoit en autres choses denié. (HT IV, 126)

A resigned acceptance of Fortune, which assumes a formulaic expression but in which Fortune is nonetheless personified:

> Parquoy face fortune ce qu'elle voudra... (HT VI, 209)

> Facent doncques fortune et l'amour comme ils entendent. (HT I, 32)

And finally the realization of death as a refuge:

> ...sçachant que la sepulture n'est autre chose qu'un fort rempart et imprenable chasteau auquel nous nous enfermons contre les assauts de la vie et furieux aboys de la fortune, lesquels il vaudroit mieux...les yeux fermez attendre au sepulchre, que les experimenter les yeux ouverts avecques tant d'angoisses sur la terre.... (HT VI, 203)

The last two solutions are dealt with in HT III. Once Rhomeo is banished, the nurse counsels Julliette to adopt a stoic attitude and patiently accept their misfortune until the tide turns again in their favor:

> Il me semble...qu'il vous sied mal...de tomber en telle extremité, car lors que la tribulation survient, c'est l'heure où mieux se doit monstrer la sagesse....Suffise-vous que Rhomeo est vif, et ses affaires sont en tel estat qu'avecques le temps il pourra estre rappellé de son exil....Parquoy armez-vous desormais de patience; car combien que la fortune le vous eslongne pour un temps, si suis-je certaine qu'elle le vous rendra au parapres avecques plus d'ayse et de contentement que vous n'eustes oncques. (HT III, 87-88)

But the inadequacy of the nurse's solution is immediately made apparent, for further complications threaten Julliette. According to Boaistuau's version of the tale, it is in Antonio's insistence that Julliette marry Comte Paris that the impetus to the tragedy lies. For Julliette, unable to reveal her marriage to her parents, ultimately risks adultery. As she explains her plight to Frere Laurens, she sees suicide as the only solution ("Tis death alone saves innocence from fortune"):

> Monsieur, parce que vous sçavez que je ne puis estre mariée deux fois, et que je n'ay qu'un Dieu, qu'un mary, et qu'une foy, je suis deliberée partant d'icy, avec ces deux mains que vous voyez joinctes devant vous, ce jourd'huy donner fin à ma douloureuse vie, à fin que mon esprit porte tesmoignage au ciel, et mon sang à la terre, de ma foy et loyauté gardée. (HT III, 97)

As Frere Laurens later explains to the magistrates, it is for this reason that he took the chance of giving the drug to Julliette, preferring to risk his soul "que de souffrir que ceste jeune damoiselle deffeist son corps et meist son ame en peril" (HT III, 117).

Suicide is clearly regarded here as a sin. And yet, just before she dies, Julliette kisses the lifeless Rhomeo and assures us of their victory over misfortune:

> Et toy...Rhomeo...reçoy celle que tu as si loyaument aimée et qui a esté cause de ta violente mort, laquelle t'offre volontairement son ame, à fin qu'autre que toy ne soit jouïssant de l'amour que si justement avois conquis, et à fin que noz esprits, sortans de ceste lumiere, soient eternellement vivans ensemble au lieu d'eternelle immortalité. (HT III, 113)

Only with the most delicate reasoning, however, can Boaistuau "save" Rhomeo and Julliette and assure their salvation. He gives the first clue in the title of the tale: "Histoire troisiesme, de deux amans, dont l'un mourut de venin, l'autre de tristesse." As he suggests in the preface to the tale, one can die from the effects of a strong passion:

> Ceux qui ont leu en Pline, Valere, Plutarque et plusieurs autres qu'anciennement il s'est retrouvé grand nombre

d'hommes et de femmes qui sont morts par une trop excessive joye, ne feront doute qu'on ne puisse mourir par les furieuses flammes du trop ardent amour; lequel s'il s'empare une fois de quelque genereux subject, et qu'il ne trouve forte resistence qui luy serve de rampart pour empescher la violence de son cours, il mine et consomme si bien peu à peu les vertuz et facultez naturelles que l'esprit succombant au faiz quitte la place à la vie. (HT III, 61-62)

In accordance with the title, Julliette "dies" before she plunges the dagger into her breast. Realizing that her former patient endurance of misfortune was to no avail, she slowly succumbs to her present grief: "Ha miserable et chetive que je suis! pensant trouver remede à mes passions, j'ay esmoulu le couteau qui a faict la cruelle playe dont je reçoy le mortel dommage" (HT III, 112). She is speaking metaphorically: the speech occurs before she seizes Rhomeo's dagger. The 'knife which she has sharpened' is the acute pain of her patient suffering. And she promises that the tomb is receiving her "derniers souspirs."

The fact that she afterwards picks up Rhomeo's knife and stabs herself therefore seems rather superfluous since she has already died from "tristesse" as the title promised. Furthermore the previous indictment of suicide would apparently deny the happy reunion of the two souls in heaven. Is Boaistuau's addition of the stabbing a concession to pathos or to the predilection for blood and horror that had such favor according to the demands of tragedy? It seems unlikely, since even the "guilty" heroes of the other two sentimental tales are pardoned and finally discover happiness on earth. The answer is to be found rather in the leitmotif of the story which insists that Rhomeo and Julliette are "parfaicts amants." Julliette's "suicide" must be seen as a symbolic gesture to assure this perfection. Dying by her own hand, and yet remaining innocent, free from sin since she has in fact already "died" from "tristesse," Julliette joins Rhomeo who likewise died by his own hand, but who remains innocent since the responsibility for his death is placed on the apothecary who provided him with the poison and who, "prins, gehenné et convaincu, fut pendu" (119). [28] Rather than a mortal sin, therefore, Julliette's suicide becomes a positive proof of her love for Rhomeo and a dramatic demonstration of the perfection which the couple represents. [29]

Boaistuau writes elsewhere of his admiration for Julliette's gesture: "Que se peult il produire de plus prodigieux en nature, que de se vouloir sacrifier soy-mesme pour accompagner à la mort la personne qu'on ayme?" [30] But he was also evidently aware of the moral implications of his addendum and was able to extricate himself from the problem only with the most delicate reasoning.

A final problem in HT III concerns the conclusion of the story. Boaistuau makes another addition to the Bandello tale with the extensive summary of events narrated by Frere Laurens to the Seigneur de l'Escale, followed by a revelation of the contents of the letter which Rhomeo wrote to his father and

---

[28] *Cf.* Arthur J. Roberts, "The Sources of Romeo and Juliet," *MLN* XVII (1902), 82: "Boisteau took large liberties with his Italian original. Besides the important difference of not having Juliet wake before Romeo dies, there are several minor differences.... In Boisteau Romeo buys his poison of an apothecary whom he tempts by a handful of gold to break the law, for selling poison was a capital crime. Romeo is careful to put the name of the apothecary in the post-mortem letter he writes his father, and the poor fellow is promptly apprehended and tortured to death. It is difficult to see why Boisteau went out of his way to make the hero of his story do so unspeakably mean a thing as to tempt a man to wrongdoing by taking advantage of his poverty, and then report him to the authorities. The Bandello Romeo takes a vial of deadly poison and goes to Verona, but nothing is said about where he got it."

[29] *Cf.* H. B. Charleton, "France as Chaperone of Romeo and Juliet," *Studies in French Language and Mediaeval Literature presented to Professor Mildred K. Pope* (Manchester: Manchester University Press, 1939), p. 49: "In Bandello, Juliet does not commit suicide; she dies of sheer grief — Boaistuau in fact puts at the head of his tale a title literally translated from Bandello, for whom, but not for Boaistuau, it was true.... Boaistuau's Juliet does not, like Bandello's, die of more grief. She kills herself with Romeo's dagger."

[30] *Histoires prodigieuses* (Paris: Club français du livre, 1961), p. 141. *Cf.* Bayet, *op. cit.*, pp. 522-523: "Quand on ne peut avoir ce qu'on aime, on se tue, on essaie au moins de se tuer. C'est ce que font à l'envi les héros et les héroines de la *Mariane* [du Philomène], du *Printemps* d'Yver, des romans d'Ollenix, de Beroalde de Verville, de Des Escuteaux, de Jean d'Intras, de Joulet, de Du Pont, de Du Verdier, de Jeanne Flore. On ne voit dans ces suicides ou ces tentatives que des preuves de loyal amour."

which repeats the same details. Although an artistic justification is difficult, these several additional pages do indicate Boaistuau's understanding of the tale. Upon hearing this pitiful narrative and out of compassion for the misfortune of their children,

> les Montesches et les Capellets rendirent tant de larmes qu'avec leurs pleurs, ils evacuerent leurs coleres, de sorte que deslors ils furent reconciliez, et ceux qui n'avoient peu estre moderez par aucune prudence ou conseil humain furent en fin vaincuz et reduicts par pitié. (HT III, 119)

At first glance the friar's summary of the complex series of events and the final catastrophe seems to have had but a meagre result. With the concentration upon the web of circumstances gradually enveloping and finally destroying the two central characters, with the heightened pathos of the death scene, the dispute between the Montesches and the Capellets had been left in the background, having been accepted as the necessary point of departure for the ensuing events. But it is nevertheless the description of the quarrel which begins the story. And the outbreak of violence during the street-fight scene precipitates the catastrophe. Rhomeo shouts at that moment: "Mes amis, c'est assez, il est temps desormais que noz querelles cessent; car outre que Dieu y est grandement offensé, nous sommes en scandale à tout le monde et mettons ceste republique en desordre" (HT III, 83). Frere Laurens insists upon the central significance of these "querelles" by recounting the tale from start to finish and readjusting the perspective so that the deaths of Rhomeo and Julliette are seen in a true relationship to the cause. The thrust of Boaistuau's conclusion therefore is not so much that the catastrophe ended the quarrel, but that such a great sacrifice was necessary in order to end a dispute which could not be solved "par aucune prudence ou conseil humain." At a time when internal strife was a constant threat and too often a painful reality, the tale was a meaningful example of the havoc wrought by any kind of disorder.

In that microcosm which is Verona, a monument is raised to honor the perfect love of Rhomeo and Julliette. Adorned with epitaphs, replete with marble columns, and adding to "toutes les plus rares excellences qui se retrouvent en la cité" (119), it dominates the city. But the monument mars the lush idyllic site described in the beginning of the tale. It becomes a grim statement of the disastrous results of man's intemperance and an ironic proof that "parfaicte amitié" can evidently not exist on earth at all.

Chapter IV

STYLE

> ...ces fleurs & ces fruictz colorez de cete grande eloquence...
>
> —Du Bellay, *Deffence et illustration*, I.3

Each of the major elements of the *Histoires tragiques* examined up to this point — history, character, theme — contribute ultimately to the avowed ethical dimension of the tales. The fourth and final aspect of tragic theory is concerned with expression and advocates that the work be composed in a noble and ornate style. Every art form has a style which is appropriate to it, Horace state in his *Ars poetica* (v. 92), and the history of the short story during the sixteenth century might be defined as the search for that style. Des Périers' oral anecdotal style, Noël du Fail's humanist discourse, and Marguerite de Navarre's Boccaccian imitation are but three examples of the effort on the part of the French Renaissance tale teller to give a meaningful expression to narrative prose.

These experiments and imitations are significant, because the short story follows a development that differs in one important respect from other literary genres cultivated by the Renaissance. The poet wishing to abide by the recommendations of the Pléiade could dismiss medieval forms such as the lai, the virelai, and the ballade, and find instead descriptions and examples of poetic forms cultivated by the Ancients. The dramatist could discard his medieval heritage of the mytsery play, the morality play, and the farce, and create tragedy and comedy patterned on ancient examples. But the short story, developing from such medieval forms as the *exemplum* and the *fabliau*, had no poetic to which its practitioners could turn. It had necessarily to develop its own theories, to define its own artistic goals. There was no authoritative pronouncement on composition. In order to achieve a degree of artistic integrity, the fictions of a Noël du Fail or a Marguerite de Navarre try to conceal the author-narrator and to project the short story into its own autonomous realm. But with the disappearance of these fictions, and the practical disappearance of the author in Boaistuau's *Histoires tragiques*, thus isolating the exemplary moral tale and making it a self-contained artistic entity, the same problem of the suitable expression and style again appears.

By working within the area of tragic convention, Boaistuau was able to contribute to the form a different concept of character and thereby refine the traditional and exemplary "type cast;" at the same time, a more complex structure mirrors the peripetetic complications arising from the strength of human passion and the very complexities of the human condition. For the expression of these stories, he turns once again to the prescriptions of tragedy.

One of the main influences of dramatic form on the *Histoires tragiques*, as well as one of the distinguishing features of the French version of Bandello, is the proliferation of dialogue, especially in the sentimental tales. We have referred to these passages throughout the preceding discussion, so it will suffice merely to summarize those observations at this point. In reality dialogue is an inappropriate term, for these highly rhetorical passages are mainly exclamatory embellishments of the narrative used to heighten privileged moments of happines or else to intensify the expression of emotional crisis. As such, direct discourse breaks the narrative progression. It elaborates upon defined situations, but generally does not introduce new elements upon which further action depends, with the notable exception occurring in HT III where Frere Laurens reveals his plan to Julliette (98-101), although the passage is not composed as dialogue, but rather as narrative in direct discourse, evoking no reaction or response from Julliette.

Direct discourse is therefore used essentially as a means of amplification and is labeled as discourse, confession, consolation, or exhortation if a listener is present, as complaint, lamentation, or deliberation if the speaker is alone. HT I is a fine example of the way in which these various oratorical embellishments can be combined to produce essentially the whole body of the story, for the narrative framework is meagre. The theme of the tale is the confrontation of lust and chastity as embodied in Edouart and Ælips. Edouart pursues and urges in the name of love, Ælips refuses and retreats in the name of honor. Each of the first three movements of the drama builds up to a confrontation of two characters who relate their attitudes in lengthy speeches. In the first movement, Edouart's confession of love is balanced by Ælips' defense of honor; the second episode pits Edouart's complaint against the discourse of the Comte, another example of the adaptation of the *inventio* in the *Histoires tragiques*. Beginning with Edouart's internal monologue, the third part concentrates on Ælips' renewed defense of honor as more important than life in answer to the Comte's report of the king's demands on her person. With the series of speeches, this tale is the closest approximation to a completely dramatic presentation in the collection, but Boaistuau insistently maintains these speeches as ornaments rather than developing a functional dialogue.

The reason lies undoubtedly in his view of characterization and in the tension that exists between the representational and illustrative character. The exemplary status of the characters predetermines their actions, or narratively, their reactions. They speak as befits the role they are chosen to play, the ethic they are called upon to illustrate. But the mimetic element is assured by the fact they do speak, that they do express the anguish they feel. All forms of direct discourse delve into the mind of the speaker and reveal his feelings. Such interiorization enhances the psychological interest of the tales, and whether the direct discourse is presented as dialogue or monologue, its value lies in the fact that it does give a direct expression to a particular emotional state. Only with the internal monologue does direct discourse probe the reasoning mind. In all other uses, it is rather a description of a state of mind in order to insist upon the reality of a particular emotional experience.

In the tragical tale where narrative predominates, shorter passages of dialogue likewise serve an emotional end, but in a somewhat different manner. As mentioned, Boaistuau generally reveals the conclusion of his tales early in the story. But before the anticipated conclusion, dialogue suspends the catastrophe. Mahomet's words to Mustapha and to the seigneurs who have gathered at the feast postpone the murder scene announced on the first page of the tale. They also assure the irony of the conclusion, as Mahomet boasts that he has finally gained control over his passions. In general, however, the profusion of complaints, confessions, and lamentations is a concession to ornamental embellishment. Stylistically smoother than the narrative passages, these speeches are the clearest examples of the noble and ornate style that was required of tragedy.

Dramatists of the sixteenth century were all in accord as to that expression suitable to tragedy. In the preface to Sophocles' *Electra* (1537), Baïf expresses his fear that his French translation did not capture the full style of the original play, "laquelle en son endroit est tant bien ornée de fleurs d'antique et aultres figures et couleurs." [1] Guillaume Bochetel's introduction to his French version of Euripides' *Hecuba* (1544) praises the original for "la sublimité du style et gravité des sentences." [2] Similar expressions are numerous. Grévin's preface to the edition of his plays considers the three Greek tragedians as the main source of inspiration for all playwrights and "le tresor auquel ils ont pris les richesses pour embellir leurs poëmes." [3] Jacques Peletier du Mans compares the two ancient dramatic forms and insists that "la Comediẹ parlẹ facilẹment... la Tragediẹ ẹt sublimẹ" and the reason he recommends the two later Greek tragedians is that he considers "Sofoclẹ plus gravẹ dẹ stilẹ e plus hautein" while Euripides is "plus santancieux e plus filosofiquẹ." [4] Finally

---

[1] In Bernard Weinberg, *Critical Prefaces of the French Renaissance* (Evanston: Northwestern University Press, 1950), p. 74.
[2] *Ibid.*, p. 108.
[3] *Ibid.*, p. 185.
[4] *L'Art poetique*, ed. André Boulanger (Paris: Les Belles Lettres, 1930), pp. 190 and 192.

it is a stylistic consideration which is at the very basis of Jean de La Taille's definition of tragedy as "un genre de Poësie non vulgaire, mais autant elegant, beau et excellent qu'il est possible." [5]

The adjectives used in these descriptions readily denote what was felt to be an essential quality of the tragic poem. It was to be elegant, sublime, ornate, sententious, embellished. [6] The gravity of tragedy demands a style which alone is appropriate to it, a Grand Style according to the distinctions made by ancient rhetorics:

> There are, then, three kinds of style, called types, to which discourse, if faultless, confines itself: the first we call the Grand; the second, the Middle; the third, the Simple. The Grand type consists of a smooth and ornate arrangement of impressive words. The Middle type consists of words of a lower, yet not of the lowest and most colloquial, class of words. The Simple type is brought down even to the most current idiom of standard speech. [7]

Such a distinction of styles continues through the Middle Ages and the Renaissance. The *ornatissima verba* of the Grand Style were felt, according to sixteenth-century definitions, to be the proper expression for tragedy. The problem was very simply how the Grand Style was to be achieved.

Again traditional rhetoric provides an answer. In the divisions of rhetorical art — *inventio, dispositio, elocutio, memoria, actio* —

---

[5] "De l'Art de la Tragédie," preface to *Saül le furieux*, ed. Elliott Forsyth (Paris: Didier, S. T. F. M., 1968), p. 3.

[6] A curious exception is Théodore de Bèze whose *Abraham sacrifiant* is credited with being "la première tragédie originale en langue française" (Lebègue, *La Tragédie française de la Renaissance*, p. 28). In the preface, Bèze states that "combien que les affections soyent des plus grandes, toutesfois je n'ay voulu user de termes ni de manieres de parler trop eslongnées du commun, encores que je sache tel avoir esté la façon des Grecs et des Latins.... Mais tant s'en faut qu'en cela je les vueille imiter, que tout au contraire je ne trouve rien plus mal seant que ces translations tant forcées et mots tirez de si long temps qu'ils ne peuvent jamais arriver à point" (in Weinberg, *op. cit.*, p. 151).

[7] *Rhetorica ad Herennium*, IV.viii.11 (trans. H. Caplan, "Loeb Classical Library" [Cambridge: Harvard University Press, London: W. Heinemann, 1954], p. 253).

the third comprises a system of stylistic rules. Figures of words, tropes, figures of thought, these contribute to the basic ingredient of style: ornamentation. "To confer distinction upon style is to render it ornate, embellishing it by variety." [8] The Grand Style, proper to tragedy, is a style that is ornate and highly embellished according to the precepts and recommendations of *elocutio*. For the Renaissance, this compendium of figures and examples, the third part of the traditional scheme of rhetoric, plays an increasingly preponderant role, gradually blurring and finally ignoring the balance which the Ancients sought to maintain with the accepted five-part system.

In the Middle Ages a shift of emphasis is already apparent. The doctrine of rhetoric, based on the *Herennium*, Cicero's *De Inventione*, and Horace's *Ars poetica*, comprises *disposition, amplification,* and *ornement*. [9] *Disposition* assimilates and combines *inventio* and *dispositio*, a distinction that was vague, if not repetitive, in ancient rhetorics. Moreover medieval rhetoricians accorded this first area a secondary role since, according to Faral, "la composition n'a pas été le souci dominant des écrivains du moyen âge." [10] But *elocutio* predominates. It is refined and given a more exaggerated importance. *Amplification* gathers together those figures which assure prolixity, while *ornement* receives the major emphasis and deals with rhetorical figures. Dante's statement in the *Convivio* that "la bellezza è ne l'ornamento de le parole" (II.xi.4) confers upon the notion of style the requirement of ornamentation and embellishment as a prerequisite of beauty.

The importance given to grammar and rhetoric in the medieval *trivium* preserves this heritage right into the Renaissance. [11] To cite only the two major theoreticians of the Pléiade,

---

[8] *Ibid.*, p. 275 (IV.xxxi, 18).

[9] Edmond Faral, *Les Arts poétiques du XIIe et du XIIIe siècles* (rpt. Paris: Champion, 1962), pp. 55-103.

[10] *Ibid.*, pp. 59-60.

[11] "Mr. Faral has shown how the writers of the Middle Ages had reduced the art of writing to the systematic, unrestrained application of a set of mechanical rules mostly derived from the *Ad Herennium*. And in some ways it might be said that the sentimental rhetoric of the *Histoires tragiques* represents the full blossoming of a tendency transmitted from medieval literature" (René Pruvost, *Matteo Bandello and Elizabethan Fiction* [Paris: Champion, 1937], p. 314).

we find that Du Bellay accepts *elocutio* as such a fundamental aspect in the background of any prospective writer that he proposes to dismiss any consideration of it at all:

> Quand aux figures des sentences & des motz, & toutes les autres parties de l'eloquution,...je n'en parle point apres si grand nombre d'excellens phylosophes & orateurs qui en ont traicté, que je veux avoir été bien leuz & releuz de nostre poëte, premier qu'il entreprenne quelque hault & excellent ouvraige. [12]

Following the traditional scheme of ancient rhetoric for his own *Abbregé de l'Art Poëtique françois*, Ronsard proposes that "elocution n'est autre choses qu'une propriété & splendeur de paroles bien choisies & ornées de graves & courtes sentences," [13] and he suggests that eloquence resides in the choice of words, in *copia*, and in such figures of thought as descriptions and comparisons.

The value of such ornamentation is emphasized in Thomas Wilson's comprehensive yet conservative statement of the *Arte of Rhetorique*. [14] Writing in 1553, Wilson devotes the majority of the text to the general areas of amplification and elocution. Fully half of the work is devoted to listing tropes and figures, illustrated by appropriate examples, all of which serve to embellish sentences and endow a work with eloquence and distinction. But Wilson also insists upon the triple purpose of rhetoric as a complete art of composition: it is to teach, to delight, and to persuade, thereby underscoring the value of the didactic, which is the informing element of the short narrative. The *dolce* must be complemented by the *utile*. "Delight" is achieved by artistic embellishments, and "persuasion" by those devices which effect an emotional response and move the affections. [15] We are in the domain of the *Histoires tragiques*

---

[12] *La Deffense & Illustration de la langue françoyse*, II.9 (*ed. cit.*, p. 159). Du Bellay does however follow this statement with an enumeration of certain figures.

[13] *Œuvres complètes*, ed. Laumonier (Paris: Didier, 1949), t. XIV, p. 15.

[14] See edition by G. H. Mair (Oxford: The Clarendon Press, 1909).

[15] The influence of Quintilian is evident. In his genial *Institutio Oratoria* he insists that the *dolce* and the *utile* are inseparable (VIII.iii.11). The former is achieved through rhetorical adornment, but this must always

STYLE   145

with its emphasis upon ornamentation and the accommodation of devices which will effect an emotional response and enhance the implied moral lesson.

The mid-sixteenth-century notion of the Grand Style may therefore be summarily defined as a combination of *elocutio* ("eloquence" or "elocution," the ornamentation by rhetorical figures and tropes) and amplification (copia, abundance), serving to embellish a work which has an ultimate seriousness of purpose.[16] The resounding acclaim given to Jodelle's *Cléopâtre captive* testifies to the importance of these aspects of style. In lieu of action, character development, tragic crisis, the play's success might more likely be attributed to the fact that the "French Sophocles" was a poet who endowed his regular play with a style that was plaintive and elegiac ("to delight"), emphatic and declamatory ("to persuade"), grave and sententious ("to teach"). Sufficiently sprinkled with rhetorical devices, its poetic "eloquence" was assured.[17]

The importance of *elocutio* during the Renaissance is evident; a definitive statement about *elocutio* is virtually impossible. There existed a veritable quarrel among Renaissance rhetoricians who had refined eloquence to such an extent that it became a complex maze of subtle distinctions.[18] For our purpose the general

---

remain appropriate to the subject matter, never artificial (VIII, Pr.). Similarly Wilson' elaboration of the three styles of expression recalls Quintilian's distinctions which he qualifies as *subtile, grande, floridum* — with their respective functions of instructing, moving, and charming (XII.x.58-60). Quintilian endorses no single style, but recommends a blend of all three for the most effective expression (XII.x.66). With the particular nature of these styles, it would appear that the *Histoires tragiques* moves between the grand, characterized by amplification and hyperbole, and the florid, which has recourse to rhetorical figures (elocution).

[16] In somewhat different terms, these are the two aspects which Alexandre Lorian finds most frequently in the prose writers of the sixteenth century: "l'*emphase*, provenant d'un désir d'amplifier et d'exagérer, d'impressioner et d''ébahir'; et l'*imbrication*, émanant du besoin de tout enchaîner, relier et réunir" (*Tendances stylistiques dans la prose narrative française au XVIe siècle* [Paris: Klincksieck, 1973], p. 9).

[17] For a description of the reception of the play and an analysis of its stylistic elements, see the introduction to the critical edition by Lowell Bryce Ellis (Philadelphia: University of Pennsylvania Studies in Romance Languages and Literatures, Extra Series No. 9, 1946).

[18] Sister Miriam Joseph (*Rhetoric in Shakespeare's Time* [New York: Harcourt, Brace & World, 1962], a reprint of sections of her *Shakespeare's*

notions of amplification and ornamentation or embellishment will suffice.

Boaistuau's prefatory comments bear repeating at this point. Insisting in his "Advertissement au lecteur" that his work is not a servile imitation of the Italian source, he criticizes Bandello because "sa phrase... a semblé tant rude, ses termes impropres, ses propos tant mal liez et ses sentences tant maigres." Boaistuau's criticisms clearly refer to the traditions just mentioned: the impropriety of Bandello's language offends the Grand Style and is lacking in eloquence; the words lacking proper transition and the weak sentences lack amplification, a basic precept of Latinate style. It is necessary to examine some of the ways in which Boaistuau intended to correct these shortcomings. [19]

To avoid "sentences tant maigres," Boaistuau turns to specific figures of diction, and most frequently to synonymy. As a device of amplification, synonymy endorses superfluous repetition in order to give weight and emphasis to the sentence. It is moreover one of the elements that was considered essential to a Latinate style and one that could be adapted into French without offending a normal syntax. Most often synonymy involves the doubling of nouns:

Use of the Arts of Language [New York: Columbia University Press, 1947]) tries to impose some order by dividing these theorists into three major groups: the Traditionalists, the Ramists, and the Figurists. Her discussion of the figures which they treat suggests that in many instances the sixteenth century had tried to refine rhetoric to such a point that there was not even common agreement, in certain instances, on the meaning of the same term.

[19] The following listing is not intended to be exhaustive. Such figures as *correctio* and *transitio*, valuable in a narrative context, are so infrequent that they have been omitted. Other figures, *praeteritio* (paralipsis), *interrogatio*, metonomy, which appear occasionally in the *Histoires tragiques*, have been mentioned earlier when relevant to passages discussed. For the same reason it is useless to repeat Boaistuau's adaptation of the *inventio* in HT I and HT II. One problem is always evident when dealing with rhetoric during the Renaissance: the subtle distinctions and refinement of rhetoric as an art present an obstacle to the definition of figures. We have therefore adopted the *Rhetorica ad Herennium* as a basis for this discussion since the work was a constant reference during both the Middle Ages and the Renaissance. Where modern terminology differs from that in the *Herennium*, definitions are given.

STYLE 147

> ...tant de la confusion et desordre de l'empire... (HT II, 50)

> ...ayant les yeux etincellans de grand ire et fureur... (HT II, 58)

> Ainsi se passa la journée en telle joye et liesse... (HT V, 146)

> ...jusques à ce que le jour, qui commençoit à poindre, leur causa la separation avec extreme dueil et tristesse. (HT III, 92)

> Et fut arresté entre eulx, par l'avis et conseil tant de ceux du Roy d'Angleterre... (HT VI, 200)

The synonymous doubling of adjectives imposes an emphatic or superlative strength upon the qualifiers:

> ...estant preste et disposée de vous obeyr... (HT III, 71)

> O charongne infaicte, qui as autrefois esté organe de la plus infidele et desloyale ame qui oncques descendit du ciel! (HT V, 163)

> De combien donc luy sommes-nous obligez et redevables... (HT VI, 231)

> Et si pitié est la seule et unique clef pour ouvrir la porte de Paradis... (HT VI, 203)

Less frequently synonymy involves the doubling of the verb:

> ...ceux que Dieu a tousjours plus aymez et cheriz... (HT VI, 214)

> ...il ne prenoit plaisir qu'à la cherir et caresser... (HT II, 50)

> ...vous excedez et surpassez en cecy la cruauté des animaux... (HT I, 34)

> ...les songes ne cessent lors de tourmenter et affliger mon ame... (HT V, 155)

It is not uncommon for several types of synonymy to occur within a single sentence or to be combined in a single phrase:

> ...me representans par leurs espovantables et horribles visions l'aise et contentement de celle qui tient ma place... (HT V, 155)

> ...par l'avis et conseil duquel il entendoit que tous les affaires de son Duché seroient regies et gouvernées durant son absence, et qu'il fust honoré et obey comme la propre personne. (HT VI, 193)

> Le Comte, entendant l'incivile et brutale demande de son seigneur, rougissant de honte et d'estonnement, remply encores d'un honneste et vertueux desdain... (HT I, 27)

The more than one hundred examples of this figure, occurring with frequency in both the tragical and sentimental tales, readily indicate Boaistuau's basic means of imposing strength and fullness upon the 'weak sentences' of his source, thereby assuring the nobility of his style.[20]

Such stylistic formality is further assured by a related means of amplification. Accumulation, the piling up of words or phrases, is not a figure of repetition, like synonymy, but rather the gathering together of different yet related words. But along with synonymy, this figure was a precious device in sixteenth-century literature which has been qualified as "une littérature de con-

---

[20] In his study of *Jacques Amyot, traducteur des "Vies parallèles" de Plutarque* (Paris: Champion, 1909), René Sturel maintains that synonymy is one of the most recurrent devices in sixteenth-century prose style: "Les auteurs les moins préoccupés de faire 'œuvre littéraire' usent et abusent comme les autres du redoublement.... Mais c'est surtout chez les traducteurs que cette habitude devient fatigante" (p. 235, n. 2). Examining the use of synonymy in the French version of Plutarch, he concludes that such repetitions "ont moins pour but chez Amyot, —comme sans doute chez beaucoup de ses contemporains, —de rendre l'idée du texte avec plus de précision ou plus de nuance, que de satisfaire au désir d'ampleur, d'harmonie et de rythme" (p. 245). J. Chocheyras suggests that synonymy was used in the sixteenth century not in imitation of Latin style but rather as a means of glossing neologisms ("Le redoublement de termes dans la prose du XVIe siècle: une explication possible," *Revue de linguistique romane* XXXIII [1969], 79-88). For a discussion of the varied effects that Montaigne achieves with synonymy, see R. A. Sayce, "The Style of Montaigne: Word-Pairs and Word-Groups," in *Literary Style: A Symposium* (London and New York: Oxford University Press, 1971), pp. 383-405.

ception énumérative et d'écriture énumérative." [21] Of the various types, the accumulation of nouns is the most frequent in the *Histoires tragiques* and serves various descriptive functions. Accumulation graphically describes the carnage resulting from the street fight in HT III where "la terre estoit toute couverte de bras, de jambes, de cuisses et de sang" (83). It suggests Edouart's frustration after his various attempts to win the favor of Ælips: ..."ne l'ayant peu vaincre par prieres, offres, presens, humilitez, ambassades et lettres" (HT I, 27). It occurs throughout the tales to portray character, social rank, or setting. Mandozze comes from a family that is "des plus opulentes en richesses, vassaux et seigneuries de toute la province" (HT VI, 171). Valencia is ironically described as "le vray sejour de foy, de justice et d'humanité" (HT V, 139).

The adjectival accumulations lavish description, often in a climactic series:

> La plus grande, cruelle et atroce injure que peut recevoir l'homme bien né... (HT IV, 121)

> Et si oncques journée fut lamentable, piteuse, malheureuse et fatale... (HT III, 106)

> ...mais bien d'un vil, pusillanime, cruel et libidineux tyran... (HT I, 30)

> ...il est bien en reputation d'estre l'un des plus roides, adroits et redoutez chevaliers de la Lombardie. (HT VI, 211)

The accumulation of verbs is rare, but used effectively it can serve as a functional embellishment. Mustapha warns Mahomet of his imminent downfall by telling him that "les plus affectionnez seigneurs de vostre empire murmurent, conspirent et conjurent contre vous" (HT II, 52). Rhomeo vows his complete devotion when he tells Julliette: ..."ne souhaitant autre plus grand bien... que de vous servir, obeyr et honorer par tout où ma vie se pourra estendre" (HT III, 71), a sentiment that he later repeats when he insists that life has no value for him "fors

---

[21] Lorian, *op. cit.*, p. 93.

que pour vous aimer, servir et honorer (HT III, 75). A cumulative series of verbs projects the blind fury of the street fighters who "n'entendoient qu'à se tuer, desmembrer et deschirer l'un l'autre" (HT III, 83).

But generally this type of accumulation includes verbs and their objects or modifiers in order to produce the more elaborate series of phrases, and thereby achieve an ample and rich period:

> La gloire de voz ancestres et majeurs, acquise par tant de sang, entretenue par si grande prudence, conservée par si heureux conseil... (HT II, 53)

> ...avec la deliberation de prendre la Comtesse prisonniere, desmolir le chasteau et de faire butin des richesses qui y estoyent. (HT I, 12)

> ...qui a aneanty mes forces et empoisonné mon sens et privé mon ame de tout bon conseil... (HT I, 27)

> ...car prononçant ces mots, il souspiroit tant à propos, et changeoit tant souvent de couleur, et avoit la face si couverte de larmes, qu'il sembloit que son ame... (HT VI, 189)

> Ce Comte de Pancalier...se voyant avoir entier commandement sur tout le pays, se trouvant quelquefois pres de la personne de la Duchesse et la voyant si belle et de si bonne grace, ne peut tant commander à luy mesme... (HT VI, 193)

Along with the accumulation of noun phrases — "mais nostre ancienne nourriture, le devoir de ma conscience, avec l'experience que vous avez tousjours eue de ma fidelité" (HT II, 52) — and of clauses — "Car puis que Dieu le veult, la nature le permet, et ma triste fortune le consent" (HT VI, 202) — Boaistuau tries to avoid the "sentences maigres" of his source. In his *consolatio* to the Duchesse, Mandozze combines several types of accumulation to achieve an ample oratorical style:

> Encores disoit-il estre peu ou rien de ce que nous endurons au regard de ce que Jesus Christ a enduré, lequel, combien qu'il eust forgé toute la machine du monde, a esté appellé fils de charpentier, preschant il a esté ca-

> lumnié, mené sur une montagne pour le precipiter, appellé gourmand, yvrongne, amateur des publicains et pecheurs, Samaritain, seducteur, demoniacle, disant qu'au nom de Belzebut il chassoit les diables. (HT VI, 214)

A final device of amplification frequently found in the *Histoires tragiques* is polysyndeton. It is a curious figure, for, like its opposite asyndeton, it is recommended as a means of suggesting movement. For this effect it is limited to a series of phrases joined by conjunctions.[22] When Mustapha warns Mahomet of the imminent danger that threatens him, since the Pope has called together all Christians to attack the sultan, he suggests the rapid collapse of the empire once the troops have arrived: ..."pour en apres te courir sus, et te ravir le sceptre des mains, et s'emparer de ton Empire" (HT II, 56). However when, instead of phrases, successive clauses are so connected, the sense of movement is lost, and the opposite effect is created. The rhythm becomes slower and more ponderous:

> Madame luy alla demander s'il luy plaisoit souper en sa chambre ou en la salle, à laquelle il fist responce... qu'il se commençoit à trouver bien, et qu'il avoit reposé toute l'apres disnée, et qu'il estoit deliberé de souper en bas; et manda ce soir mesme ce jeune gentil-homme pour luy faire compagnie à souper, et sceut tant bien dissimuler son juste courroux que ny sa femme ny le gentil-homme ne s'en apperceurent aucunement. (HT IV, 129)

In this case the accumulation of subordinate clauses creates a slow and deliberate rhythm suggesting the careful step by step plotting by the Seigneur whose act of vengeance has been painstakingly formulated.

With the proliferation of dialogue in the *Histoires tragiques*, Boaistuau turns readily to anaphora, another figure of repetition used "for both the embellishment and the amplification of style."[23] It occurs twice in successive passages of Violente's letter

---

[22] In his article on "Polysyndeton" in the *Encyclopedia of Poetry and Poetics* (Princeton: Princeton University Press, 1965), Haydn C. Bell limits the figure to this type of example alone.

[23] *Rhetorica ad Herennium*, IV.xiii.19 (*ed. cit.*, p. 277).

to Didaco as the betrayed wife feigns extreme grief in order to lure her husband back home to his death:

> Helas! combien de millions de fois le jour l'ay-je appellée sans la pouvoir rendre ployable à mes crys? Helas! combien de fois me suis-je veue vaincue par l'aspre tourment de ma douleur prendre de vous l'extreme congé et dernier à-dieu, pensant estre arrivée au but limité de ma vie? Voila mes delices ordinaires, Didaco, voila mes plaisirs, voila tout mon passetemps.... (HT V, 154-155)

Whereas Violente uses anaphora, as well as *interrogatio*, synonymy, and hyperbole, to reinforce the pathos of her letter, the Comte employs this figure to enhance the strong tone of accusation in his speech to Edouart:

> C'est vous, c'est vous, Roy Edouart, qui ravissez à ma fille l'honneur, à moy le contentement, à mes enfants la hardiesse de se trouver en public, à toute nostre maison son ancienne gloire. C'est vous qui obscurcissez la clarté de mon sang avec une tache si deshonneste et detestable que la memoire n'en sera jamais esteincte. C'est vous qui me contraignez d'estre le ministre infame de la ruine totale de ma maison et d'estre le ruffien effronté de l'honneur de ma fille. (HT I, 28)

Anaphora is eminently suited to the plaintive and oratorical styles, the two styles of the majority of passages in direct discourse. In his large sample of sixteenth-century prose writers, Professor Lorian finds that Boaistuau in particular favors this type of "répétition emphatique" so common to the "style fleuri." [24] Boaistuau handles the device deftly, without exaggeration, and derives maximum benefit from its ornamental value.

Since the short story has a professed ethical goal during the Renaissance, the maxim was a serviceable ornament. The concise statement of a general truth undoubtedly had an esthetic appeal, but throughout the century copybooks were filled with these brief capsules of ancient wisdom for their ethical value. It was in this manner that Seneca was first known as a dramatist — as

---

[24] *Op. cit.*, p. 124.

a writer of sententious statements sprinkled throughout his plays — even before editions of the plays were published. Erasmus admits the value of maxims in narration, and advises that "if they are employed appropriately, they contribute a no small copia to a speech, and that not without weight or charm." [25]

In his introductory remarks to HT IV, Boaistuau speaks about the Roman law which allowed husbands to kill unfaithful wives, a law he feels is "tresequitable " since most often "la crainte du supplice amorstist et esteinct le desir" (HT IV, 121). The sententious formula succinctly summarizes his prefatory comments and provides a perspective for understanding the tale he is about to relate. When Boaistuau makes an authorial appearance within the narrative, it is often in the disguise of such generalized truths. Suggesting that Edouart's lust for Ælips is not to be assuaged by his secretary's counsel, Boaistuau intercedes with the assertion that love is the "ennemy mortel de tout bon conseil" (HT I, 23).

Most often the maxim is used in passages of direct discourse; the purpose, however, varies considerably. In HT III a humorous note is sounded as Boaistuau prefigures Shakespeare's fully developed characterization of the nurse. Recommending to Rhomeo and Julliette that they enjoy the pleasures of their wedding night instead of continuing such elaborate discussions, *la vieille* departs with the warning: "Qui a temps à propos et le perd, trop tard le recouvre" (HT III, 81). More frequently characters use the maxim in the same way that Boaistuau does in the beginning of HT IV: to conclude a speech, to summarize the details they have just uttered and present them in the form of a concise and simple general truth. Mustapha's long discourse concludes with the observation that "les plaisirs interrompuz sont plus grands que ceux qu'on reçoit à toute heure" (HT II, 57). Comparing Edouart's political fortunes to the passion that now rages within his soul, Ælips assures the king that "la victoire qui s'acquiert sans effusion de sang humain est toujours la plus noble et plus acceptable devant Dieu" (HT I, 16). Confronted by the choice of yielding to Edouart's passionate demands and thereby losing

---

[25] Erasmus, *On Copia of Words and Ideas,* trans. King and Rix (Milwaukee: Marquette University Press, 1963), p. 80.

her honor or saving her honor only to endanger her family, Ælips is advised by the Comte that "de deux maulx le moindre toujours doit estre esleu" (HT I, 32). Ælips concludes the announcement of her decision to the Comte with the rationalization that "la mort honneste honore la vie passée" (HT I, 36).

Not only do maxims conclude arguments, but as general truths, they help a character to make a decision. Torn between allegiance to family honor and her love for the slayer of Thibault, Julliette no longer imagines that she was being used to further the Montesche cause once she realizes that "la face est la loyale messagiere des conceptions de l'esprit" (HT III, 73), and her faith is restored in Rhomeo's earlier expression of love and devotion. Edouart utters a maxim in order to deceive the Comte and enlist his help in securing the concession of Ælips. Feigning control over his lust, he announces self-righteously that "celuy seul est heureux qui avecques raison peut gouverner ses sens sans se laisser transporter à ses effrenez desirs" (HT I, 23).

To avoid the unpolished style and "les termes impropres" of his source, Boaistuau employs certain tropes and figures of thought which all pointedly seek to embellish his tales and assure their eloquence. Antonomasia *(pronominatio)* gives a capsule characterization and avoids the repetition of a proper name in the narrative. Thus Mahomet is cast as "le barbare cruel" (HT II, 59) and Didaco as a "faulseur de foy" (HT V, 152). Hyperbole frequently reinforces moments of pathos or the sentimental crisis experienced by a character:

> ...lesquels...menerent tel dueil que qui eust veu lors leurs contenances, il eust peu aisément juger que c'estoit la journée d'ire et de pitié. (HT III, 105) [26]

> ...laquelle, avertie tant de la mort de son cousin Thibault que du bannissement de son mary, faisoit retentir l'air par une infinité de cruelles plainctes et miserables lamentations. (HT III, 85)

---

[26] "Chez les conteurs fleuris, la consécutive d'intensité est en honneur surtout parce qu'elle permet d'exagérer les quantités et les qualités" (Lorian, *op. cit.*, p. 181); for a discussion of the widespread use of the intensive result clause in Renaissance prose, see, in the same study, pp. 58-61, and 171 ff.

Periphrasis is consistently used to avoid the verb *mourir*. It may refer to an actual death of which the paraphrase attempts to attenuate the pain:

> Et ces propos achevez, elle rendit l'esprit. (HT III, 113)

> ...depuis hier matin mademoiselle Julliette a laissé ce monde pour chercher repos en l'autre. (HT III, 108)

> ...apres avoir receu dix ou douze coups mortels, l'un apres l'autre, sa pauvre ame martyre feist le departement d'avec son triste corps. (HT V, 162)

Or else the death may be figurative, an expression of extreme pain beyond physical endurance which the characters in the *Histoires tragiques* inevitably suffer as a result of their excessive passion:

> ...il sembloit que son ame, pressée de trop grand ennuy, deust à l'instant abandonner son corps. (HT VI, 189)

> Rhomeo commença à mener tel dueil qu'il sembloit que ses esprits, ennuyez du martyre de sa passion, deussent à l'instant abandonner son corps. (HT III, 108)

> Combien de fois me suis-je veue...prendre de vous l'extreme congé et dernier à-dieu... (HT V, 154)

> ...je lamenteray le reste de ma triste vie avec tant de larmes que mon corps, espuisé de toute humidité, cherchera en brief son refrigere en terre. (HT III, 86)

Other examples of periphrasis defer to a sense of propriety, especially when describing the act of love: "Ils feirent en fin ouverture de ce qui les passionnoit si fort" (HT IV, 125). And finally, while speaking to the Duchesse, Æmilie avoids pronouncing the name of Mandozze in order not to cause her mistress further pain: ..."j'espere y pourveoir par si bon moyen que verrez en brief celuy qui, sans que l'ayez en rien offensé, vous cause tant de mal" (HT VI, 177).

In general, however, Boaistuau is more successful in syntactic embellishment than he is with rhetorical figures. His metaphors are either traditional or banal. The basic themes of the sentimental tales are summarily treated by making the analogy of bad fortune and a "tempeste" (HT VI, 227), while the "labirinthe" (HT I, 24) suggests the inevitable entanglement of the passion of love.[27] The extended metaphors *(allegoria)* deal almost without exception with daybreak and nightfall and are the most artificial of all the embellishments:

> ...si tost que la nuict avec son brun manteau avoit couvert la terre... (HT III, 74)

> Et comme l'aube du jour commençoit à mettre la teste hors de son Orient... (HT III, 105)

> ...avant que le soleil ait circuit le zodiaque... (HT II, 58)

> ...passa la nuit jusques à ce que le jour commençant à esclairer avec sa lampe ardente les contraignit de se lever. (HT VI, 176)

Boaistuau generally ignores the important recommendation of the *Herennium* that "a metaphor ought to be restrained, so as to be a transition with good reason to a kindred thing, and not seem an indiscriminate, reckless, and precipitate leap to an unlike thing."[28] The more successful metaphors are found in the introductions to the stories,[29] although his effective indictment of English royalty in HT I, where he insists that "les Roys d'Angleterre... se sont si bien laissez transporter à l'amour que la lascivité a esté le sceptre de leurs royaumes" (11), is an obvious debt to the talent of Marguerite de Navarre (*Heptaméron*, I.3).

Far more frequent than the metaphors are the similes, the greatest number of which are comparisons with animals:

> Mais elle, non plus esmeue qu'un fier lyon environné des cruels animaux... (HT I, 42)

---

[27] Cf. Lorian, *op. cit.*, pp. 133-134: ..."la métaphore [chez les conteurs du XVIe siècle] est en général banale et beaucoup moins fréquente que la comparaison proprement dite. C'est [qu'ils] hésitent devant la substitution complète, devant l'identification totale de l'objet avec l'étalon. Ils préfèrent la démarche plus analytique, plus intellectuelle, à la fois plus timide et plus brutale, de la similitude... ou la simple comparaison de degré...."

[28] IV.xxxiv.45 (*ed. cit.*, p. 345).

[29] See, for example, the preface to HT VI, quoted *supra*, pp. 59-60.

> ...puis que ma triste fortune m'a icy amenée comme l'aigneau innocent au sacrifice... (HT I, 42)

> ...laquelle, effrenée comme un tigre qui a perdu ses faons... (HT III, 105)

> Puis acharnée sur ce corps mort comme un lyon affamé sur sa proye... (HT V, 163)

> Marcucio, hardy entre les vierges comme un lyon entre les aigneaux... (HT III, 70)

Boaistuau seems more comfortable with similes than with metaphors, perhaps because they accommodate the visual more completely by an explanatory phrase. A simile such as "tremblante comme la fueille agitée des vens" (HT I, 41) establishes a relationship between mood or psychological state and image in a manner similar to the tradition of the emblemata. The extended similes constantly exploit this storehouse of comparisons. Julliette's anxiety is likened at one point to a shipwreck:

> Ceste journée doncques se passa comme font celles des mariniers, lesquels, apres avoir esté agitez de grosses tempestes, voyans quelque rayon de Soleil penetrer le ciel pour illuminer la terre, se rasseurent, et pensant avoir evité naufrage, soudain apres la mer vient à s'enfler et mutiner les vagues par telle impetuosité qu'ils retombent en plus grand peril qu'ils n'avoient esté au precedent. (HT III, 88)

Elsewhere the effects of the blinding strength of passion are compared to a hunter lost in a forest:

> ...je me recognois estre semblable à celuy qui, poursuivant sa proye par l'espoisseur d'un bois, s'eslance indifferemment par tout sans qu'il puisse retrouver le sentier par lequel il estoit entré; ains tant plus il cuide suyvre la trace, il s'en eslongne plus avant, demeurant à la fin intrinqué. (HT I, 24)

Other similes are less elaborate and more associative, especially those which compare characters to legendary, mythic, or historical figures. At the height of her vengeful fury, Violente is presented as "enflammée comme une Medée" (HT V, 162). Mandozze, disguised as a friar in order to ascertain the innocence or guilt of the Duchesse, "ressembloit trop mieux un sainct Hierosme mortifié en quelque desert qu'un grand seigneur genereux et vaillant comme il estoit" (HT VI, 212).

Antithesis is frequently used in the more expansive sentimental tale to describe the anguish, frustration, and confusion of passion after a character has been victim of "le doux venin amoureux" (HT III, 68):

> Je la suis par tout, et elle me fuit; je ne puis vivre si je ne suis aupres d'elle, et elle n'a contentement aucun, sinon quand elle est absente de moy. (HT III, 65)
>
> ...je suis tellement envelopé au labirinthe de mon effréné vouloir qu'encores que je voye ce qui est de meilleur, helas! je suys le pire. (HT I, 24)
>
> Si la main qui me devoit guerir est celle qui me blesse, où sera l'esperance de mon remede? (HT I, 28)

Such antithetical expressions of the torment of love reflect the influence of the poetic tradition where the lover, "flottant ainsi entre esperance et desespoir" (HT I, 32), laments his endless and unbearable suffering as he remains at the mercy of the woman who makes him both "vivre et mourir" (HT III, 71 and 80).

The formality of style is further assured by the use of certain constructions prevalent in Latin prose. It has been observed that one of the distinctive goals of the Renaissance writer was to endow prose in the vulgate with an artistic quality:

> Jusqu'à la fin du XVe siècle et au début du siècle suivant, nos écrivains ne concevaient que deux moyens de composer une œuvre vraiment littéraire et capable d'immortaliser leur nom: la langue latine et le vers français. Seuls les mémorialistes ou les écrivains populaires se servaient de la prose vulgaire. [30]

As Sturel's examples illustrate, there was common agreement, especially in the first half of the sixteenth century, that the best

---

[30] René Sturel, "La prose poétique au XVIe siècle," in *Mélanges offerts à Gustave Lanson* (Paris: Hachette, 1922), p. 51.

way to achieve a "literary" quality in prose was to pattern expression precisely on Latin models. Since Latin alone was considered elegant, French tried to imitate the Latin period and syntax — the so-called "Ciceronian" style: ..."cette imitation du latin était...un moyen de créer une prose raffinée et savante qui fût digne d'exprimer des idées et des sentiments réservés jusque-là au latin ou à la poésie." [31]

Such a conclusion was especially important for the short story. The increasing gravity of its purpose demanded a refinement of expression, and the Latin period seemed admirably suited to this end. The extremes to which this practice went are well known. Pantagruel's punishment of the Limousin student and the examples of François Habert and others cited by Sturel all suggest that abuse was common, that certain writers could not quite resist the proliferation of rare and unusual words, the abundance of epithets, and the emphasis upon aspects of Latin syntax which could not be comfortably accommodated to French. But whether the practice is satirized or dismissed entirely as completely lacking in artistry, [32] it does denote a significant stylistic awareness and a faith that French prose is capable, with a certain amount of enrichment through imitation, of achieving literary status.

Like other *prosateurs* of the sixteenth century, Boaistuau exploits the absolute participial phrase. The narrative passages rely on it heavily. Used with increasing frequency since the fourteenth century, [33] this construction is often used in the *Histoires tragiques* as a transition between passages of dialogue and narrative on the pattern of "ces propos finiz." It is also a formulaic means

---

[31] *Ibid.*, p. 56; *cf.* Lorian, *op. cit.*, p. 142: ..."l'imitation superficielle de la période latine — superficielle, puisque le calque ne réussit qu'à créer une phrase longue et pleine d'articulations (plutôt que réellement articulée), qu'à donner naissance à un corps qui a des dimensions importantes et d'innombrables cartilèges et vertèbres, sans pour autant posséder la structure, les nerfs, l'élégance ou le rythme du modèle."

[32] This negative view is expressed by Charles Bruneau, "La phrase des traducteurs du XVIe siècle," in *Mélanges offerts à Henri Chamard* (Paris: Nizet, 1951), pp. 275-284.

[33] Ferdinand Brunot, *Histoire de la langue française*, t. II (Paris: Colin, 1906), pp. 466-467.

of summarizing previous action or events before introducing new developments in the narrative:

> Et ses obseques parachevées honorablement,... (HT III, 107)
>
> Ceste pantiere tendue,... (HT IV, 128)
>
> Le sort des armes tombé,... (HT VI, 172)
>
> Leur mariage ainsi consommé,... (HT III, 82)

In the interest of narrative conciseness and in order to eliminate a detailed exposition of necessary but secondary events, the absolute participial phrase summarizes these events and, by its brevity, advances the narrative rapidly to moments of more genuine import:

> Le conseil assemblé et les tesmoings ouys d'une part et d'autre,... (HT III, 85)
>
> La retraicte sonnée et les affaires de l'empire reduicts en plus seur estat,... (HT II, 50)
>
> Le courrier du Duc arrivé et la matiere proposée au conseil,... (HT VI, 201)

Finally it is used to designate the temporal lapse between successive events in the narrative:

> L'heure de l'assignation venue,... (HT III, 80 and 88)
>
> Le jour venu,... (HT I, 46)
>
> Et le temps du delay expiré,... (HT VI, 177)

Charles Bruneau complains that prose writers of the sixteenth century abused relative constructions.[34] Of this Boaistuau is definitely guilty: Alexandre Lorian qualifies Boaistuau as one of the "grands artistes de la phrase à rallonges relatives complexes."[35] The inflected relative *lequel*, "l'outil conjonctif le plus

---

[34] "La phrase des traducteurs...", p. 282.
[35] *Op. cit.*, p. 244.

caractéristique au XVIᵉ siècle," [36] is used throughout the *Histoires tragiques*, and although it is sometimes of value, given certain passages of syntactic complexity, it can be cumbersome and appear at times merely as a concession to Boaistuau's preference for the complex rather than the simple sentence:

> ...retournons reprendre noz erres du Duc, lequel, quelques dix ou douze jours apres que la Duchesse son espouse fut partie, commença à sentir son absence, laquelle ne pouvant supporter pour la grande amitié qu'il luy portoit, et mesme cognoissant la grande faute qu'il avoit commise (estant sœur de Roy et femme de tel Prince) de l'avoir ainsi laissée aller comme un traict desempenné en un loingtain voyage, se delibera... (HT VI, 191)

Lequel, as an adjective or pronoun, as well as the indefinite relative *ce que* and the older form *de quoy,* are often used to link separate sentences and serve thereby as a transitional element. These relatives are frequently combined with past participles to form absolute participial phrases:

> Lesquelles choses estans profondement considerées par sainct Paul,... (HT VI, 214)

> Ce que entendu par le Comte de Pancalier, il print congé d'elle... (HT VI, 194)

> Ce qu'estant mal practiqué par celle de laquelle nous descrirons l'histoire,... (HT IV, 121)

> Dequoy Didaco averty, la vint trouver... (HT V, 156)

An elaboration of this pattern that is peculiar to the sixteenth century — a clause beginning with a relative and followed by a conjunction — appears occasionally, as in HT II: "Lesquelles choses s'elles advenoient (comme Dieu ne permette) ton empire s'en iroit en fumée (56), and in HT VI: ..."on l'avoit averty de l'infortune de la Duchesse, laquelle s'il pensoit estre innocente... il la voudroit defendre" (211).

---

[36] Lorian, *op. cit.*, p. 236.

In general, however, Boaistuau shows a fair degree of restraint in his choice of constructions and accepts those which had already passed into the language through example. He avoids those Latin constructions for which there were precedents but which could not be accommodated easily to French syntax, such as verbs following objects or coming at the end of a clause. The major influence of the so-called Latinate style is evident in his preference for the long complex sentence, and he adopts those features of Latin which will allow him to combine several phrases and clauses into one elaborate period that is sufficiently embellished by rhetorical devices that the result is a Grand Style properly befitting the tragic mood of the tales.

His efforts were not unappreciated. It is precisely the style of the *Histoires tragiques* that his collaborator François de Belleforest praises so highly in a sonnet which was added as the concluding piece to Boaistuau's volume:

> Celuy, qui sanglamment a chanté les erreurs
>   Des humains, et a fait tristes les plus joyeux:
>   Et qui des bien-vivans a humectez les yeux
> De ris, d'ennuy, de dueil, en liesse, et frayeurs:
> Celuy, qui de l'amour exprime les fureurs
>   Sous le nom des Amans fortunez-malheureux,
>   S'en vient plus hardiment, sanglant et furieux,
> De ces Amans chanter les mortelles horreurs.
> Et quoy que des saincts vers des Grecs, Latins on die,
>   Et qu'on loue, sans pris, d'eux tous la Tragedie,
> La prose de Launay nonobstant les surmonte.
> Car espandant le sang, privant d'ame le corps,
>   Il accorde si bien des nombres les discors,
>   Que sa prose tragique, aux vers tragiq' fait honte.

PART THREE

PIERRE BOAISTUAU AND THE TRAGIC WORLD OF 1560

Chapter I

LE THEATRE DU MONDE: A PROLOGUE

> The life of man entire is misery:
> he finds no resting place, no haven from calamity.
>
> Euripides, *Hippolytus*, 189-190

Contemporary observations in the middle years of the sixteenth century, paying little heed to France's cultural achievements, depict a land that is besieged from without and torn from within. "Ce royaume, autrefois si formidable aux plus grandes puissances du monde," writes Suriano, "est maintenant si faible, si infirme et si malade, que pas une seule partie de ce grand corps ne s'est conservée saine." [1] The country whose tradition of Christian rulers, whose military power, autonomy, demographic superiority, territorial expanse, wealth, and natural defenses should assure her glory, is now reduced to "le misérable état d'un pays plein de troubles, d'ambitions, de partis, endetté, pauvre, épuisé par une guerre longue et coûteuse." [2] Peering beneath the veneer of military glory, heroic idealism, artistic achievement, and luxuriant life, "on dirait que tous les fléaux qui peuvent contribuer à la décadence d'un pays se soient réunis pour la destruction de la France." [3]

---

[1] Michel Suriano, "Commentaire sur le royaume de France" [1561], in *Relations des ambassadeurs vénitiens sur les affaires de France au 16ᵉ siècle*, ed. N. Tommaseo (Paris, 1838), t. I, p. 559 (in the "Collection des documents inédits sur l'histoire de France," t. 47).

[2] *Ibid.*, p. 543.

[3] *Ibid.*, p. 541.

Such is the state that writers will deplore with increasing frequency during the latter decades of the century as a new mood of unrest emerges with explosive prominence. The turbulent political and religious crises which shook the very soul of France challenged the enthusiastic confidence of the early humanists. The sixteenth century became increasingly preoccupied with the relationship of man to an ill-defined world in which a veritable competition of systems and doctrines had wrought an untenable confusion. No longer dominated by established doctrine, liberated from the restrictions of dogma, thought was free to choose its own direction. But with the various currents of rationalism, naturalism, skepticism, mysticism, epicurianism, stoicism, the Renaissance faced not only the dissolution of unity, but the prominence of diversity. Intellectual and religious liberation brought about a profusion of doctrines, all proposed and formulated with the enthusiasm of absolutes. The answer of reconciliation and accommodation was not to come until the closing decades of the century. Meanwhile in this world of multiple ideologies, thinking moved inevitably to an extreme in order to counteract another extreme, all in the desperate hope of finding some satisfactory answer to a world that had lost all harmony and proportion.

Boaistuau gives his own interpretation of this critical moment of French history in his humanist compendium of 1558. Drawing heavily on the writings of Pliny, Plutarch, and Cardano, the work interprets the nature and causes of the crisis and serves as a succinct thematic preface to the concept of the tragic in the *Histoires tragiques*.

The complete title of the work readily suggests Boaistuau's theme: *Le Theatre du monde, où il est faict un ample discours de toutes les miseres de l'homme, ensemble de plusieurs vices qui regnent pour le jourd'huy en tous les estats de la terre*. Boaistuau's metaphorical world-stage is the setting for his drama dealing with the universal manifestation of vice and wretchedness. He no longer sees the world imbued with an optimistic fatality guiding mankind to a state of absolute perfection. In his introductory letter "Au lecteur," he emphatically denies such a positive view:

> Mais quelle occasion auroient les docteurs, philosophes, Prophetes, & Apostres de s'escarmoucher, s'ils avoient rencontré un tel siecle que le nostre, qui est si corrompu, depravé & conflct en toutes especes de vices et abominations, qu'il semble proprement que soit le retraict & l'esgoust où toutes les immundicitez des autres siecles & aages se soient venues espurer & vuyder.[4]

Within this bleak setting, Boaistuau's drama unfolds, and in every scene, he repeats his subject: *la misère humaine*. The major character is man, man in every rank and profession, man from his miserable birth to his wretched death. Yet Boaistuau must ask the reasons for this misery. His central character is a powerful figure, and Boaistuau has his century's pride in human potential as well as an admiration for the "celerité de son esprit" which "recherche l'essence, nature, & ressort de tout ce qui est contenu en l'univers." With a Faustian propensity for knowledge, man has sought to understand the heavens and dominate all life on earth. But the outcome of this drama is tragic. In his search for knowledge, man has failed to come to grips with himself and he remains not only an impenetrable mystery but the cause of his own misfortune:

> Il a descouvert par sa diligence & vivacité, la proprieté des herbes & plantes, les vertus secrettes des pierres, la calcination des metaux. Et neantmoins il est si bien masqué & deguisé, qu'il se descognoist soy mesme. C'est le herault, truchement, & oracle de toutes les choses contenues au pourpris de ce monde, & si est aveugle & muet en ses propres affaires. Il voltige & discourt par tous les elemens, il reforme, ordonne, compasse & balance ce qui se voit sous la concavité des cieux, & si est confuz & retif en luy mesme. (TM, dédicace)

Boaistuau's purpose is therefore to reveal man to himself in all of his abject misery, to tear aside the mask of pretense and grandeur and show that ambition and achievement are mere folly. Once death puts an end to "ceste sanglante tragedie," life

---

[4] All references to this work are taken from the 1559 edition published in Paris by Gilles Robinot and will hereafter be included in the text with the abbreviation TM followed by a page reference.

has been nothing but "une infinité de calamitez & miseres, desquelles [l'homme] est envelopé depuis sa naissance jusques au tombeau."

The first book begins in good humanist fashion as Boaistuau culls examples from the Ancients to support the general theme of his work. From the compassionate complaints of a Heraclitus and the sardonic laughter of a Democritus to the stoic meditations of Marcus Aurelius, all concur with Boaistuau's view of man as "vil & abject" (TM, 5v). But these laments are merely an introduction to the basic theme of the section: nature and man's role in the order of nature. Following Pliny's argument, Boaistuau compares the human with the natural and animal realms and concludes that the latter has definitely been favored. An animal is born clothed, while man's nakedness at birth testifies to nature's contempt for him. The crying and wailing which signal his birth also presage his future calamities. Man must labor to make his dwelling, while nature provides a habitat for other animals and protection for plants. Victim of his passions, man is his own enemy while other species can live in peace. A delicate creature, man is subject to illness, while nature has given instinctive remedies to the other animals.

However Boaistuau's purpose is not to criticize nature, as do those authorities he cites, "l'appellant cruelle marastre, au lieu de gracieuse mere" (TM, 1r). Nature is still a benevolent force. The animal world cannot be considered superior, for human ingenuity has compensated for all the shortcomings of natural gifts. However the realm of man falls far short of the natural world insofar as the latter exemplifies a moral virtue and harmony non-existent among men:

> ...il est evidemment monstré qu'en la contemplation des animaulx il se peult trouver une armonie de philosophie tant morale que naturelle: car en contemplant les mœurs & actions d'iceux tant bien ordonnées selon les usages de nature, leur justice, temperance, fortitude, œconomie en l'administration de leurs petites republiques, leur continence aux œuvres de nature, & quelques autres parties de vertu qu'ilz exercent, par la diligente consideration desquelles l'homme descend & entre en luy mesme, & advisant, comme estant vaincu & surpassé d'iceux en plusieurs choses, & considerant sa misere &

> piteuse Metamorphose, & comme il degenere de son excellence & dignité, il est esmeu, & a sa vie en horreur, se trouvant inferieur d'iceulx, lesquels il doit autant exceller, qu'il les surpasse en honneur & dignité. (TM, 19v-20r)

Boaistuau's logic is simplistic, but his conclusion is important. The animal world represents nature's law and harmony; but man represents the opposite of nature's law. He is the "meurdrier tant ennemy de nature" (TM, 16v), for "luy seul ose repugner à tout ordre de nature, & à son office, auquel toutes creatures demeurent" (TM, 21v). The incarnation of anti-nature, man is so proud that he dares even to blaspheme and challenge God, "auquel toutes autres creatures, ciel, terre, mer, estoilles, planettes, tous elemens, bestes, anges, diables obeissent" (TM, 21v).

As the propagator of the unnatural, man is the cause of his own misery and suffering. Disdaining natural laws which maintain order in the universe, he has placed his own destiny beyond the order of nature and created not a paradise, but a terrestrial hell which resounds with "tromperies, fraudes, blasphemes, adulteres, raps, incestes, guerres, effusion de sang, violences, rapines, ambition, avarice, haynes, rancunes & vengences" (TM, 4r). The positive creative force of nature has been perverted and replaced by a negative force which destroys the traditional cosmic hierarchy. Ironically the creator of this unnatural world of confusion and chaos is placed at the very bottom of a new chain of being, for "l'homme...n'est qu'un miserable ver de terre, qui à peine se peut trainer" (TM, 21v). Formerly a creature of magnificent potential, man becomes a mere toy in the hands of a fatality which he himself has determined and created. And he must still answer to an ultimate authority:

> ...il est en la main de Dieu, ainsi que l'argille & le vaisseau de terre en la main du potier, lequel il peut faire, defaire, former, rompre, casser & reparer ainsi que bon luy semble, sans luy faire tort ou injure: Car qu'est ce autre chose que l'homme, sinon un simulachre ou statue en ce monde, qui est une vraye boutique des œuvres de Dieu, lequel il ne fault que pousser qu'il ne tombe du hault de soy pour estre brisé & rompu, & toutesfois quelque misere qui le puisse acabler, il se

> mescongnoit, & ne se peut abaisser soubs le joug de son Dieu. (TM, 5v)

Man's lowly entrance into life is nature's warning that he retain this humility; but his pride thwarts nature's purpose, and it is therefore man who calls forth divine retribution. As the creator of his own life, man has created his own suffering.

The second book of the *Theatre du monde* elaborates upon these themes, proposing to "penetrer plus avant, & continuer ceste piteuse tragedie de la vie de l'homme" by following him from his "miserable entree...en ce monde" to "son triste & estrange depart" (TM, 22r). Brevity is not one of Boaistuau's virtues, and he begins with a repetition of the afflictions imposed upon man from birth: the pains of childbirth, the infant's frailty, the numerous possible difformities, the child's first song: "larmes, pleurs & gemissemens" (TM, 25v). This helpless creature, this "petit monstre hideux & masse de chair" (TM, 26r) is little more than the image of that misery which will pursue him during the whole course of his existence. Adolescence is hardly more favorable, for the youth is besieged by all the vices of the world:

> ...c'est la saison où nature luy dresse un combat plus furieux, le sang luy commence à bouillir, la chair l'appelle et semond à faire son plaisir, la sensualité le meine, le monde malin l'espie, le diable le tente, la jeunesse le convie, & si est impossible que ce qui est combatu de plusieurs vices, & n'est secouru d'aucun, ne soit en fin desconfit ou abbatu: car au corps où jeunesse, liberté, richesses, & delices abondent, tous les vices du monde... y mettent le siege. (TM, 31r)

Youth is all the more unable to resist temptation because his training has been entrusted to the care of "ignares & vicieux precepteurs" (TM, 31v). Moreover if this "mal fortuné" should seek some kind of salutary assistance from the world about him, he would find in every walk of life no other example than that which encourages his indulgence of passion and vice.

The latter half of the second book reveals the misery inherent in every rank and every profession of life. Boaistuau methodically attacks each ideal the Renaissance had postulated, and in each case, it is destroyed, its mythic and poetic appeal blatantly contradicted. The rustic retreat no longer promises a simple and pure life; Boaistuau cannot find the gentleman who has turned away from the turmoil of business cares to enjoy peaceful calm and reflection. He discovers instead the farmer who toils in extreme heat and cold, who is at the mercy of flood, drought, and insects, whose harvest is destroyed by winds and storms, whose cattle die, whose produce is stolen, who returns home to a family crying from hunger. Hardship, suffering, and misfortune are the sole fruits of man's labor on earth. For these he traded paradise.

As Boaistuau examines each level of society, his conclusions are always the same. The professional soldier no longer fights honorably and gloriously, but is forced to endure unheroically his military servitude, which promises no grandeur in return but merely a life of hardship and bloodshed. No longer a *chevalier sans paour et sans reproche*, he is "transformé en beste brute, pour exercer sa rage contre son prochain" (TM, 41r). And in his path he leaves only destruction, violence, and death.

The soldier's inhumanity is encouraged by the ruler's warped ambition for territorial gain, by kings who spend extravagant sums on the patient preparation and practice of this man-made pestilence from which there can come no meaningful gain:

> Encor si nostre rage s'exerçoit contre l'estranger ou barbare, la victoire duquel peust raporter quelque contentement au victeur. Mais bon Dieu, voulons nous sçavoir quelles sont les gloires & trophées des guerres entre les princes chrestiens? Leur salut & conservation c'est la ruïne de leur prochain, leurs richesses sont les pauvretez & despouilles des autres. Leur joye est le dueil & les larmes d'autruy. (TM, 42r)

The prodigious thirst for blood and destruction reduces man to a level below that of the animal who has at least a respect for his own kind.

The courtier moves away from the natural hardships which the farmer and the soldier must endure and into the luxuriant comfort of the castle. His only concern is to return the favor of his prince. But his life is no better for its surroundings. He is forced to submit to the caprice of the ruler, to live amid the hypocrisy, corruption, and depravity of the court. He sacrifices his liberty for a life of ease, and must accept servile obeisance or death as the only rewards for his services. Not even kings, princes, or monarchs fare any better in this unnatural world, for their supposed happiness, based upon wealth, land, and power, cannot dispel their fears of treachery. Moreover they must accept the weight of responsibility to thousands of subjects, a task not a little hampered by their advisers who indulge their weaknesses and flatter their pride so that all true perspective on truth and purpose is lost:

> Leur folie & temerité ils l'appellent prudence, leur cruauté justice, leur luxure, dissolutions & paillardises, passetemps & gaietez: s'ils sont avaricieux, ils les appellent bon mesnagers, s'ils sont prodigues, ils les nomment liberaux: de sorte qu'il n'y a vice au prince qu'ils ne pallient, masquent & desguisent soubs le pretexte de quelque vertu. (TM, 49r)

Ruling becomes exploitation, and in the kingdom vice becomes rampant. Judges are so corrupted by fear, passion, hatred, and bribery that they readily consider "le mal estre bien & le bien mal" (TM, 59v). Integrity is foreign even to the pope and his priests. Honored and revered by the rulers, they nevertheless exude corruption. Rich and opulent, they preach the virtues of poverty. Ignorance prevents some from reading the Mass; others are more adept at pleasure and sin than they are at explaining the Scriptures:

> Brief, sont les vrayes censues qui ne servent de rien qu'à tirer le sang & la substance des pauvres brebis, & employer les biens de l'eglise en pompes, delices, & exces, au lieu de maintenir les pauvres, & d'entretenir la jeunesse aux arts liberaulx & autres disciplines divines & humaines. (TM, 55v)

In a world in which nature has been corrupted, the reality which man creates constantly belies the mythic and the ideal which he has formulated. All values have been reversed. Virtue has no meaning in a world where corruption prevails, where a depraved humanity has perverted all nature. The priest's cassock, the king's crown, the courtier's finery, the soldier's weapons and armor are all masks and disguises which conceal a bestial corruption, a corruption which perpetuates itself as each generation is swept up by a tide of vice, sin, and inquity. The perversion of all ethical norms creates a world in which every value has been turned upside-down.

The ultimate expression of this blind adherence to the unnatural is to be found in man's attempt to challenge God, a presumptuous act which provokes divine wrath and punishment. This is the theme of the third book of the *Theatre du monde* in which the causes of human corruption receive their tragic reward. Boaistuau bemoans man's greatest error: his attack upon God's Church. The only institution which could bring solace to the afflicted is torn by diversity of opinion and internal corruption:

> Ce n'estoit pas assez qu'il y eust corruption en tous les estats, & en la masse mesme de l'homme, qui n'est qu'une charoigne puante & orde, s'il ne s'eslevoit encore contre son Dieu, s'il ne luy dressoit bataille en camp ouvert, s'il ne luy deschiroit sa robe & divisoit la religion.... Encore ce qui nous doit donner plus grand terreur, sont les diversitez des opinions qui sont entre nous, & les erreurs, desquelles nous sommes envelopez: car ce que l'un dict estre blanc, l'autre le dict estre noir: ce que l'un appelle jour, l'autre appelle nuict. Ce qui est lumiere à l'un, est tenebres à l'autre. Ce que l'un trouve doux, l'autre le juge amer. Ce qui est Jesus Christ, verité, & Paradis à l'un, est Antechrist, mensonge & enfer à l'autre. (TM, 65v-66r)

Heresy is the greatest sin of which man is guilty, for it has divided Christendom against itself and brought about death and destruction in the name of the Church. Boaistuau cannot deal with diversity in any way other than to condemn it as a sin. He makes no effort to reconcile or to synthesize. Very simply, disparity of opinion has caused the convulsive upheaval of all order, and its effects are everywhere apparent. Despite man's effort to define and comprehend, the very insufficiency of his reason has led him blindly to heresy. There is no possible defense for man's ultimate challenge. Placing his faith totally in himself, he has disrupted the whole course of nature, submitted to base motives in the name of an ultimate justice, and applied his faulty reason to realms which supersede its capacity. Man has perverted himself, nature, and the Church.

The tragic in Boaistuau's world results from man's loss of humility, from his persistent refusal of moderation, from his audacious attacks upon the natural and divine realms. His corruption causes his own suffering in the unnatural world he has created; but most fearful of all, it calls forth the retributive justice of God. God turns the unnatural back upon man to induce humility by reminding him of "la fragilité & misere de [sa] condition humaine" (TM, 68r). His rigorous justice torments all men with the corrupt nature they have created. Divine wrath inflicts plague, famine, and conflagration as the "tesmoings & ministres de [sa] vengeance" (TM, 82r).

It is at this point that Boaistuau becomes his most eloquent. The moralist seems almost to relish the prolonged descriptions of God's supreme power as He increases the already prevalent misery of the human lot. At God's command, all of the elements conspire against this pathetic creature. Water, no longer associated with growth and fertility, becomes a destructive flood. Fire razes whole cities. The air "se putrifie & corrompt" (TM, 84r), while by the upheavals of the earth, "plusieurs villes ont esté demolies, & plusieurs milliers d'hommes engloutiz aux profonditez de ses abismes" (TM, 84v). The earth, which is to provide for man's sustenance, produces poisonous herbs and nurtures venimous animals. Rampant pestilence destroys indiscriminately, sparing neither king nor peasant, parent nor child. And he who survives perishes from famine.

One of the most striking passages in the *Theatre du monde* is Boaistuau's description of the famine of 1528, which serves as a precise example of the manner in which the moralist accommodates and exaggerates historical fact to suit his ideological purpose. In that year, he writes, vice and sin were so rampant that God's wrath and vengeance were provoked:

> ...l'an mil cinq cens vingt & huict, le monde lascha si bien la bride à tous vices, & estoit si mal conditionné, plein de peché & vilenie, que non seulement il ne s'estoit point humilié & amendé, pour les furieux assaults & grande effusion de sang des guerres precedentes: mais au contraire, qu'il estoit empiré, & totalement depravé.

> Au moyen dequoy la bonde de l'ire de Dieu estoit laschée & desbordée en ce pauvre Royaume de France de telle maniere, qu'on estimoit tout estre reduict à la fin & dernier periode: car il advint si grande calamité, pauvreté & misere, qu'il n'est nouvelle par la memoire des temps de telle punition, tant ès corps humains, qu'ès fruictz & revenuz de la terre. (TM, 74r-74v)

The statement of the immediate and ultimate causes is a necessary preamble to the succeeding description. Some reason must be given for the devastation that follows. And in the hands of the moralist, this "historical proof" serves as well as a warning for the future: if man sins, God's fearsome vengeance is imminent. This warning is emphatically pronounced in the next lines which describe the cosmic disorder resulting from man's willful indulgence of every vice. Nature's disorder mirrors moral disorder:

> ...car durant l'espace des cinq ans entiers, qui commencerent l'an mil cinq cens vingt huict, le temps vint en telle indisposition & desordre, que les quatre saisons laisserent leurs cours naturels, & se monstrerent toutes confuses, perverties & preposterées entre elles, se monstrant le Printemps en Autonne, Autonne en Printemps, Esté en Hyver, Hyver en Esté. (TM, 74v)

As the adjectives describing the four seasons become applicable to both sides of the man-nature equation, the chiasmus in the final phrases suggests the reversal of the whole order of nature.

Now instead of being a beneficial force, nature produces only that which destroys and kills, leaving a world that is barren and naked. Nature's fertility becomes the sterility of an anti-nature:

> Car en cinq ans il n'avint gueres gelée qui durast plus d'un jour ou deux, encore n'estoit-ce chose dont l'eau se peut geler, & par ceste grande chaleur inacoustumée, se maintenoit & nourrissoit la vermine de la terre, comme limaces, chenilles, en telle quantité, que le jeune & tendre germe des bledz nouveaux, n'estoit pas si tost né, & dehors du grain, qu'il estoit incontinent rongé & devoré, qui fut cause que les bledz qui devoient multiplier, fueilleter, jetter plusieurs tiges & espiz d'une mesme racine, n'en produisoient qu'un ou deux, encore bien steriles, & pleins de nielle & morfondus, de sorte que

> quand ils furent cueillys, la pluspart ne revenoit qu'à la quantité de la semence, & le plus souvent à moins. (TM, 75r)

By an irony which is repeated throughout Boaistuau's writings, man becomes the unwitting victim of that destructive force which he himself has created and unleashed. The bold figure who indulged himself with every extravagant pleasure is reduced to a foul and putrid beggar groveling for roots:

> ...& croissoit le nombre des pauvres mendians en telle maniere, que c'estoit chose espoventable de les veoir en troupe, insupportable à leur subvenir, & plus dangereuse à les endurer: car oultre la crainte qu'il y avoit d'estre pillé...il sortoit une grande puanteur & infection d'air de leurs corps, pource qu'ils emplissoient leurs ventres de toutes sortes d'herbes, bonnes, mauvaises, saines, venimeuses... (TM, 75v)

The sterility of all of nature can have but one result as disease and death add the final tragic note to God's vengeance:

> ...le Seigneur Dieu, ...indigné contre l'ordure de noz pechez, ...permettoit...que les hommes fussent reduicts en necessité de manger & banqueter avecques les pourceaux, dont il s'ensuivit une infinité de maladies, & le monde tomba en grand effroy, voyant grand trouppe d'hommes & femmes, jeunes & vieulx, tremblans par les rues: les autres, ayant la peau enflée comme tabourins, d'hydropisie: les autres couchez (à demy morts) par terre, tirer les derniers souspirs. (TM, 76v)

Boaistuau's tragic world is set in a cosmos which is destructive. The ravaging force of the unnatural leaves only the desolate quiet of death. The theme of sterility is the underlying motif of every page, and the cause is man's weakness, malice, and corruption. "Voyla comme sa fierté, arrogance & audace, est cause de toutes les playes & maledictions de tout le genre humain" (TM, 87r).

The end of Boaistuau's tragedy has been anticipated from the beginning: "Apres que l'homme a ahanné & souspiré toute sa vie sous l'insupportable faix & fardeau de tous malheurs" (TM,

99v), he can anticipate only death, "le plus espouventable de tous les espouventables, le plus terrible de tous les terribles" (TM, 100r). Drawing upon the naturalistic view of the putrifying corpse, Boaistuau suggests the final unmasking of all earthly pretense, as man is finally reduced to the image of humility into which he was born:

> Mais regardons l'homme caché en son sepulchre: qui veit oncques un monstre plus hideux? qu'y a il plus horrible & vil que la creature morte? Voila la saincteté, l'excellence, majesté & dignité couverte d'un morceau de terre: voila celuy qui estoit chery, caressé & honoré jusques à luy baiser les pieds & les mains, & toutesfois par une soudaine mutation, il est devenu si abominable, que tous les beaulx tombeaux de marbre, de Porphire & de Bronze, toutes leurs belles statues, piramides, epitaphes, & autres pompes funebres, ne le sçauroient si bien masquer ou desguiser, qu'on ne sçache bien que ce n'est autre chose qu'une charoigne vile & puante. (TM, 101v)

Man cannot even hope for salvation; on the day of final judgment, his soul will appear before God in apprehension and terror. In the final words concluding this human tragedy, Boaistuau assembles his whole cast. Kings and princes, magistrates and judges, priests, merchants, and usurers "seront comptables de leurs corruptions & iniquitez" (TM, 109r). Boaistuau does not purposely denigrate man, for indeed he recognizes and reveres the strength of this creature that allows him to persevere despite the malevolent forces which constantly besiege him. But the responsibility for this misery is placed not on God, not on nature as the "cruelle marastre," but on man himself who has created by his own evil a world which is the very antithesis of God and nature's order, a world which is the very image of himself.

Boaistuau's censure of his contemporaries and his times must be considered from two points of view. Living in the middle years of his century, he shares the prevalent mood of deception. The betrayal of chivalric political ventures, the deterioration of social and religious reform, the dichotomy between human potential and its realization all greatly temper an earlier enthusiasm.[5] For Boaistuau the moralist, each observation tends to add to an increasing number of examples which support his defined and categorical viewpoint. He depicts the world and its inhabitants in somber tones. On a literal level, the day of wrath and judgment is at hand, and man can anticipate only his immediate damnation. Such exaggeration is understandable in a moral treatise. But while Boaistuau admires human ability, he insists that man recognize his limitations and failings. He pleads for a readjustment of perspective, and to this end, his warnings become ominous, his condemnations vitriolic.

To convey the disparity which is everywhere observable and which threatens the very fabric of human society, he tries to induce a humility which will allow the realization of man's aspirations within the specific context of his creative freedom. This is a freedom with definite restrictions; to deny them is mere presumption. Yet such presumption is rampant, challenging the ultimate authority of nature and God. The logic of his orthodox conclusions is evident, but it is made graphic by examples. The denial of limit may incur God's wrath, but for the moralist it is even more meaningful to depict the disorder created by man himself. For this reason Boaistuau's "tragic vision" concentrates on the havoc wrought by human presumption and excess.

As the framework for the tragic, Boaistuau uses a *topos* which Curtius labels as "the world upsidedown," a motif which had currency since ancient times. Originally a complaint about the state of affairs, it developed into the notion that the "whole world is topsy-turvy," that "the order of things is changed into its opposite."[6] The expression given to this *topos* can range from the comic to the serious. The traditional ribald tale exploits the reversal of natural order for comic effect. Rabelais "relies upon the simple parodic pattern of the world upside-down" in order

---

[5] See Lionello Sozzi, "La 'Dignitas hominis' dans la littérature française de la Renaissance," p. 188: "Vers [le milieu] du XVIe siècle, en pleine crise des valeurs élaborées par l'humanisme, ...un *tropos* dont on se servait d'habitude pour exalter l'excellence de l'homme devient, paradoxalement, le point d'appui pour un revirement, il est réabsorbé et capturé dans les filets de l'ancienne thématique de la *miseria humanae conditionis*, il ne devient que l'instrument d'un retour à ce thème du 'mépris de la vie'...."

[6] *European Literature and the Latin Middle Ages*, trans. Willard R. Trask (New York: Bollingen Foundation, 1953), p. 96.

to create his equivocal world which hovers between truth and nontruth.[7] This ambivalence allows the comic world to expand in order to accommodate the satirical. It serves as a critical dimension whereby the author can combat those who accept appearances as truth, and attack those who would endorse the artificial and thereby upset nature's harmony or prevent the full integration of the individual within nature.[8]

Boaistuau's use of the *topos* ignores the comic disparity. Moving to the opposite pole, he enlarges the framework again to encompass a general criticism of his times and of man in general instead of limiting it to individuals, types, or attitudes. As a moralist with an ethic to propose, it might be said that Boaistuau does not have a tragic view of the world at all. The world may have gone awry, but he has a solution to set it once again aright. While with one hand he threatens, with the other he indicates the path to salvation. The tragic resides initially in man's persistent refusal to accept Boaistuau's answer. Therefore, just as he accommodates the formalities of tragic theory to the form of the short story, so he dons the garb of the tragedian for his theme. His heroes suffer the reversal of fortune in a world of contingency. The fall of the great and the ideal is his tragic frame of reference. The impossibility of combatting the ill tide of fortune is common to all of his characters who by necessity succumb to misery and suffering because of their helplessness to control the passion which guides them to their destruction. And in their wake, they leave in ruins the formulation of many a Renaissance ideal. This is the truth Boaistuau insists upon and superficially it is the nature of the tragic in the tales. The corruption of man corrupts the world and nature. A moral disharmony effects a natural disharmony, throwing the world out of balance, and leaving no refuge except the desolate quiet of death. For Boaistuau, tragedy lies in man's blind acceptance of this inevitable necessity. And as he observes in the *Theatre du monde*, the ultimate responsibility lies with man himself.

---

[7] Rosalie Colie, *Paradoxia Epidemica: The Renaissance Tradition of Paradox* (Princeton: Princeton University Press, 1966), p. 45.

[8] See Stanley G. Eskin, "Physis and Antiphysie: The Idea of Nature in Rabelais and Calcagnini," *CL* XIV (1962), 167-173.

CHAPTER II

THE REVERSAL OF ORDER IN THE *HISTOIRES TRAGIQUES*

> ...unnatural deeds
> Do breed unnatural troubles...
>
> —*Macbeth*, V.1

i. LOVE

The *Histoires tragiques* is not a fictional transcription of the *Theatre du monde*, but the essay does provide an ideological setting for the tales which are an elaboration and refinement of select themes and examples. As only the first part of a larger work that Belleforest was to continue, Boaistuau's collection does not present the whole range of suffering humanity. However he did choose specific stories to translate, and these follow no definite order from Bandello's *Novelle*.[1] It is therefore likely that Boaistuau's selection and organization are significant. Certain patterns have already been observable: the movement from the historical tale to the *nouvelle*, and finally to the chronicle tale, with a tragical and sentimental tale in each category. Furthermore, there is a general thematic unity in the collection, which offers a series of examples dealing with the effects of passion. Against his defined background of the tragic, Boaistuau selects a single cause of human suffering and gives several examples of its destructive effects in order to make his solution irrefutable.

---

[1] See "Introduction," p. 25, n. 32.

In the *Theatre du monde* Boaistuau states that the "maladies de l'esprit" are far more dangerous than "celles du corps" (TM, 87v). And of these, the most dangerous of all, the 'sin' about which he discourses at greatest length, is love, which destroys all sense of justice, honor, and moderation as it ensnares its helpless victim, blinds him to reason, and plunges him into an abyss of misery and suffering. This theme pervades all of the *Histoires tragiques* as Boaistuau seeks the causes of love, describes its effects, and demonstrates how it is capable of perverting the normal order of the world and destroying all established values.

For Boaistuau, the world is filled with wonders, and his gaze is invariably drawn to the exceptional and the extraordinary. Yet, as an indefatigable seeker of causes, he tries to understand the reason for the prodigious; his inquisitive mind needs an answer. A great deal of the charm of Boaistuau's writings resides in the innocent faith he places upon the judgments and observations of others. His writings are a storehouse of theories formulated by the Ancients and well as his contemporaries. In the accumulation of evidence an answer must lie. With a choice between two improbabilities, he simply accepts the less incredible. But there exists a tension nevertheless. Boaistuau is fascinated by the discoveries of a burgeoning empirical science. Yet as a moralist, he cannot quite accept the full import of these discoveries, and he is quite satisfied to use the results of such inquiries to confirm the hypotheses of the Christian apologist. Boaistuau's treatment of love is no different: the sensational always captures his attention. Love's fury is apparent, given the numerous testimonies he has read; its calm is rare. Therefore love is depicted as a dangerous malady capable of making men "frenetiques & transportez de leurs sens" (TM, 93v).

The "quêteur de prodiges" could hardly fail to be impressed with the numerous treatises concerning the origin of this passion. His ideas are an amalgam of contemporary theories which had such currency in the poetry and prose of his time. Platonic, Petrarchan, and courtly motifs abound and interpenetrate. His scientific mind appreciated the physiological explanations of the sudden birth of this debilitating passion:

> Autres philosophes ont dit, que quand nous venons à jetter nostre veue sur la chose que nous desirons, soudain quelques esprits, lesquels sont engendrez de la plus subtile & parfaicte partie du sang, partent du cueur de la chose que nous aymons, & montent jusques aux yeux, & puis apres s'eslancent en vapeurs invisibles & entrent en noz yeulx, lesquels sont disposez à les recevoir, tout ainsi qu'il demeure quelque tasche sur un miroir apres y avoir regardé, & puis de là penetrent jusques au cueur, & petit à petit se dilatent par tout. Et partant le miserable amant attiré par les nouveaux esprits, lesquels desirent tousjours se rejoindre & approcher avec leur principale ou naturelle demeure, est constrainct à se douloir & lamenter sa liberté perdue. (TM, 94r-94v)

This blend of the Platonic and Petrarchan notions of love, penetrating from the eyes and infecting the victim with a venimous humor which spreads and affects the whole body, is repeated throughout the tales. Seeing Julliette for the first time at the Capellet ball, Rhomeo wants only to "repaistre ses yeux de la veue d'icelle, par lesquels il humoit le doux venin amoureux, duquel il fut en fin... bien empoisonné..." (HT III, 68-69) But at this point the similarity ends. Love follows a specific and defined route in the *Histoires tragiques*. Sight of physical beauty does not permit a progression to the beauty of the soul, to the beauty of pure ideas, to the divine unity which is the source of all beauty. Nor is it possible to draw from the suffering of the heroes of these stories the unity of a superior good. The vocabulary is the same: *feu, martyre, flammes, larmes, pleurs, mort, tempeste, playe, servitude;* but the results are not those of theory.

Boaistuau presents a love which is tainted. Inevitably the preconceived notions of the moralist color his statements, for love is a corrupt humor, a grievous passion, incurable. And it is all the more fearful because of the merciless rapidity with which it possesses and destroys its victim. All of the descriptions of nascent love progress with the same rapidity that moves Rhomeo from seeing Julliette to being *empoisonné*. From the image of Mandozze described by Ysabeau, the Duchesse "ne pouvoit dormir, et avoit si bien la beauté de ce chevalier incogneu gravée au plus profond de son cueur que, cuidant clorre les yeux, il luy sembloit avis qu'il voletoit incessamment devant elle" (HT VI, 175).

The longest description of the birth of love is found in the first tale where Edouart

> commença peu à peu à se sentir *saisy d'une nouvelle flamme*, à laquelle tant plus il s'efforçoit de resister, s'enflamboit d'avantage; et sentant ceste nouvelle mutation en luy, projettoit une infinité de diverses choses, balançant entre *esperance et crainte*, faisant estat ores de luy communiquer ses passions, ores de les retrencher du tout, de peur que, succombant aux faiz, les urgens affaires desquels il estoit enveloppé des guerres, eussent mauvaise yssue. Mais à la fin, *vaincu de l'amour*, proposa de sonder le cœur de la Comtesse; ...et l'entretenant ce pendant d'une infinité de divers propos...les petits tiges d'amour qui n'estoient qu'à peine entez commencerent à penetrer si avant que les racines demeurerent gravées au plus profond de son cœur. Et...pressé du *mal*, s'appuya sur une fenestre, pensant et repensant par quel moyen il pourroit jouyr de celle qui estoit cause de son *tourment*. (HT I, 14-15; italics added)

In this passage, Boaistuau describes the merciless rapidity with which love renders its victim helpless. At the first glimpse of Ælips, Edouart is powerless to arrest its fatal course. Love is born irresistibly. The internal struggle between hope and fear, suggested by the correlative *ores... ores*, is short-lived. His concerns over the affairs of state lose their immediacy as he surrenders to a cancerous passion. The traditional love vocabulary is used throughout, but it assumes a new meaning in Boaistuau's world. The *mal* and *tourment* from which he suffers and which prevent his peace of mind are of no value in themselves. There is no *voluptas dolendi*. Nor are Boaistuau's heroes satisfied to lament their misfortune. They must strike out actively in an effort to placate this torment. It is at this point that Boaistuau departs most definitively from theory and myth, and since each tale has its authentic source, testimony and history confirm that poetic fabrication has misrepresented love. The *Histoires tragiques* attacks and reverses the poetic. Love no longer seeks anything beyond its own satisfaction, and to this end, there are no limits to human ingenuity. Love is synonymous with self-interest, but in its pursuit of satisfaction, it accomplishes only the deterioration and destruction of the individual.

Boaistuau repeatedly describes the effects of love upon man once the venom has permeated the body. Powerless to resist its force, love's victims have little recourse but to submit to the resulting misery:

> ...la Duchesse, pensant amortir ce nouveau feu, l'enflammoit d'avantage, & tant plus l'esperance luy manquoit, tant plus luy croissoit son desir; et apres une infinité de divers pensemens, la victoire demeura du costé de l'amour... (HT VI, 176)
>
> ...cognoissant mes forces diminuer, je ne sçay à qui me plaindre de ma liberté perdue...sinon à vous... (HT I, 17)
>
> ...ceste mienne vie, ou plustost mort, est confitte en tant d'angoisses et peines mortelles que je suis le propre siege de tous maux et unique receptacle de toutes miseres. (HT I, 24)

The play of antithesis suggests the impossibility of overcoming this passion. And the resulting helplessness deprives man of his strength, leaving him to lament during a life which is no more than death for all of its anguish. These are the motifs popularized by the Petrarchan poets and repeated until they became clichés. These are the *concetti* which depict the internal suffering of the poetic pose.

But the moralist cannot allow man a whole life of lamentation without results far more serious than personal unhappiness. For the exemplary hero, the pathos of such complaints assumes a new meaning and dimension. The king and emperor cannot play the role of a Rhomeo who "abandonna toutes ses autres occupations pour... servir et honorer" (HT III, 65). Just as Edouart admits to Comte de Varuccio that after so many victories on land and sea, "maintenant suis lié et veincu d'un si desordonné appetit que je ne m'en puis relever" (HT I, 24), Mustapha accuses Mahomet, "ensevely en ses delices," of the same "desordonnée affection" (HT II, 52). The adjective *desordonné* gives a distinctive coloration to the passion described in the *Histoires tragiques:* this is a love which is excessive, lacking in moderation. But the lover is no longer admirable for his complete and total devotion to the object of his passion; rather he is guilty of incontinence and immoderation. This is the first major moral imperative that recurs in every tale and which is in each one ignored:

> Toutesfois par traict de temps ils ne peurent si bien maistriser leurs passions ne les moderer par telle discretion... (HT IV, 126)

> ...pour le regard seulement d'une trop ardente et demesurée amytié que je vous portois... (HT VI, 203)

> ...les excessifs delices... (HT II, 52)

> Dequoy Violente passionnée outre mesure... (HT V, 150)

Counselors such as the Comte and Mustapha inveigh against such excess, but to no avail. No balance can be achieved given the strength of the emotional disorder. Mahomet's love for Hyrenée controls him to such an extent "que plustost eust-il consenty la ruine de l'empire que se separer d'avec elle" (HT II, 51). The Comte de Varuccio warns Edouart that his inordinate love endangers all England, and that unless he show some restraint, "ceste Isle perdra son nom de Royaume et ne sera plus qu'un receptacle de brigants et voleurs" (HT I, 30); but the king is deaf to such advice and continues his vain pursuit.

Therefore it is not only man's helplessness before love which concerns Boaistuau; the results of this helplessness are more important. The suffering is so severe that the victim shuns all obligations in order to try to satisfy an insatiable desire. He becomes increasingly entangled in the web of passion. Love ceases to be a complement to a purposeful life and becomes the sole objective of life itself. But this objective has lost all meaning; it is not directed to a higher good. The victim merely obeys the dictates of a selfish passion whose obsessive and excessive nature destroys the delicate balance within him and within his world, for his emotional imbalance results in a civil imbalance. The exemplary hero, representing all men, will permit even the destruction of his realm, the microcosm in a series of symbolic relationships. The world order is threatened, its harmony untuned, its balance destroyed. Man has committed the secular sin of immoderation.

ii. Love and Reason

As Edouart tries to convince Varuccio that his intentions towards Ælips are honorable, the voice of deception ironically speaks the moralist's truth. He insists that man differs from animals since the latter are governed only by a natural instinct and appetite. Man, on the other hand, is endowed with reason to temper the demands of the senses:

> ...nous, avec la mesure de raison, pouvons et devons moderer noz actions avec telle providence que sans desvoyer nous elisions le sentier d'equité et de justice; et si quelque fois la chair infirme succombe, nous n'en devons accuser que nous mesmes qui, deceuz par une ombre fuyarde et faulse apparence des choses, trebuchons en la fosse que nous nous estions preparée. (HT I, 23)

This passage is of capital importance to an understanding of Boaistuau's tragic world. In the first clause, Edouart utters the humanist prescription for an upright and worthy life. Reason, which distinguishes man from all other living creatures, enables man to rise above that wretched condition into which he was born, to direct and control his actions in order to create a life of perfect integrity. Such is man's moral obligation ("devons"), and it is fully within his capacity ("pouvons"), given the divine gift of reason which can effectively moderate any instinctive desires threatening to divert man from this single purpose. The responsibility to realize human potential lies with man himself. He has the choice in the creation of his own life and salvation, but the decision need not be pondered. To deny reason's authority and thus accept the senses as a guide is mere self-deception since such a choice would deny truth for the illusory appeal of appearance. In that case, the only result could be the denial and destruction of human dignity.

The irony of Edouart's speech lies in its context. He appropriates a secular credo and ideal for the purpose of achieving that which he condemns. The moral imperative of the first clause is ignored, and as is true of all of Boaistuau's suffering heroes, the hypothetical "si quelque fois" becomes the general rule which is followed repeatedly to the anticipated result. The *Histoires tragiques* relentlessly contradicts this ethical ideal as its heroes persistently refuse to tread the path of "equité" and "justice."

The formula is applicable to all the tales where the strength of passion blinds the one whom it controls:

> ...ayant maintenant les yeux bandez du voile de vostre desordonnée affection... (HT II, 52)

> ...en la chambre de madame, où amour les aveugla si bien qu'ils se coucherent ensemble au lict où monseigneur avoit accoustumé de coucher.... (HT IV, 131)

> Esveille-toy de ce profond sommeil lequel t'a sillé les yeux. (HT II, 56)

> Oste ce voile amoureux qui te bande les yeux et qui t'empesche de suyvre le droict sentier par lequel tes ancestres ont cheminé (HT III, 66)

> Amour, estant en pleine possession du cueur de ces deux amans, les aveugla si bien que, laschant la bride trop longue à leur honneur.... (HT IV, 126)

Blindness, the natural effect of love, prohibits the functioning of right reason. The victim is a *desvoyé*. He grows impatient with reason's insistence upon a moderation which would deny his sole objective. After reading Ælips' letter which refuses his advances again, Edouart, "se consumant peu à peu en cest amoureux feu, commença à sortir hors des gonds de raison" (HT I, 22). Under the imperious sway of passion, he has fallen victim to a new and destructive fatality which he has created but over which he has absolutely no dominion as he is led blindly to his own destruction:

> Mais tu sçais quelle liberté a celuy qui est subject sous la puissance d'autruy, estant quelquefois contrainct faire beaucoup de choses non seulement contre son vouloir, mais (qui pis est) contre sa propre conscience.... (HT I, 33)

Reason does not disappear; it is summoned in moments of despair. But at such times it is deformed and becomes a simple rationalization, the objective of which is not integrity but rather the fullest expression of passion. In desperation the Duchesse tries to find a rational means of combatting her obsession for a man she has never seen and whom she knows only by an act of fortune:

> Et lors la Duchesse luy declara privéement que depuis le departement de ma dame Ysabeau, elle n'avoit eu repos en son ame, et comme elle estoit enamourée d'un chevalier sans l'avoir veu, la beauté et bonne grace duquel la sollicitoit si pres que, ne pouvant plus resister à son mal, elle ne sçavoit à qui avoir recours qu'à la fidelité de son conseil; adjoustant pour conclusion qu'elle ne l'aymoit point impudiquement ne pour esperance qu'elle eust de satisfaire à quelque vouloir lascif, mais seulement pour en avoir la veue, laquelle (ce luy sembloit) luy apporteroit tel contentement que son mal prendroit fin. (HT VI, 177)

But any such attempt to find a logical answer for human suffering is doomed to failure, for the very foundation of that logic is destroyed by the blindness caused by passion. Faith in its power is belied by human weakness. The deformation of reason removes one of the powerful resources against contingency. And man becomes the pitiful victim not only of an external fortune but also of an inner fatality as well, a fatality which he has created and to which he yields helplessly. The heroic image slowly deteriorates. What Edouart hails as the distinctive feature of man over the beast is nothing but a myth which has no more meaning than the deceptive lip service he pays to it. The hierarchy becomes an equation.

But Boaistuau does not stop at this point. He plunges man further into the abyss of wretchedness by denying him equality with animals. The equation is destroyed and replaced by a new hierarchy in which man's rightful place is at the bottom. Since his love is selfish, it is impure and therefore becomes a mortal sin. Lust is the only possible definition of the "desordonnée affection" which blindly entices. But it is also a corrosive cancer which corrupts not only the body but also the soul. The *desvoyé* now becomes a *damné:*

> Quand le malheureux vice de l'impudique amour prend une fois racine, il ne cesse de ramper par toutes les plus saines parties du corps humain, jusques à ce qu'il ayt engendré en noz cœurs un tige si puant et infaict que le fruict qui en resort est l'entiere corruption de noz vies et de noz ames. Et combien que pour quelque temps il entretienne ses vassaux en delices, si est-ce que les dernieres confitures qu'il leur appreste sont si difficiles à digerer que les uns perdent le sens, les autres la vie.... (HT II, 47)

The initial pleonasm establishes the moralist's focus and expresses his final condemnation. His statement completes the destruction of the myth of love. The amorous venom which penetrates the eyes of the lover is a poison which infects the body, corrupts the mind, and destroys the soul. Love is merely the disguise of lust.

Lust will not accept servitude however. When unsatisfied it strikes out at the cause of its frustration, and in order to dominate, it becomes a destructive fury. Pancalier's blind love for the Duchesse turns to hatred as a result of her constant refusals:

> Le Comte, se sentant refusé, injurié et en doute que la princesse ne feist entendre son faict au Duc,...changeant ceste grande amour en une hayne plus que mortelle, se delibera (quoy qu'il en deust advenir) d'inventer tous les moyens qu'il luy seroit possible pour ruyner du tout la Duchesse. (HT VI, 194-195)

A perverted reason is summoned to help construct an intricate plot which Pancalier elaborates with diabolical joy, the same joy that posseses the Seigneur du Piedmont as he plans the punishment of his unfaithful wife. The "tige si puant et infaict" has corrupted all sense of moral values, and the act of vengeance, the most frequent expression of this perverted affection, leads only to a figurative (HT IV) or actual (HT II, V, VI) death. Boaistuau completes his destruction of the hero. The painful pleasures of love, the docile servitude of the lover, the higher good which love reflects, these are myths which cannot be sustained in the world of the *Histoires tragiques*. Man's creative potential, assured by the gift of reason, is concerned only with destruction. The heroic figure who delves into the mysteries of the microcosm and the macrocosm is reduced from gigantic proportions to a pitiful creature who bemoans his helplessness.

The most serious consequence of this passion is its effect upon the ruler of the state. Mustapha's reasoned plea suggests the two qualities most necessary to assure the success and glory of the king:

> ...degenerant de vostre ancienne generosité et grandeur, vous vous estes si bien donné en proye à une simple femme que vous dependez entierement de ses blandices et mignotises sans que raison ou conseil puissent trouver place en vostre cueur passionné... (HT II, 52-53)

It is *generosité* and *raison* which should assure not only his *gloire*, but all of those qualities associated with the successful king such as *magnanimité, valeur,* and *justice*. But *generosité* and *raison* are pointedly denied in both of the historical tales. Against the ideal of *generosité* (courage, valor, gallantry) is the portrait of Edouart who

> tomba en tel desespoir de son amour qu'il en cuida forcener de dueil, faisant les nuicts egales aux jours, sans prendre aucun repos, mettant à part les armes, l'administration de la justice, le deduict de la chasse, où le temps passé il s'estoit tant delecté; et toute son estude n'estoit qu'à passer et repasser plusieurs fois devant la porte de la Comtesse pour espier s'il en pourroit tirer quelque traict d'œil. (HT I, 37)

The political ideals of the humanists are meaningless formulations for the ruler. The theories are eloquent, the formulas tempting, but the ideal appears unattainable. The ethic which would "discover happiness in the practice of virtue, through a life carried on in accordance with reason and the Aristotelian golden mean" [2] becomes an impossibility, for it relies upon man's rational

---

[2] Hiram Haydn, *The Counter-Renaissance* (New York: Charles Scribner's Sons, 1950), p. 53.

nature, and that is imperfect and fallible. The rational ideal for earthly happiness assumes a noble creature with a natural impulse for virtue. But in the world of the *Histoires tragiques*, that natural impulse is directed solely towards the satisfaction of the passions, and reason is perverted to this single end. The struggle is not upward; there is instead a steady fall into a pit of vice in accordance with the fatality of passion itself. Indeed all nature is contaminated by this passion: as the incarnation of the unnatural, the king corrupts the world about him.

In his *Histoires prodigieuses* Boaistuau makes a similar appeal that the king exemplify reason and moderation: "Qu'ils mettent donc peine & s'esvertuent de si bien modérer leurs actions, & si bien reigler l'estat de leur vie, qu'ils rendent un jour loyal compte au seigneur de leur troupeau." Kings control the moral climate of their realms, for they are "comme les Fontaines publiques, où tout le monde boyt, les Théatres où tout le monde regarde, & les torches qui esclairent à tous." Therefore the sins they commit are the examples they transmit to their subjects. Their corruption becomes that of their realm. But ruling is a task, Boaistuau continues, that virtually surpasses human capacity, "car l'affluence des biens & honneurs esquels les princes sont coustumièrement conficts, liberté de mal faire sans estre repris, la corruption du conseil de ceux qui leur assistent, sont les vrayes allumettes pour les enflammer es vices." The examples of corruption are too numerous to be ignored. Boaistuau recalls "la bonté de Saul" that way "perverty & gasté;" Salomon who "se donna en proye aux femmes;" Caligula, Mithridates, and Nero who infected "toute la terre… de leurs tirannies, & cruautés;" and "une infinité d'autres, tous consommés en vices, & cruautés." In his concluding portrait of Nebuchadnezzar, Boaistuau finds the fitting image of the dethroned king who has yielded to the passions and been "precipité en un eternel Labyrinthe de vices:

> …le miserable Roy Nabuchodonosor…sentit la fureur de la justice divine si aspre, qu'il fut l'espace de sept ans chassé & exillé de son royaulme, vagant par les deserts avec les bestes brutes, vivant de semblable pasture, & demeura nud en tel estat, battu du chault, du froid, de la gresle & rousée, jusques à ce que le poil luy creut comme celuy de l'Aigle, & ses ongles comme ceux des

> oyseaux.... Quel prodige pour ceux qui commandent! de voir celuy qui estoit si somptueusement servy de délicates viandes, oster aux desers la nourriture aux bestes, & banqueter avec elles: Celuy qui souloit estre vestu de pourpre, & aorné de joyaux precieux, estre si bien abaissé par la main forte de Dieu, qu'il n'est plus couvert que de poil, qui est la parure des bestes. [3]

Glory, courage, valor, and reason have no meaning for this blind creature who can aspire only to the lowest ranks in the hierarchy of creation. The Comte describes the result of the supposedly natural impulse to virtue in Edouart:

> ...non seulement toutes les loix de nature sont esteintes et amorties en vous, mais qui pis est, vous excedez et surpassez en cecy la cruauté des animaux, lesquels, quelque brutalité qu'ils ayent, si ne sont-ils point si desnaturez de faire tort à leurs faons ou d'exposer leur fruit à la mercy d'autruy, comme vous faites le vostre sous le plaisir d'un Roy. (HT I, 34)

The passion which destroys the individual lashes out at those around him and leaves only a path of devastation. Love's poison spreads rampantly throughout the world, destroying every refuge of man's creation. And because of his willing acquiescence, man's nobility becomes nothing more than a meaningless title which masks a bestial brutality.

iii. Love and Honor

With the impossibility of the rational and humanist ethic in Boaistuau's tragic world, there remained nevertheless the answer provided by the social code. In place of reason and moderation, the ethic of honor provided another means of regulating life. "Under the names of Honor and Love, two related yet essentially courtly ethical codes (or codes of conduct) sprang up in the Counter-Renaissance to challenge the supremacy of the traditionalist-humanists' allegiance to Virtue and Reason." [4] Although

---

[3] *Histoires prodigieuses* (Paris: Club Français du Livre, 1961), pp. 18-22.

[4] Haydn, *op. cit.*, p. 555.

condemned by the humanists as a permissive rationalization of anger and lust, the courtly tradition of the sixteenth century intended to give an artistic and ethical form to social conduct.

Honor promised to succeed where reason had failed, for as Rabelais suggests, "gens liberes, bien nez, bien instruicts, conversans en compaignies honnestes, ont par nature un instinct et agillon qui tousjours les poulse à faictz vertueux et retire de vice, lequel ilz nommoient honneur." [5] The instinct to honor among the well-born was to assure the validity of the ethic, as well as its vitality and utility, and to prohibit any act that would be vicious and dishonorable. Since the theory of honor was founded upon a natural instinct inherited through noble birth, in the final analysis it dismissed any dependency upon reason as an essential ingredient in achieving true virtue. [6] Indeed the aristocratic ethic displaced reason to a subordinate if not to an almost negligible position. "Honor becomes 'the ruling principle of ... conduct,' instead of reason; it replaces reason as the guide to virtue; and it becomes the natural 'spur' that leads men away

---

[5] *Gargantua*, chp. LVII. *Cf.* C. B. Watson, *Shakespeare and the Renaissance Concept of Honor* (Princeton: Princeton University Press, 1960), pp. 3-4: "Honor...was often considered inseparable from virtue itself. Instead of being the loosely defined secular morality it had been for the medieval aristocracy, it was now a fully conceived, carefully rationalized and articulated, formal philosophical code. In the Renaissance, honor, basically a pagan idea, has become almost a religion."

[6] As Hiram Haydn points out, the social ethic as developed by Castiglione was intended to complement the humanist ethic "in its acknowledgement of the claims of reason and virtue and the traditional Christian values — consonant, also, with the traditionalist concepts of limit: moderation, degree, and balance" (*op. cit.*, p. 564). Later exponents of this aristocratic ideal and privilege, however, tipped the balance of the rational foundation, and the ennobling force of love gradually evolved to a physical passion dominated by natural instinct rather than reason. In the extreme, desire itself could be defended as Nature's design and therefore physical love became an act honorable in itself. The perversion of the original doctrine comes quite obviously from the various definitions given to Nature and honor. Both were accounted for in the humanist doctrine. Nature was equated not with the fulfillment of instinctive impulse, but with obedience to a divinely inspired plan or order best pursued through moderation. Honor was "the deserved reputation accompanying a virtuous action, and [was] dependent upon 'Conscience.' It [was] not however to be the director of our lives and actions, ... for the guiding principle [was] Reason" (Haydn, *op. cit.*, p. 572).

from vice — usurping natural reason's prerogative."[7] Ideally honor could perform the function of natural reason, given its definition as public esteem and self-esteem. The balance maintained by Castiglione was lost. Honor was called upon to condone any action as its prerogative. Just as lust could be rationalized as obedience to nature, so honor could justify anger as a means of preserving personal and public esteem.

The inconsistencies of the social ethic are evident. As a formulation which dismisses the validity of reason as the controlling factor in human action, it calls upon reason to condone any unnatural act that may be committed. As a separate code distinct from the humanist ethic, which love invalidates, it is held in greater esteem by Boaistuau's heroes who all defend their actions according to its precepts.

Honor is a theme which occurs in every story. It is considered as an ideal and an absolute:

> ...j'ayme mieux perdre la vie avec la plus cruelle de toutes les honteuses morts qu'il sçauroit inventer que de consentir une chose tant deshonneste, ayant de long temps imprimé cecy en mon ame, que la mort honneste honore la vie passée. (HT I, 36)

> ...mon honneur, que j'ay plus cher que ma vie... (HT III, 74)

> ...aymant trop mieux mourir en honneur pauvre et desherité que vivre puissant, malheureux et pusillanime. (HT VI, 209)

All of the commonplaces are repeated by the heroes, especially the idea of honor as more important than life itself (HT I, 17; 35; HT IV, 133). For the characters, if not of royal birth, all lay claim to a certain nobility: they are all presented as *genereux*. Pancalier is an "homme genereux, fort prudent en ses affaires" (HT VI, 193). Mandozze is "l'un des plus genereux et accompliz gentils-hommes qui vivent" (HT VI, 175). The Seigneur du Piedmont is "vaillant et genereux" (HT IV, 124). But in each tale Boaistuau attacks some aspect of the myth. Pancalier is the court-

---

[7] Haydn, *op. cit.*, p. 573.

ier who turns into a vengeful tyrant and murderer, for his is not an anger controlled by reason nor in any way justifiable. Mustapha warns Mahomet that he is a man "degenerant de [son] ancienne generosité et grandeur" (HT II, 52), but his vain efforts to recapture his glory and reputation, his personal and public esteem, result only in an example of "la cruauté inhumaine d'un infidele amant envers sa dame" (HT II, 49). The Seigneur du Piedmont tries to preserve his honor by seeking revenge against his wife for her infidelity: "La plus grande, cruelle et atroce injure que peut recevoir l'homme bien né et nourry en vertu est celle qui se commet en l'honneur de sa femme" (HT IV, 121). Here reason is called to the service of vengeance as the seigneur plots a just retribution. But it is a reason deformed by the force of passion and which ultimately destroys both the husband and the wife.

The courtly ethic is no more valid in Boaistuau's world than the humanist ethic. Its absurdity is indicated early in the collection. When Edouart flatters Ælips in lofty superlatives and states that the beauty of her eyes alone would have halted the invader, the Comtesse replies with a disarming frankness: "Et quant à mon regard, je m'asseure qui si j'eusse faict l'essay de ce que m'avez dit, et que je me feusse sumise à leur misericorde, mon crops feust maintenant reduit en cendre" (HT I, 14).

Gallantry as a social code of decorum, honor as an instinctive impulse to virtue, defense of honor as an ultimate good, all these motifs are blatantly denied by the *Histoires tragiques*. The faithful lover becomes a wrathful avenger. Nobility is contaminated by a destructive lust. Honor is compromised or forgotten entirely, as by the wife of the Seigneur du Piedmont, "laquelle, oubliant l'honneur qui accompagne ordinairement les grandes dames" (HT IV, 125), surrenders willingly to adultery. The Duchesse realizes that her failure to obey the code of honor is most likely the reason for Mandozze's cool reception as she admits to him: ..."j'ay jugé... que m'eussiez pensé (peut estre) par trop liberale de mon honneur d'avoir abandonné le pays où je commande pour me rendre esclave de voz bonnes graces" (HT VI, 190).

Boaistuau condemns the courtly code as a meaningless convention, an absolute which has no validity since its proponents are not led instinctively to virtue but to vice. Weak and helpless before a dominating passion, the notion of honor is perverted; it serves as a mask to conceal a consuming lust and to condone the unnatural. When Pancalier stabs his nephew as part of his involved plot of vengeance against the Duchesse, the King of England and the Duc have only praise for the murderer, "louans en eux-mesmes grandement la fidelité du Comte, lequel n'avoit pardonné à son propre sang pour garder le devoir et honneur de son seigneur" (HT VI, 200). All of these motifs and themes are stated and carefully examined in HT V which is Boaistuau's most eloquent indictment of the courtly ethic.

"The new tradition," writes Haydn, "is one of aristocratic chivalry."[8] This condition Didaco faithfully meets: he is descended from "une famille fort ancienne, nommée de Ventimiglia, de laquelle sont sortiz un grand nombre de riches et honorables chevaliers" (HT V, 139). His heritage is assured. Noble blood flows through his body, and his rank of "chevalier" is immediately qualified by "honorable." The fatality of blood produces a man "renommé de tous pour le plus liberal et courtoys gentil-homme de la cité" (139). This rapid characterization lists all the qualifications essential to the aristocratic code: *chevalier, courtois, gentil-homme.* Didaco is to be the perfect exemplar of the code of honor. Moreover since the courtly code is concerned with love, Didaco willingly fulfills this requirement, for he "consommoit... sa jeunesse en triomphes, masques et autres despenses communes à tels pelerins, dressant l'amour à toutes les femmes indifferemment, sans qu'il eust l'une plus affectée que l'autre" (140-141).

Obviously Boaistuau's insinuations are attacking the myth from the very beginning of the tale. If the courtly conception makes love an ennobling force, it becomes in Didaco's case a mere pastime and amusement for the idle. His dedication to the game is "par deffaut de meilleures occupations" (139). Thus the chevalier himself is a figure of pure ornamentation with a complete

---

[8] *Op. cit.,* p. 556.

devotion to empty self-indulgence. But he is certain nevertheless that he has satisfied at least one essential aspect of the code of honor:

> Honor, in one of its meanings, is an exclusively social virtue. Honor, in this sense, may refer to one's *reputation* in the community, to one's *credit* as a man of integrity, to the *honors* or *rewards* which are bestowed publicly as a testimony to one's virtue, to the *glory* and *fame* which one acquires as the result of exceptional or heroic accomplishments, or to the *good name* which is gained when one consistently behaves in a fashion which gains the *respect* and *esteem* of one's fellows. [9]

Boaistuau's implicit commentary concentrates initially on the superficiality of the public side of the ethic. Didaco's amorous conquests have enhanced his name and reputation: they are regarded with admiration, thus making him "renommé de tous" as a courtly gentleman. But public esteem is divorced from personal integrity, and the public is a poor judge of the worth of a man's actions. These are based on appearance only, and the code of honor thereby serves merely as a convenient mask to gain public admiration. As such, honor is condemned for its falseness. This is the first theme of the story which Boaistuau introduces. The ethic of honor has little validity since the mask itself is too readily accepted as a reliable testimony of truth, a truth founded only on appearances. Another absolute has been deformed.

Fulfilling the role expected of the courtly chevalier, Didaco does experience the exhilaration of true love. Like Rhomeo, he spends his youth in a meaningless series of conquests until he discovers the one woman who can inspire a true passion, "une jeune fille de moyen aage, mais de beauté fort exquise" (140). Here the second element of the courtly code comes into play, since "the chief influence upon the courtier, the ennobling and refining influence, is that of a beautiful woman." [10] And Didaco succumbs in the prescribed fashion before Violente, "de laquelle,

---

[9] Watson, *op. cit.*, p. 11.
[10] Haydn, *op. cit.*, p. 556.

ayant receu un traict d'œil au despourveu, ne se sceut si bien garantir que de là en avant elle ne luy touchast plus pres du cueur que les autres" (140). This time Boaistuau presents the same progression of love, not to destroy reason and moderation as he had done in the case of the ruler (HT I, II), but to show its effects on the courtly lover. The motifs are the same however: the first stunning glance, the endless days Didaco spends wandering back and forth in front of her door, hoping to catch a glimpse of the one woman alone for whom he now yearns. With each glance he is reduced to further misery, for "son pauvre cueur... ne pouvoit endurer ceste nouvelle charge" (141).

Didaco follows all of the conventions: "presens, lettres et messages, lesquels il continua l'espace de demy an ou plus" (141). But it is his purpose which belies the gesture: "il voulut tenter sa pudicité" (141). The nobility of the courtly pose is destroyed. Instead of a respectful submission to the incarnation of honor, the uplifting quality of love is lost, and love becomes merely desire which craves satisfaction. Again myth is helpless before lust, and the ideal is coincidentally perverted. For Didaco, honor, in this case Violente's chastity, is not something admirable in itself nor worthy of respect; it is only an obstacle to the satisfaction of desire. The illustrative purpose of the tale therefore becomes evident: Didaco represents the hypocritical mask of honor, Violente true honor which is gradually eroded and finally destroyed.

This confrontation of truth and appearance is exploited during the first third of the story which relates Didaco's vain attempts to convince Violente of his sincere affection and Violente's total defense of her chastity. The result is an impasse. But as Didaco tries to maintain his public image and satisfy a raging lust, he readily embraces any means since personal honor is merely a synonym for pride. The fallacy of the ethic of honor is summarily presented in this single character whose only concern is overcoming an obstacle worthy of his efforts as his public image defines him. Such a departure from the ethical absolutes of the courtly code creates a distance between hero and heroine which cannot be bridged.

The futility of his letters and gifts brings Didaco to his first verbal encounter with Violente. With each keeping a firm and unyielding commitment to his own views, their conversations are little more than meaningless exercises in rhetorical verbosity. Assuming the pose of the suffering lover, Didaco follows the formula which had worked so successfully in the past. His words are accompanied by "tant de larmes, sanglots et souspirs qu'il donnoit assez suffisant tesmoignage que sa langue estoit la vraye et fidele messagere de son cueur" (142). He speaks at length of the "amitié" he bears Violente, and she replies in the only fashion suitable to that which she represents, an answer fully in character as she defends her "honnesteté." Yet Violente is extremely perspicacious. She understands the intentions which the courtly tradition is supposed to conceal; she pierces the mask of reputation. Evoking the disparity between his "vie passée" and his supposed expression of love, she fully realizes that they obey two codes of conduct whereby her adherence to honor is seen by Didaco only as "rudesse ou cruauté."

Violente speaks well within the confines of the myth. She assumes a haughty pose of proud disdain as she insists to Didaco that "vostre mal... ne peut prendre fin par le moyen que vous pretendez" (142). And with patronizing sympathy, she tries to redirect Didaco's attitude to a proper appreciation of that ethic by which he professes to live:

> ...combien que je doive plaindre avec raison ceux qui sont en semblable peine, si est-ce que je ne veulx tellement lascher la bride à ma passion que mon honneur en demeure au pouvoir d'autruy, et (peut estre) à la mercy de ceux, lesquels, ne sçachant combien il m'est cher, penseroient avoir fait petite conqueste. (HT V, 142)

Honor as a virtue encounters honor as appearance. The first is unyielding. Violente spouts all of the commonplaces of the doctrine: honor is the finest possession in life; honor is to be guarded with one's life; and "si vous... esperiez quelque chose de moy qui fust alienée de l'honneur, vous vivriez en tresgrande erreur" (143). Finally she offers Didaco the only thing her honor will allow, her "honneste amitié, de laquelle vous me trouverez à l'avenir tant liberale en tout ce que l'honneur pourra permettre" (143).

Their conversations are carried out on two different planes. Violente speaks of a sense of honor that is incomprehensible to the chevalier. Her defense is eloquent, her words truthful, their meaning inescapable. But dialogue becomes a useless formality. Didaco lives his lies. Just as honor masks his pride, so his plaintive words are a mere concession to formality. The deception of the mask is the same deception which inspires the lover's lamentation. Boaistuau condemns the whole tradition. True honor pierces this mask and discovers the pride and hypocrisy which lie beneath.

But pride will not accept defeat lest the public reputation be likewise tarnished. It turns to deception in order to preserve the falseness of appearances. Since conventional formulas obtained for him only what convention formally allows, having offered "amitié" and received only "honneste amitié" in return, Didaco decides to bend convention to his purpose. Assuming the mask of "ceux qui aiment parfaictement," he "resolut en fin que c'estoit le plus profitable pour le repos de son esprit de l'espouser" (145). The feigned marriage satisfies his lust, but, according to Boaistuau, the logical result of a love based on desire alone is boredom. Didaco's satisfaction is short-lived, due especially to Violente's blind and complete devotion, and "se voyant en pleine possession de son cueur, [il] commença peu à peu à se refroidir et à s'ennuyer de ce qu'il avoit eu si cher par le passé" (149). The only effect of his love and "marriage" has been the destruction of Violente's honor and virtue.

The second half of the tale concentrates on Violente. In Boaistuau's collection, she is the most complete representative of the code of honor as it concerns not only a public but also a personal image. In Renaissance theory, "honor also refers to one's *private* and *personal* judgment of one's *own* actions, one's *inner* conviction of *innate* moral rectitude. Honor, in other words, relates to *self-esteem* as much as to public approbation."[11] This personal sense of honor is denied by Didaco whose actions are governed

---

[11] Watson, *op. cit.*, p. 12.

by a self-exalting pride which endorses hypocrisy to maintain public approval. And if Didaco is representative of the courtly gentleman, Boaistuau's condemnation falls upon the whole class, for the most perfect example of the total sense of honor is to be found not among the nobility, but among the bourgeois. For Violente is the "fille d'un orfevre" (140) who spends her days in "l'exercice des ouvrages de l'aiguille, propres aux filles qui tenoient son rang" (140). But morally her devotion to honor elevates her to the highest position, and since "il y avoit peu de damoiselles et dames en la ville qui la peussent egaler en vertu et gentillesse" (140), Didaco easily convinces himself that "combien qu'elle ne fust de telle maison et moindre encores en biens qu'il meritoit, si est-ce que sa beauté et vertu et autres dons de graces... la rendoient digne d'un grand seigneur" (145).

Violente's defense of her honor was well known in Valencia and thereby ensures her public image: ..."elle estoit reputée tant chaste et spirituelle qu'il ne se trouvoit encores aucun qui eust eu le bruit d'avoir fait breche à son honneur, encores qu'elle eust esté poursuyvie de plusieurs" (140). She defends her honor as virtue and virtue as chastity, a viewpoint that was frequently criticized by the detractors of the courtly code. Haydn observes that the naturalists of the sixteenth century objected that such a definition of personal honor was mere hypocrisy. [12] But Boaistuau does not permit the attack upon Violente's sense of honor to occur because it was a hypocritical mask. Violente represents an absolute and she is admired for the eloquent defense of her principles.

But even true honor is powerless before deceit. Violente succumbs to the very thing she holds in such abhorrence. The delicate balance between self-esteem and public esteem is destroyed. Didaco has convinced her to keep their marriage secret until he has set his private affairs in order, and assured her that

---

[12] "This is all pretense, the naturalists claim — hypocrisy and guile. What 'the ladies' are really thinking of, when they refuse their favors to honest men, is their reputations. That is all 'honor' means to them; it has no connection with virtue or conscience — and if one of them feels sure that her 'fair name' will not suffer, all her scruples disappear. 'Art' of the worst sort" (op. cit., p. 574).

although he will be detained during the day, he will return faithfully to her each night. However Violente's faith in Didaco's words ultimately destroys her public reputation as "les voisins commencerent à soupçonner qu'il entretenoit ceste fille impudiquement" (147). Her commitment to honor is strong, but a poor defense against its determined destruction, and the 'portraict et exemplaire de chasteté' cannot survive the tide of opinion which maintains that, "degenerant de son ancienne vertu, elle estoit devenue si effrontée qu'elle dependoit du tout de la lascive amitié d'un homme" (148). Boaistuau is insistent that any secular ethic is invalid because of those who represent it. It is in vain that Violente defends her chastity and honor; she is helpless before those who are devoted to a principle which is only the rationalization of pride and lust. Against deceit honor cannot survive. Those who are to be the finest examples of honor — the nobility, the aristocracy — have simply exploited its formalities and lustre in order to mask their own base inclinations, and they willingly destroy those who defend a principle for which they have no sympathy.

The rest of the ethic is likewise condemned. "It is possible," says Watson, "that a man may paradoxically risk the loss of 'honor' (i.e., may fail to conform to the norms established by a given society which will win him the praise and esteem of his fellows) in order to preserve his 'honor' (i.e., avoid becoming dishonored in his own eyes)." [13] At this point revenge enters the code as a defense of the personal sense of honor; but it is to "be carried out in a spirit of just anger, controlled by reason." Violente tries to abide by the code of revenge, but reason is valid in terms of theory only. In reality passion and anger have full sway. Upon learning of Didaco's marriage, Violente, "passionnée outre mesure, pressée d'ire et de fureur... commença à faire une cruelle guerre à sa face et à ses cheveux (150). Janique makes a vain appeal for some sort of rational control over her rage:

> Et apres plusieurs remonstrances particulieres, luy mist devant les yeux que si elle se vouloit moderer quelque

---

[13] *Op. cit.*, p. 12.

> peu, elle iroit parler au Chevalier Didaco et luy remonstreroit si bien sa faute qu'elle le convertiroit à retourner à la maison, et qu'elle se devoit fortifier contre son mal et le dissimuler pour un temps pour s'en venger au parapres. (151)

But a rational revenge is a meaningless concept, a contradiction which Violente pointedly underscores with her sententious reply to Janique: "Le mal est trop leger où le conseil est receu" (151). The only reason that is evident is a perverted reason controlled by passion, a reason which allows Violente to formulate her plan of revenge with a terrifying calm and lucidity:

> Janique, si tu as donné bon commencement à nostre entreprise, aussi n'ay-je pas dormy de mon costé, car j'ay avisé qu'il nous fault faire provision d'une forte corde, laquelle nous attacherons au pied du chevet du lict; et si tost qu'il sera endormy, je te getteray l'autre bout de la corde en la ruelle, que tu tireras de ta force, et avant que tu commences à tirer, je luy auray donné le coup de la mort en la gorge. Parquoy donne ordre d'avoir deux grands couteaux, quoy qu'ils coustent; mais je te prie qu'il n'y ayt que moy qui donne fin à sa vie, ainsi que luy seul a donné la premiere attaincte à mon honneur. (158)

Every detail is carefully planned as Violente pursues her revenge with a logic and purpose which hatred alone can inspire. Her "honneste amitié" has deteriorated to a violent hatred that lashes out to destroy. The blindness of her passion corrupts all sense of values. She easily rationalizes her act, stating that "les dieux m'ont esleue pour executer moy-mesme la vengeance de leur ire et de la perte de mon honneur" (152). Her vengeance is to be a public defense of her personal sense of integrity, since all that remains of her reputation now is "le tiltre de vile et abominable putain" (152).

Boaistuau insists repeatedly upon the paradoxes of this ethic. It appears that the only means of maintaining integrity are treacherous and contemptible in themselves. And such vengeance is all the more fearful in the hands of a woman, as he suggests in his prefatory comment to the story:

> Combien qu'entre toutes les creatures de Dieu il ne se trouve rien plus traictable et humain que les femmes, de sorte qu'il semble qu'elles soient envoiées du ciel pour le soulagement de nostre humanité, si est-ce que depuis qu'elles degenerent de leur naturel et que leur colere s'allume et s'enflamme, elles deviennent quelque fois furieuses et entreprennent des choses que les cruels tyrans auroient horreur d'exercer. (137)

In the code of honor, there is a certain fatality which drags an individual ever further into corruption. To avenge her honor, Violente turns to the same deception that had served Didaco so well. In the letter she sends to the chevalier to lure him to his death, she uses all of the phrases and terms which Didaco had spoken to her in their first conversation. "Conficte en tant de larmes, souspirs, tourmens et ennuyz" (154), she relates the unhappiness of her life and invokes death as the only end to her "martyre:"

> ...s'il advient que mes pauvres yeux, lassez d'avoir presque sans intervalle espuisé une vive source de larmes, se veulent clorre, les songes ne cessent lors de tourmenter et affliger mon ame par les plus cruels tourmens qu'il leur est possible, me representans par leurs espovantables et horribles visions l'aise et contentement de celle qui tient ma place. (155)

Ironically the conventional phrases of the plaintive suffering hero may be taken at a literal level. The torment that Violente relates is the torment she feels at Didaco's offence towards her honor. Her tears and complaints move the chevalier to respond to Violente's invitation to love. But the bed of love becomes a bed of death. And Violente's wrath is not easily assuaged. She prolongs the horror of the murder with the mutilation of Didaco's body, and to each severed part she addresses an invocation, a series of "contre-blasons:" "Ah! trahistres yeux...;" "Ah! langue abominable et parjure...;" "Ah! cueur diamantin...;" and concludes her savage butchery with a speech to the unmasked remains of aristocratic honor: "O charongne infaicte, qui as autrefois esté organe de la plus infidele et desloyale ame qui oncques descendit du ciel! Or es-tu maintenant payée de desserte condigne à tes merites" (163).

The death of Violente is Boaistuau's final judgment on the social code of honor. Most often it is only a mask, and once the mask is torn aside, he finds not a heroic chevalier, but only raw pride. The chevalier is the very opposite of what the code demands. His loyalty and fidelity are conveniences to feed his pride which is the source of all his actions. If honor can exist in its true sense, it is short-lived, for once attacked, it cannot withstand deceit, and falls victim to its own definition once defended by means dishonorable in themselves. Again the hero is left weak and helpless, and can only complain as does Edouart:

> ...l'amour...m'a tellement aliené ma liberté et offusqué le meilleur de moy que, sortant maintenant hors des loix d'honneur et de raison...et ne pouvant chasser le venin mortifere hors de mon cœur, qui a aneanty mes forces et empoisonné mon sens et privé mon ame de tout bon conseil, je ne sçay que faire... (HT I, 26-27)

The power of passion invalidates any formulated secular ethic. Honor, reason, and moderation are all equally far from the grasp of man. Theorizing appears to be a meaningless and futile pastime, for these codes and ethics are insignificant for the individual who has in Boaistuau's tragic world lost all heroic proportions. They presume a man of nobility, but nobility is only a mask. They are directed toward a creature of strength, but all strength is dissipated by the force of lust. They are intended for a man of reason, but reason is useless in the face of passion. Man's only expression of power is the force which destroys. Unable to live by an ideal, his only act is to corrupt it, to reverse the ideal so that it is a faithful reflection of his own nature. Grandeur, nobility, and virtue are readily sacrificed by man's monstrous nature, a nature which accepts no restraint that would prohibit its fullest expression.

iv. Love and Nature

Against the ravages of fortune and the corruption of man, a retreat to the pure and simple life of the country was an honored notion in the Renaissance. Nature was a refuge from the activity of the city or court, an escape from worldly concerns, a haven for the afflicted. The theme of peace, calm, and repose in a simple natural world became a commonplace for poet and moralist.[14] For our purposes it is necessary to consider two specific concepts associated with the pleasance. First, as its bucolic origin suggests, it is associated with love. The poets of the Renaissance exploited and developed the bucolic setting as a luxuriant framework for love: nature is the ideal setting, it is the refuge where the lover can try to calm his torment. As a springtime world it provides an image of his beloved, echoes her name, induces a sweet reverie in which each natural image corresponds to some aspect of her beauty. Or else it sympathetically bemoans the poet's grief.[15]

From the pastoral setting developed a second concept which was especially important to the Renaissance humanist. The calm associated with country life could not be found in city or town. The country promises a simple life, a life that is virtuous, for it avoids the sins endemic in city life with its vain pursuit of riches and success. As the moral overtone supersedes the amorous, the city becomes synonymous with vice and sin, the country with virtue and goodness.

The humanists found such equations irresistible. Petrarch writes to the Bishop of Viterbo inviting him to come to Vaucluse, for there "Niccolò will find no tyranny, insolence, backbiting, wrath, faction, complaining, deceit, clamor, shouting, blaring of trumpets, clash of arms, avarice, jealousy, ambition, servility, guile, or offense." The rustic retreat offers instead "a quiet, humble, and gentle manner of life, a peaceful coun-

---

[14] The theme is of course not new. Curtius traces the appeal of the ideal landscape back to Homer where scattered references suggest an image of a luxuriant nature with trees, springs, and meadows, as well as the springtime world of Elysium. Theocritus developed these motifs into a bucolic world where nature was linked to love. But it was Virgil who moved the locale of Theocritus' pastoral world from Sicily to a more distant Arcadia. With Virgil's elaboration, the description of the ideal landscape assumed full metaphoric and rhetorical value as a *topos*: the *locus amoenus* which, "from the Empire to the sixteenth century ... forms the principal motif of all nature description" (*European Literature and the Latin Middle Ages*, p. 195).

[15] These aspects are examined in detail by Henri Weber, *La Création poétique au XVIe siècle en France* (Paris: Nizet, 1956), t. I, pp. 307-333.

tryside, soft air, sweet breezes, sunny swards, clear springs, a river full of fish, flowery banks, leafy woods, dewy caverns, green meadows, the lowing of cattle, the song of birds, and the murmuring of waters." [16]

Nature preaches moral wisdom. It is a refuge, a teacher, and offers a setting in which one can find serenity:

> Nature is not silent but speaks to us everywhere and teaches the observant man many things if she finds him attentive and receptive. What else does the charming countenance of blooming Nature proclaim than that God the Creator's wisdom is equal to his goodness. [17]

The pleasance is the earthly representation of a paradise that is accessible and morally edifying. Therefore it is the ideal locale favored by the humanist for his discussions. The pleasance is adapted as the framework for the moral treatise. The gathering under the trees, in the garden, at a country villa, is a conventional setting for dialogue. It is the setting of Noël du Fail's humanist tales, *Les Propos rustiques,* for the natural surroundings are conducive to thought, a place where the four elderly *devisants* can "à l'ayse philosopher," and move toward the discovery of "une pure vérité." Similarly, Marguerite de Navarre's ten travelers decide to relate and discuss their tales in a "beau pré le long de la riviere du Gave, où les arbres sont si foeillez que le soleil ne sçauroit percer l'ombre ny eschauffer la frescheur." [18]

The humanist pleasance adapts the pastoral appeal that had enticed the poet to the ethical ideals pronounced in moral discourse. For the Ancients the pastoral setting was an escape, but an escape into the imaginary realm of literature, opposing literary truth and the truth of reality. However, "the renaissance humanist could not accept this facile dichotomy which fragmented man rather than making him whole. He wanted real literature as well as an ideal life. Literature, like life, must take form within the

---

[16] E. H. Wilkins, *Life of Petrarch* (Chicago: University of Chicago Press, 1961), p. 124.
[17] Erasmus, "The Godly Feast," in *The Colloquies of Erasmus,* trans. Craig Thompson (Chicago: University of Chicago Press, 1965), p. 48.
[18] *Heptaméron,* "Prologue."

human sphere; yet it should reflect the perfection glimpsed by the poet in his moment of ecstasy."[19] The pleasance is the realization of that ideal. It represents in a symbolic fashion those virtues elaborated upon in the humanist discourse. The *locus amoenus* is an escape from worldly confusion and disappointment, a temporary refuge from a despairing reality. As such it is a symbol of simplicity and order, and serves as the very image according to which man should pattern his life. The ideal is given reality and becomes an accessible Eden.

The pleasance is evoked twice in the *Histoires tragiques*. In the two *nouvelles*, it promises an ideal retreat for love. But the idyllic quality is lost. Julliette's father arranges for the wedding feast to take place not in his town house where he had given the masked ball, but at Villefranche, "un lieu de plaisance où le seigneur Antonio se souloit souvent recréer, qui estoit à un mille ou deux de Veronne" (HT III, 103). The setting is well chosen by Antonio who believes that Julliette's marriage to Comte Paris will put an end to her sorrow and tears. Villefranche is to be a prelude to the happiness he anticipates for his daughter.

But in the sentimental tale, one cannot put unquestioned faith in any ideal, given the limitations of human perception and the complexity of human motivation. One can lament in private or to a confidant, but true sentiment is not divulged beyond such private confessions. Characters unwittingly erect insurmountable

---

[19] S. K. Heninger, Jr., "The Renaissance Perversion of the Pastoral," *JHI* XXII (1961), 261. Heninger states that the exploitation of bucolic motifs for satirical and allegorical purposes is a "perversion" of the pastoral which is typical of the Renaissance. The juxtaposition of the ideal and the real provided a meaningful criticism of actuality. He also suggests that the Renaissance pastoral introduced the theme of death and mutability in Arcadia. Erwin Panofsky credits Virgil with this motif: see "Et in Arcadia ego: On the Conception of Transience in Poussin and Watteau," in *Philosophy and History: Essays presented to Ernst Cassirer* (Oxford: The Clarendon Press, 1936), pp. 223-254. For an eloquent summary of the tradition of the pleasance, see David Evett, " 'Paradise's Only Map': The *Topos* of the *Locus Amoenus* and the Structure of Marvell's *Upon Appleton House*," *PMLA* 85 (1970), 504-513. Thomas G. Rosenmeyer brings a wealth of detail and a number of refinements to the notion of the pleasance in his study, *The Green Cabinet: Theocritus and the European Pastoral Lyric* (Berkeley and Los Angeles: The University of California Press, 1969), pp. 179-205.

barriers around themselves and force others to act out of blindness to the truth. Antonio's plans are based upon mere assumption and without knowledge of the reasons for Julliette's unhappiness. His exasperation over her grief precipitated his arrangements for the marriage to Paris; but he acted in the belief that Julliette was bemoaning the death of Thibault. Blindness and false assumption lead ultimately to tragedy. And the site of happiness, the "lieu de plaisance," becomes the scene of Julliette's fears and apprehensions, her doubts and hesitation, her macabre nightmare and simulated death.

While HT III suggests certain inconsistencies between setting and its mythic significance, HT IV blatantly perverts the concept of the pleasance. Boaistuau's purpose is made clear in the introduction to the tale:

> L'ancienne et generale coustume des gentils-homme Piedmontois et damoiselles a tousjours esté d'abandonner les villes fameuses et murmures de republiques pour se retirer aux champs en leurs chasteaux et autres lieux de plaisance, afin de decevoir les ennuyeuses parties de la vie avec plus grand repos et contentement que ceux qui s'occupent à desmeller les troubles de la chose publique. (HT IV, 123)

The basic elements of the moral concept of the pleasance are all duly recognized: a refuge from the city, a temporary escape from public duty, a site of peace and calm. The country is an invitation to leisure, a leisure which is to be beneficial and instructive:

> ...ains se retiroient tous en leurs maisons champestres avec leurs familles, lesquelles estoient si bien ordonnées et dressées que vous partiriez aussi content et bien edifié de la maison d'un simple gentil-homme que vous feriez en quelque grosse ville de celle de quelque sage et prudent Senateur. (HT IV, 123)

But this peace and harmony existed "avant que les guerres eussent preposteré l'ordre de l'ancienne police" (HT IV, 123), and now all values are completely reversed. The city is now the site of leisure and pleasure, the labels given to idleness and vice:

> ...la pluspart des villes ne sont pour le jourd'huy peuplées que de gentils-hommes oysifs qui y font sejour,

> non pour y profiter, mais pour augmenter leurs delices; et ne se corrompent pas seulement eux mesmes, mais qui pis est, ils infectent ceux avec lesquels ils frequentent. (HT IV, 123-124)

The country, moreover, no longer provides pleasure or instruction. The seigneur's wife, "nourrie aux villes en grande compagnie," complains of boredom and "l'incommodité de la solitude" which become synonymous with the rustic retreat. The ideal landscape may still serve a stylized role as a setting for love, but love loses its purity and becomes instead an adulterous passion. And a new element is added to the description of the pleasance: the wife and her lover meet in the garden, but the setting is overshadowed by the tower in which the jealous husband is hidden, spying on the scene of love-making and plotting his revenge.

The nature which consoled a languishing poet now incites a jealous wrath. The nature which carried the memory of the poet's beloved now conveys proof of her deception. The springtime freshness of the pleasance is now traded for the mysterious shadow of the castle where the vengeful punishment can be exacted. The corruption of man has infected even the purity of the idyllic retreat. He has blatantly refused the refuge of a poetic Arcadia, shamelessly perverted the *locus amoenus*, and created instead a *locus mortis*.

The *Histoires tragiques* is a work of devastation. With the same vengeful wrath of the God he portrays in the *Theatre du monde*, Boaistuau mercilessly attacks man and his world along with all of those myths and ideals created to assure their poetic appeal. The weakness of man belies the heroic image that he would like to propagate. In reality he is but a helpless creature, ever victim to the ravaging effects of passion. His acquiescence to temptation releases the instinctive brutality of his nature, a brutality which redefines the whole world as it destroys sentimental myth, social myth, geographic myth, and moral postulations. Continuously pitting the poetic against the unpoetic, Boaistuau proves unfailingly the devastating strength of his anti-hero in a world in which love and creation mean nothing more than lust, destruction, and death.

CHAPTER III

THE *HISTOIRES PRODIGIEUSES*: AN EPILOGUE

> Is man no more than this?
> *King Lear*, III.4

According to the portrait that emerges from the *Histoires tragiques*, man, devoid of any instinct toward virtue, deprived of the mask of honor and nobility, is nothing more than the physical representation of a bestial lust, his sole directive force. He has recast his noble and divine image in favor of that which is defective and perverse. And recreating nature in his own image, he has destroyed even that generating force which now begets only the monstrous, the image of man's own perversity. Boaistuau dedicates a great portion of his last complete work, the *Histoires prodigieuses*, to a description of those monsters so prevalent in this new man-made creation. It serves as a final commentary on his tragic world. [1]

---

[1] All references to the *Histoires prodigieuses* are taken from the edition published by "Le Club Français du Livre" (Paris, 1961), a reproduction of the original edition of 1560. Quotations are followed by an abbreviated reference HP and the page number. This edition contains a useful introduction by Yves Florenne that was also published in the *Mercure de France* 342 (1961), 657-668: "Un quêteur de prodiges." Rudolf Schenda studies the HP in his work, *Die französische Prodigienliteratur in der zweiten Hälfte des 16. Jahrhunderts* (Munich: M. Hueber, 1961). He has also compiled a bibliography of similar collections published during this period which appears in ZFSL 69 (1959), 150-167. Jean Céard's forthcoming study of *La Nature et les prodiges: L'Insolite à la Renaissance* (Genève: Droz) is summarily presented in "La Nature et les prodiges au XVIe siècle," *Information littéraire* 28 (1976), 151-156.

The work describes the world that man's perversity has created, a terrestrial hell where monsters are legion. The deformed and the fantastic, the terrifying and the abominable are all examples "esquels nous voyons les œuvres de Nature...préposterées, renversées, mutilées & tronquées" (dédicace). In 1543, Boaistuau reports, in the city of Cracow, the following monster was seen:

> ...il estoit fort horrible, difforme & espouvantable, ayant les yeulx de couleur de feu, la bouche & le nez semblable au muffle d'un beuf avec une corne approchant du promuscide & trompe de l'Elephant, tout le derriere du corps estoit velu comme un chien. Et au lieu où les autres ont coustume d'avoir les tetins situés, il avoit deux testes de Singes, & au dessus du nombril le caractere de deux yeux de chat: aux joinctures des genoux & des bras, quatre testes de chien avec leur mine truculente & furieuse. Les paulmes de ses pieds & de ses mains estoient comme ceulx d'un Signe, & si avoit avec tout cela une queüe retroussée en haut, de la haulteur d'une demye aulne... (HP, 31)

Similarly, during the early years of the century when war engulfed all of Italy, the brutality and inhumanity of man was graphically represented in another monster:

> ...il fut engendré à Ravenne...un monstre ayant une corne en la teste, deux aeles, & un pied semblable à celuy d'un oyseau ravissant & avec un œil au genoil, il estoit double quant au sexe, participant de l'homme & de la femme, il avoit en l'estomac la figure d'un ypsilon, & la figure d'une croix, & si n'avoit aucuns bras. (HP, 309)

For Boaistuau the veracity of these reports is unimportant. They are recorded and are therefore authentic. If imagination delights in creating the monstrous, if superstition becomes authoritative assertion, there is a truth in these fantastic creations. Reality is that which exists in man's mind, and Boaistuau gives entire faith to these reports. This is a luxury he can well afford, for he can offer an explanation for the continual occurrence of the unnatural in the world.

Boaistuau gives token recognition to the various theories about the origin of monsters: "une ardente & obstinée Imagination que peult avoir la femme pendant qu'elle conçoit, laquelle a tant de puissance sur le fruict, que le rayon & caractere en demeure sur la chose enfantée" (HP, 24); "la superabondance ou deffault & corruption de semence" (HP, 25); "la corruption des viandes ordes & salles" (HP, 25); and even "les diables...[qui] peuvent...abuser des hommes & des femmes" (HP, 34). But it is the religious explanation which Boaistuau asserts authoritatively:

> Il est tout certain que le plus souvent ces creatures monstreuses procedent du jugement, justice, chastiment, & malediction de Dieu, lequel permet que les peres & meres produisent telles abhominations, en l'horreur de leur peché, parce qu'ils se precipitent indifferemment, comme bestes brutes où leur appetit les guide, sans respect ou observation d'aage, de lieu, de temps, ou autres Loix ordonnées de nature. (HP, 23)

The monstrous may be the result of God's vengeance, but the cause for His wrath is "l'incontinence & peché" of man himself. [2]

This explanation allows Boaistuau to regard these unnatural phenomena not in terror, not in order to justify the ways of a vengeful God to man, but as a sober warning of a final justice that admits no departure from God's defined moral truth. Boaistuau can narrate with the detachment of the moralist who has deduced the causes and can therefore accept in awe and wonderment these examples of God's power. [3] Yet, as his collection

---

[2] This explanation of unnatural phenomena is not uncommon at this time. Even Ambroise Paré, suggesting thirteen causes for monstres, places "la gloire de Dieu" and "son ire" as the first two (see *Œuvres complètes d'Ambroise Paré*, ed. J.-F. Malgaigne [Paris: J.-B. Baillière, 1841], t. III, chap. 1). In his "dix-neufième livre traitant des monstres et prodiges," Paré cites Boaistuau as one of his major sources. He offers in the preface the following distinctions: "*Monstres* sont choses qui apparoissent outre le cours de Nature (et sont le plus souvent signes de quelque malheur à advenir)... *Prodiges*, ce sont choses qui viennent de tout contre Nature..." (*op. cit.*, pp. 1-2). Boaistuau's terminology is not so rigid, although he does appear to distinguish between the 'unnatural' and the 'anti-natural': the first produces wonderment, the second horror and revulsion. For an indication of Paré's debt to Boaistuau, see Jean Céard's edition of Ambroise Paré, *Des Monstres et prodiges* (Genève: Droz, 1971).

[3] According to Jean Céard, Boaistuau, who 'invented' the genre of the *histoire prodigieuse*, imposed upon his collection of monsters and marvels

progresses, one has the feeling that there is a certain fascination which develops independently of the moralist's central preoccupation. Culling examples indiscriminately from sources biblical and secular, ancient and contemporary, and confirming whatever he can from his own experience and observation, Boaistuau asserts that many of the curiosities in the world are due to natural causes. He can offer a "scientific" explanation for the man from Milan who washed his face and hands with melted lead, and for the terrifying prospect of earthquakes he turns to Aristotle and Pliny who "attribuent les causes de ce malheur aux vapeurs & exhalations qui sont encloses aux entrailles de la terre, lesquelles cherchant à sortir, & à s'évaporer la secouent, mouvent, & agitent" (HP, 68). Comets, flames in the heavens, showers of blood all have their natural explanations (HP, 124-126), and Boaistuau maintains with calm authority that they "engendrent grand terreur & estonnement" only "à ceux qui en ignorent les causes" (HP, 124). But there is no real inconsistency. The scientist is not competing with the moralist. The two are complementary. That which can be explained with logic and reason is an example of God's design and exists to His greater glory.

It is the unknown which is fearful. Some reason must be imposed. Here the moralist can complement the work of the scientist, and admiration and wonder turn to threat and warning. Man's delight in those sins expressly forbidden by God's word, his addiction to gluttony (HP, chp. 25), avarice (HP, chp. 39), lust (HP, chp. 37), anger and hatred (HP, chp. 36), create a monstrous distortion of man's divine nature. For this reason the monster of Ravenna, like so many others in Boaistuau's collection, is a symbolic amalgam of the sins of mankind. It is the visible projection of the perverted nature created by man himself through his own weakness and his heedless delight in the unnatural. So the author suggests in his summary of the conclusions drawn up by "quel-

---

this unified view which was not, however, to be endorced by his successors who "choisissent de raconter 'sans rien asseurer', et ne s'estiment même plus tenus par l'exactitude historique: ainsi peu à peu l'histoire prodigieuse cesse d'être une récréation et une méditation en marge de la science de la nature pour devenir un mode et l'art de conter" (art. cit., p. 155).

ques hommes doctes & celebres" about this particular phenomenon:

> ...lesquels disoient que par la corne estoit figuré l'orgueil & l'ambition: par les aeles, la legereté & inconstance: par le default des bras, le deffaut des bonnes œuvres: par le pied ravissant, rapine usure & avarice: par l'œil qui estoit au genoil, l'affection des choses terrestres: par les deux sexes, la Sodomie: & que pour tous ces pechés qui regnoient de ce temps in Italie, elle estoit ainsi affligée de guerres. (HP, 309)

For Boaistuau, the monster of Ravenna represents the tragic paradox of mankind: that of a divine creation which persistently denies its divine heritage:

> ...sommes tous composés de semblables elemens, sommes incorporés en une Eglise, avons un mesme chef Jesus Christ, sommes tous enfans d'un pere celeste, sommes vivifiés d'un mesme esprit, sommes racheptés d'un sang, regenerés d'un baptesme, nourris de pareils Sacremens, participons d'un mesme Calice, & bataillons tous soubs la Croix & Baniere de Jesus Christ, avons un commun ennemy Sathan, sommes tous appelés à pareil heritage. (HP, 280)

And yet men more willingly follow the dictates of their 'common enemy.' "Nous n'avons point de honte de nous desmembrer & deschirer...nous voulongs combattre contre nature, & espuiser la terre de sang humain, & la laisser desormais deserte" (HP, 280). With an overt denial of God, man becomes the "bourreau de Sathan" (HP, 284), reversing all of nature to his unnatural purposes.

The greatest mystery is still man himself, for his choice is incomprehensible. Not only does he accomplish Satan's bidding, he becomes the very incarnation of Satan on earth. The "prodiges de Sathan" begin Boaistuau's compendium and define each aberration. The *Histoires prodigieuses* is cast as a cosmic struggle between God and Satan, between God's wonders and Satan's destruction. "L'un édifie, l'autre ruyne, l'un veult perdre, dissiper & gaster, l'autre conserver, réparer, & vivifier" (HP, 7). And man readily allies himself with the forces of destruction and perverts

God's purpose. The twenty-second chapter is a clear example. Divine purpose has compensated for man's mortality:

> ...pource qu'il estoit impossible que l'homme nay mortel, vescust perpetuellement, Dieu a supplié ce default par continue & perpetuelle generation, afin que la terre fust multipliée, les Republiques peuplées, & les societés humaines conservées. (HP, 146)

But pleasure, lust, and bestiality prevail instead of obedience to God's ordinance. And Boaistuau can only warn about "toutes les generations qui se font contre l'ordonnance de nature,

> par-ce que le plus souvent le fruict qui en sort est immunde, miserable, monstrueux, vicieux, odieux & detestable aux esprits, aux Daemons, aux hommes & familles. Et de tels attouchements illicites naissent quelquefois plusieurs enfantements monstrueux, comme celuy...du ventre duquel il sortoit un autre homme, bien formé de tous ses membres, reservé la teste. (HP, 146)

In the face of such defiance, God's wrath is provoked. He rains destruction upon a helpless creature who is cast into the same abyss of suffering as was the idol he worships:

> ...nous sommes instruicts que lors que la justice de Dieu s'enflamme contre nos pechés, & qu'il fouldroie les flèches de son ire contre nos vices, les pusilles & abjects animaulx sont les bourreaux exécuteurs & ministres de la peine qui nous est preparée, laquelle ne s'estend pas seulement sur le vulgaire, mais sur les plus grands. (HP, 14)

Obeying the unnatural designs of Satan, man can anticipate only the punitive vengeance of God.

In all of his works Boaistuau tries to offer some explanation for the misery prevalent in his time. What he discovers is a world that has lost all order and balance because its noblest inhabitant has willingly sacrificed all reason and honor. His pride, passion, and presumption have deformed him until he has become the very incarnation of his monstrous nature, joyfully inflicting suffering on his own kind, helplessly enduring the suffering he himself has created. There seems to be no refuge. All nature assumes man's perverted image. And those who strive to live virtuously struggle in vain to discover that elusive thing called happiness, for a contrary fortune takes pleasure in completing the devastation that man has begun. The unknown is fully as fearful as that misery which man inflicts upon his own kind. It appears that the only certainty is the inevitable evolution of pleasure to pain, happiness to sorrow. This is a world in which malice and destruction are the only laws, a world, as Donne suggests, "quite out of joynt."

PART FOUR

A TRAGIC WORLD IN SEARCH OF SALVATION

A TRAGIC WORLD IN SEARCH OF SALVATION

> Au fort de l'eloquence de Cicero, plusieurs en entroient en admiration; mais Caton, n'en faisant que rire: "Nous avons, disoit-il, un plaisant consul."
>
> —Montaigne, *Essais*, I.26

Boaistuau's world of suffering and unhappiness, of the strange and the incomprehensible, of the monstrous and the unnatural, is but one response to that era André Chastel has called an 'age of crisis,' a period "emportée par une tension qui, rendant tout avenir incertain, brise sans cesse les illusions intellectuelles et entraîne un flux presque intolérable de sacrifices, de cruautés, d'espérances et d'erreurs."[1] Yet despite the overwhelming evidence, Boaistuau does not find cause for total resignation and despair. Writing at a time before the full impact of civil strife destroys all hope of salvation from a benevolent deity, he looks toward a traditional yet proven means of restoring balance and order to his world.

Boaistuau's faith in an omniscient and omnipotent God lends a paradoxical tone to his writings. In the *Histoires prodigieuses* he shifts capriciously from monsters to marvels, from threatening man and his satanic propensities to praising his accomplishments, from condemning his presumption to lauding his reason. He concludes the *Theatre du monde* in a predicant style, warning that the suffering man experiences on earth is nothing compared to the eternal tortures of hell which await him:

---

[1] *La Crise de la Renaissance* (Genève: Skira, 1968), p. 9.

> Tenons nous doncques sur noz gardes (Chrestiens) & mettons peine d'estre point comprins sous l'arrest & sentence de la plus grande misere de toutes les miseres du monde, & au regard de laquelle toutes les calamitez humaines par nous descrites, ne seront que voluptez & delices. (TM, 109v)

However his stern admonition disappears on the following pages where he praises a God of infinite mercy whose only concern is the well-being of man. Leaving the sources which demean man and deplore his wretchedness, Boaistuau turns to those which laud his perfection in order to compose his *Bref Discours de l'excellence et dignité de l'homme,* added as a conclusion to the *Theatre du monde.* [2] In the light of God's love, which bathes this whole essay, all of the darkness of the *Histoires tragiques* and the *Theatre du monde* is dispelled. Boaistuau pleads for a complete and total faith in divine wisdom and power, for with this faith, what gave cause for complaint is merely another reason for ecstatic wonderment. God alone has the power to reconcile those aspects of the world, of nature, and of fortune which surpass man's comprehension and control.

The *Bref Discours* provides a total readjustment of perspective. It answers every complaint uttered in the *Theatre du monde;* it rationalizes every misery inflicted upon man; it sets aright a world that had gone awry. For in God's creation, the world is not a scene of tragedy, but "une boutique en laquelle reluisent & sont manifestez les rayons de sa sapience" (BD, 4r). And this wisdom created not monsters and perversions of the natural, but a noble creature, "à fin qu'il fust Roy & Empereur de tout ce qui estoit contenu en cest univers, & que contemplant l'excellence d'un tel ouvrage, il eust en admiration & reverence l'architecte & auteur d'iceluy" (BD, 4r). Boaistuau's tragic world disappears in favor of a harmony and balance between divine

---

[2] All references are taken from the 1559 edition published in Paris by Gilles Robinot, and will be included in the text with the abbreviation BD followed by a page number. For a more detailed examination of the *Bref Discours,* see the "Introduction" to the critical edition of the *Histoires tragiques,* pp. xxviii-xxxiv.

creator and divine creation, each looking upon the other with love and reverence.

Boaistuau has found his means of combatting human misery and suffering. God's grace has given man advantages denied all other aspects of creation. He alone can aspire to "ceste felicité de la vie eternelle, de laquelle nous sommes asseurez par foy" (BD, 7r). He alone receives the constant protection of God: ..."dès sa naissance [Dieu] l'a commis en la garde des anges, lesquels comme fideles ministres luy assistent, le conseillent, accompagnent & deffendent tant des incursions des malings esprits, que des autres aguets de la chair & du monde" (BD, 8r). Moreover man alone is blessed with beauty, and Boaistuau writes at length in admiration of the eyes, nose, lips, tongue, chin, ears, of this noble subject who has "une beauté si grande, qu'aucunefoys nous desirons mourir de nostre bon gré, & sacrifierions voluntiers nous mesmes, pour cause de la beauté d'aucunes personnes" (BD, 12v). In this way he can explain the obsessive madness of love experienced by those who are "agitez jusque à devinir insensez par les stimules & agillons de ceste belle face" (BD, 12v). Love is no longer a destructive lust, but an overwhelming admiration for the perfection of God's most marvelous creation. [3]

---

[3] The theme of Boaistuau's *Bref Discours* is certainly not new; for a succinct statement of the "long and rather complex history" of the notion of the dignity of man, see P. O. Kristeller, *The Renaissance Philosophy of Man* (Chicago: University of Chicago Press, 1948), p. 219. Boaistuau, in composing his *Bref Discours*, draws at random from ancient and contemporary writings, and presents an amalgam of ideas and theories which have an ideological relationship with both Plato and Aristotle, with the patristic philosophers, with both Florentine and Paduan thinkers, all with a heavy dose of Cardano and Pliny. It is for this reason that Henri Busson, somewhat perplexed by such an indiscriminate display of authorities, includes Boaistuau's writings among those of his "apologistes suspects" (*Les Sources et le développement du rationalisme dans la littérature française de la Renaissance* [Paris: Letouzey et Ané, 1922], pp. 427-428). Elsewhere Busson places Boaistuau more directly in the camp of the Paduan rationalists by indicating the similarities between certain aspects of his thought and those explanations of miracles offered by Pomponazzi ("L'influence du *De Incantationibus* de P. Pomponazzi sur la pensée française (1560-1650)," *RLC* IX [1929], 322-323). But neither Villey nor Busson, who examine the sources of Boaistuau's moral essays, mention the one philosopher with whom Boaistuau was most deeply involved: Saint Augustine. It is Augustinian theology that offers the real foundation for Boaistuau's writings. It is not

Yet Boaistuau is not being inconsistent; his ideas do not change from one moment to the next. The dual themes do not detract from his singleness of purpose. In a Christian world, disorder brings about a heightened sense of sin, but the sense of sin itself gives meaning to human suffering. Man cannot be subjected to the whim of a blind fatality if God can provide an ultimate answer. And this is the answer that Boaistuau seizes upon in order to begin the restoration of an upside-down world.

His faith does not falter. As he insists in his *Histoires prodigieuses,* by "me submettant en toutes ces choses au jugement de l'Eglise catholique, auquel je veux persister immuable, jusques au dernier souspir de ma vie" (HP, 199), he is able to offer not only a means of understanding apparent misfortune, but also a dependable refuge from the misery man has experienced and to which he has been subjected. All things become answerable in the light of faith, especially since his God is the incarnation of goodness and mercy:

> ...combien grande & esmerveillable est la bonté & clemence de nostre Dieu, lequel jaçoit que l'ayons offencé par une infinie multitude d'execrables pechés, neantmoins il nous tend sa main, nous appelle, admoneste & convie de retourner à luy, ores par maladies & autres particulieres afflictions, quelquefois par signes & Prodiges, qui sont le plus souvent les héraulx, trompettes & avant-coureurs de sa justice. (HP, 7-8)

The statement is a significant rationalization of everything Boaistuau has decried. It allows him to reconsider all the examples he has gathered from a different angle. The monster is still there, but as a sinner, he has hope of redemption. Affliction still

---

a question of a systematic transposition, but he does receive an imprint of Augustinian thought that is undeniable: man as soul inhabiting a body; the soul as a spiritual substance living on after the death and decay of the body; man's inheritance of original sin which is his responsibility; sin as the rebellion of the body against the soul; the possibility of redemption by redirecting reason to God who is love; the implicit ideal of men living together in a common bond of love for God and a pursuit of divine grace, creating of the temporal city of man a true City of God; the very juxtaposition of the *Theatre du monde* and the *Bref Discours* as an example of divine justice and divine mercy.

rains upon humanity, but it is not sent by fortune or fate, but rather from God who pleads with man to return to the fold. And though man is so weak that he is dragged helplessly into a pit of sin and vice, he has the strength of God to raise him up once again. The God of wrath and vengeance in the *Theatre du monde* becomes a God of mercy, love, and understanding. In this light the monsters of the *Histoires prodigieuses* are those who have turned away from God's beckoning and allied themselves with Satan. The marvels are those who have sought and received God's protection and who will receive God's grace.

The dichotomy is clearly established in the *Histoires tragiques*. The tragical tales all evolve in a world without God, and the only possible conclusion is death. The sentimental tales all appeal for God's help, and conclude with an ultimate happiness. Boaistuau does not dismiss honor, reason, and moderation outright. HT I, III, IV prove that they can be serviceable guides. But they are fallible. They cannot exist by and for themselves. Reason exclusive of God is presumption. Honor exclusive of God is pride. Neither exclusive of God can achieve happiness. As moral imperatives by themselves, they have no value. But complemented and directed by a superior religious ethic, they are a means to humanity and dignity. Of this Boaistuau appears to be optimistically certain. It is perhaps for this reason that the two stories that contain ardent pleas for divine assistance, HT I and HT VI, frame his collection, leaving a final impression not of despair but of hope.

The tragic paradox between man's potential greatness and his present misery is resolved, for he can turn to the outstretched hand of God: "Entre toutes les plus grandes merveilles...il ne se trouve rien de plus admirable ès œuvres de Dieu...que sa misericorde et grace" (HT VI, 169). If man will only look to God for salvation, grace is inescapable: ..."il n'y a astuce, machine, invention humaine ou diabolique qui luy puissent faire telle resistance qu'elle ne parvienne en fin jusques en son poinct et periode determiné" (HT VI, 169). If there is a single unifying theme to Boaistuau's collection, it lies in his exposition of a religious ethic: the impossibility of living life divorced from divine guidance (the tragical tales), and the happiness gained by living in compliance with divine law (the sentimental tales).

The basic outline of this ethic appears simplistic, yet Boaistuau is not trying to vindicate man entirely. He is too willing to admit human failings. Rather he is offering a plausible answer which he supports by example, an answer which can dispel the tragic potential of human action. For each "sin" that wreaks destruction because of man's reliance upon himself, he proposes an example of redemption from that sin once God is allowed to play a role. In this way the tales may be paired, each tragical tale being complemented by a sentimental tale that avoids the tragic conclusion that would otherwise be inevitable. The heroes of the sentimental tale do not automatically avoid suffering. But they avoid tragedy in the light of God's favor, and their suffering is merely the necessary prelude to a happiness that will occur if faith continues unfailingly. Therefore the prayers that recur throughout the sentimental tales are not meaningless ornamentations. They are ardent pleas for divine aid in a situation that has become untenable.

HT I establishes the religious tone of the whole collection. The two major characters are the most absolute, indeed allegorical, that Boaistuau presents. The story is clearly a confrontation of lust and chastity. Edouard is the type of anti-hero who appears in the other tales with more subtle modulations: he is the incarnation of lust, the veritable monster of sin. Ælips is not only a "portraict et exemplaire de chasteté"; her unswerving devotion to honor is based upon an unquestioned respect for God's commandment. By word and deed she becomes the complete realization of absolute virtue.

At the end of their first meeting, Edouart announces his departure to combat his political enemies: ..."à quoy la Comtesse luy fist response que non seulement elle prioit Dieu incessamment luy donner victoire de ses ennemis exterieurs, mais aussi luy faire la grace de dompter ceste passion charnelle qui le tourmentoit ainsi" (HT I, 19). The underlying theme of the story is the mysterious workings of God's grace as a result of this prayer. Therefore the plot is less concerned with the danger Ælips risks by refusing to submit to the king, since she is under

God's protection, than with the gradual degradation of Edouart before he is redeemed. The scene in the king's castle, when Edouart believes he has finally been successful in forcing the Comtesse's submission, is the true point of horror in the tale, for here pure lust, the monstrous sin of which Edouart is the incarnation, speaks in the refined and polished tone of the dutiful servant and the respectful lover:

> L'unique maistresse et seule gardienne de mon cueur, puis que de vostre grace vous avez daigné venir à mon palais pour me requerir d'une seule faveur, laquelle dès maintenant, sans revocation, je consens et octroye, vous jurant par la dignité du sacrement de baptesme, par laquelle je fus incorporé en l'Eglise de Dieu, et par l'amour que je vous porte...que ne serez refusée de chose qui soit en mon pouvoir... (HT I, 43)

Ælips' request of death and threat of suicide provide the turning point at which time the full miracle of God's grace descends with suddenness and rapidity:

> Le Roy, qui brusloit d'une ardeur amoureuse, advisant ce piteux spectacle et considerant l'invincible constance et chasteté d'Ælips, vaincu d'un remors de conscience, accompagné d'une juste pitié, luy dist...: "Levez-vous, dame Ælips, et vivez desormais asseurée, car je ne veux ny ne pretends jour de ma vie prendre chose de vous outre vostre gré." (HT I, 44)

Through divine grace, Edouart recovers that reason which he had lost because of his obsession. Lust, the major threat to order in the *Histoires tragiques*, cannot survive against absolute devotion to God and His law.

In comparison with the first tale, where the theme of grace is treated in subtle terms, HT VI is written as a veritable apology. We have seen that despite his development of the conflict of love and honor, Boaistuau insists upon a religious interpretation in order to justify the events of the story. The tale thereby assumes a structural progression of sin committed, repentance, expiation, and absolution. HT VI is another example of the "grandeur des œuvres de Dieu," and throughout the tale Boaistuau gives many a statement of the glory and omniscience of

God. While the Duchesse may blame fortune for her initial encounter with Ysabeau, from which results her love for Mandozze, it is true that the whole development of the story is in the hands of divine providence. Ysabeau's trip to Turin results from a prayer to God that He intercede in the war her brother was waging. She promises a pilgrimage to Rome if Mandozze is victorious. The answer to the prayer sets the action in motion.

The Duchesse is a more living portrayal than Ælips. Guilty of adulterous desire, she is representative of human weakness which even man's noble heritage cannot dispel. And if fortune brings the Duc to Spain, thereby causing the Duchesse's remorse after her three days' visit with Mandozze, she realizes that her struggle is not so much between love and honor as it is the effect of God's strength and protection against man's weakness and inability to resist passion:

> ...ils entrerent en l'eglise avecques tresgrande devotion où...la Duchesse...commença à cognoistre que Dieu resistoit à sa lascive volonté, et qu'ayant prins compassion de la bonté du bon Duc son espoux, il n'avoit voulu permettre qu'il eust esté ainsi desloyalement deceu; et pleurant à grosses larmes, elle commença à se repentir amerement de sa faute passée, et se sentant pressée en son ame d'un remors de conscience, gagna sur elle qu'elle se delibera du tout oublier Mandozze et sa beauté, louant toutesfois Dieu de ce qu'il luy avoit pleu luy faire la grace de si bien borner les choses que les affections n'avoient point passé les limites de l'honneur. (HT VI, 192)

Similarly her suffering in prison is not the result of blind chance by which Pancalier, in the absence of the Duc, was able to avenge himself upon the Duchesse for her refusal to submit to his lust. In speaking about Mandozze, the Duchesse confesses her own responsibility for her shameful accusation and imprisonment:

> ...or cognois-je bien maintenant...que de l'extreme amitié que je t'ay portée naist la premiere source de mon mal, lequel n'est point accidental ou fortuit, mais procede de la celeste dispensation et divine providence de mon

Dieu, lequel permet ores que mon hypocrisie et simulée devotion reçoive condigne chastiment de son peché. (HT VI, 207)

God's justice is rigorous, but the suffering He imposes is not cause for despair. If it serves to purge man of his sin, it is at the same time a sign of His favor, for human endurance of such affliction is the visible sign that faith has not diminished, and faith is the requisite for obtaining the consolation of divine grace. Æmilie tries to console the Duchesse with such assurance:

> ...vous sçavez que toutes les afflictions que nous recevons du ciel ne sont que preuves de notre fidelité, où vous mesme recognoissez par voz plaintes justes chastimens de noz pechez. Or doncques, soit l'un ou l'autre, vous vous devez fortifier contre le dur assaut de vostre ennuy et remettre le tout à la misericorde de Dieu, lequel par sa saincte grace vous delivrera de vostre tribulation comme il a faict beaucoup d'autres, lesquels se pensoient abandonnez de tout secours lors qu'il faisoit pleuvoir quelque rayon de pitié sur eux. (HT VI, 207-208)

Boaistuau's rationalization of human suffering depends upon a stoic forbearance. In his long *consolatio,* Mandozze insists upon this paradox of Christian faith. "Soyez asseurée," he tells the Duchesse, "que les tribulations sont les signes des predestinez et esleuz de Dieu, et les vrayes erres de nostre salut" (HT VI, 213). And this faith alleviates the pain of any present misfortune, for it is in reality a sign of God's love: "ceux que Dieu a tousjours plus aymez et cheriz, il a voulu qu'ils beussent au calice de sa passion et qu'ils feussent plus affligez que les autres" (HT VI, 214). This manifestation of God's love and mercy is beyond human comprehension, but one must remember that God sacrificed Himself to redeem mankind, and faith in this single aspect of Christian doctrine is sufficient to dissipate the tragic in human life:

> Mais considerons un peu, ma dame, quel il a esté faict, nous le verrons nud pour nous vestir, prisonnier et lié pour nous deslier du lien du diable, faict sacrifice pour nous purifier de toute macule interieure, nous le verrons

> qu'il s'est laissé ouvrir le costé pour nous clorre l'enfer...
> (HT VI, 214)

The mystery of the redemption offers hope in place of despair. In a new but positive series of antitheses, man can anticipate an eternal happiness, for "de sa douleur vient nostre joye, nostre santé naist de son infirmité, de sa mort derive nostre vie" (HT VI, 214). Against this reward, the complaint of present suffering becomes outrageous, because "si nous n'avions autre esperance en Jesus Christ sinon en la vie presente, il nous faudroit inferer que nous serions les plus miserables de tous les hommes" (HT VI, 214).

The consolation has its proper effect on the Duchesse who ends her "dueil" and, "se sentant allegée," can anticipate the "celestes delices" which await her. But it also contains the long-sought answer to the tragic world Boaistuau has described. Boaistuau casts the story as a type of "spiritual exercise," which relates the "Passion of Man" as he relives the drama of temptation and sin, suffering and repentance, and moves finally to expiation and grace. The stoic faith of a Mandozze insists upon a disciplined manipulation of the soul whereby the reflectively induced detestation of sin will effect a new humility and allow the immersion of the human will with the divine will. Man thereby regains heroic proportions through a revitalized religious idealism. The dangers of the world of the *Theatre du monde* are answerable in terms of faith, and the tragic mood of the six tales is dispelled when reconsidered in the light of God's wisdom. Each story presents a further example of the happiness won by living according to God's word, or conversely, the misery resulting from disobeying divine law.

The same attitude prevails in the *Histoires prodigieuses* where each "prodige" is comprehensible in terms of the mysterious workings of God's will:

> Ce qui doibt servir d'exemple & miroir perpetuel à ceulx qui sont illustrés de la lumiere de Dieu, afin qu'ils mettent peine de faire fructifier leur talent & conserver le trésor de la grace qui leur est faicte, considéré que le serviteur sachant la volonté de son maistre ne l'executant point, est beaucoup plus reprehensible devant Dieu, que celuy qui l'ignore. (HP, 6)

Living in accordance with divine law, man can restore a balance to reason which is serviceable only in the light of the limitations imposed by God. And when Æmilie suggests to the Duchesse: "Laissons desormais le soing de l'honneur entre les mains de Dieu" (HT VI, 202), she posits the only way in which the social ethic is valid and does not risk becoming the pure manifestation of pride. True honor is the obedience to God's law, not to an artificial code created by man. Divine law is likewise the single guiding principle of love, as Julliette tells Rhomeo:

> ...si vous pretendez autre privauté de moy que l'honneur ne le commande, vous vivez en tresgrand erreur; mais si votre volonté est saincte, et que l'amitié, laquelle vous dictes me porter, soit fondée sur la vertu, et qu'elle se consomme par mariage, me recevant pour vostre femme et legitime espouse, vous aurez telle part en moy que, sans avoir egard à l'obeyssance et reverence que je doy à mes parens, ny aux anciennes inimitiez de vostre famille et de la mienne, je vous feray maistre et seigneur perpetuel de moy et de tout ce que je possede, estant preste et appareillée de vous suyvre par tout où vous me commanderez. (HT III, 75)

In this light, love gains God's sanction and avoids the misery which inevitably results from lust. And divine mercy is ready to receive even the sinner for whom there is hope if he is willing to repent (HT I, VI).

For Boaistuau, God's law remains the single absolute. It offers him a new perspective by means of which every complaint of mankind assumes a new and positive significance. He can raise man up from the mire and offer him the sole means of achieving happiness, "car Dieu, qui est droicturier, ne permet jamais injustice sans la vengeance, quoy qu'il tarde" (HT VI, 228). Faith in this ultimate justice makes misery a temporary state. Elliott Forsyth notices that the words "quoy qu'il tarde — *tam sera reddi jura* — s'appliquent avec une fréquence étonnante" in the moral treatises of the sixteenth century.[4] It is a qualification

---

[4] *La Tragédie française de Jodelle à Corneille*, p. 109. Forsyth traces this notion back to Seneca's *Thyestes* and shows its relationship to sixteenth-century stoicism.

necessitated perhaps by the disparity between religious hope and actuality experienced. For this reason both Æmilie and Mandozze repeat the stoic precept of "fortifiez-vous donc" — endure patiently while awaiting true felicity.

It may be said that the acceptance of a Christian stoicism is one concession that Boaistuau has to make in order to maintain his unified ethic. Yet there is another problem which seems irreconcilable. HT III is cast as the story of "parfaicte amitié," yet both Rhomeo and Julliette helplessly combat a contradictory fortune. They encounter every possible obstacle to happiness. Nor does HT III seem consistent with the statement by Mandozze who insists to the Duchesse: ..."vous n'ignorez point que les calamitez et tribulations qui viennent aux creatures ne sont point par accident ou par cas fortuit, mais par la providence ou dispensation de Dieu" (HT VI, 213). Boaistuau quite obviously recognizes two instances of fortune, the one, the working of God's mysterious grace, the other, fortune in the sense of a capricious external force. He feels no need to offer any explanation for the occurrence of fortune, but suggests very simply that it too can be overcome by God's aid. For Rhomeo and Julliette do achieve immortal happiness together after their deaths. This is perhaps little consolation for those who protest that infinite wisdom could allow the most perfect example of love to exist on earth. But Boaistuau would reply that such happiness did exist, if only briefly, and this is more than a life not directed toward God can provide. He offers very simply a clear choice between the world without God and the world with God, the world of the tragical tale and that of the sentimental tale.

But man's choice is really no choice at all. Against the misery and suffering which he inflicts upon himself by encouraging God's wrath, against the bestial and subhuman proportions to which he is reduced as a result of his irresistible penchant for vice and sin, against the fallibility of secular ethics which tend to depravity instead of nobility, man cannot help but choose to abide by the ennobling ethic which derives from God's love and which alone assures him of the dignity and excellence for which he was created. Armed with faith, Boaistuau can assure man of the imminence of the City of God:

> Faisons comme Platon, congoissans les biens que nostre
> Dieu nous a faictz, rendons luy grace de ce que nous
> sommes nez hommes & non bestes, & si nous trouvons
> quelques espines en ceste vie caduque, ...& que nous
> sentions quelques batailles en nostre ame...mettons pei-
> ne de nous preparer d'aller en la saincte cité de Hieru-
> salem, où nous serons exempts de faim, froid, chauld &
> soif. Et generallement de toutes infirmitez & larmes...&
> lors estans impassibles, immortels, en eternel repos, com-
> blez de toute gloire, nous jouyrons de nostre premier
> degré de dignité. (BD, 30v)

Boaistuau's answer does not scintillate by its novelty. Indeed, as Villey points out, "cette question de la grandeur et de la misère de l'homme est une des questions les plus goûtées des auteurs à la mode," [5] for it clearly coincided with Christian dogma by showing the effects of original sin and indicating the happiness of man in the natural state into which he was born. But if this idea had great currency, Villey credits Boaistuau for its popularity, for "plus que tout autre, Boaistuau l'avait mise en faveur." [6]

Boaistuau's plea rises at times to eloquence, but more important is the faith he seems to put in his solution. He does offer an answer to a world menaced with chaos and destruction. Against this threat he envisions a return to the order with which God endowed His creation, an order which man has corrupted by usurping the power that is God's alone. Man's presumption has brought about catastrophe. But at least Boaistuau can peer through the rubble to glimpse the remains of the divine inspiration which created man and his world. And the glimpse is sufficient to enable him to maintain that the nobility of man's nature can shine forth to dispel all suffering. All things become comprehensible in the light of faith, but only as long as God is allowed to keep His place of prominence in the hierarchy of creation. A respect for this ordered plan of the universe permits the fullest possible manifestation of any way of life or of any code of life that man may propose, for under God's guidance,

---

[5] Pierre Villey, *Les Sources et l'évolution des Essais de Montaigne* (Paris: Hachette, 1933), t. II, pp. 29-30.

[6] *Ibid.*, pp. 74-75.

pride will become an admirable humility and presumption a functional reason. The unnatural will disappear, the destructive penchant will become creative and productive.

Boaistuau is possessed by a Utopian vision which recurs with frequency in the history of mankind. He shares his century's pride in its accomplishments. He reveres the Ancients for their wisdom, but is quick to point out the superiority of his contemporaries. For with all their wisdom, the Ancients did not realize that the true reason for man's greatness is that he is God's masterpiece. But even admitting such failings among the Ancients, Boaistuau's world is not yet ready to assert its independence from their wise counsel. He is not ready to quarrel about the superiority of the moderns until this superiority is indeed manifest in all aspects of life. The single solution he can offer remains eclectic: to assemble all those distinct accomplishments from the whole history of mankind, to subject them to the ordered advantages of Christian faith, to pursue with man's natural gifts the dignity of his own kind. The unknown is therefore no longer terrifying, but a challenge, and that which cannot be explained by reason assumes its meaning through faith. Even contingency is greatly controlled, while its infelicitous occurrences are meaningfully combatted or absorbed by a stoic faith in a future of eternal bliss.

The consolation of faith offers a tempting solution to the threat of a tragic world, but the logic is not impeccable. It cannot eradicate the innumerable examples of man's failure to realize his perfection. Ever haunted by a divine vision, Boaistuau is at the same time obsessed by the blindness of mankind to a solution which to the apologist seems so apparent. He does not posit the ideal without reservations about its accomplishment. Furthermore there are gaping holes in his logic which not even his rationalizations can cover. If, as he insists, God's protection follows man throughout his life, it appears that those ministering angels have been somewhat lax in their assigned task. Boaistuau makes every effort to fight such overt skepticism, but it becomes increasingly difficult. The doubts persist. He concedes that although man's ingenuity has created canons and war machines, their use "apporte plus de ruine & detriment, que de decoration & ornement à nostre genre humain" (BD, 18v). The pieces do not all fit into a coherent pattern. Blatant contradictions forbid an ultimate harmony.

Perhaps for this reason Boaistuau, in his final work, turns back to the role of the moralist who repeats his threats of the dire consequences that are inevitable if man continues to incur the wrath of God. But there is not even any consistency in this posture. The surface calm of the *Histoires prodigieuses* is betrayed by the chaotic impression of the work as a whole. At times Boaistuau points with pride to the accomplishments of science in providing reasons for the phenomena which have plagued man throughout his history; but as an ultimate answer, reason encounters obstacles which force Boaistuau back to the Christian pose at the end of the work. Now he points more despairingly to the path of salvation. His optimism is greatly tempered. On the eve of bloody civil strife, his ideal remains elusive.

The opposition in the *Histoires tragiques* is resolved in theory only. And even here, more than once Boaistuau's doubts pierce the solidity of a Christian framework. The very fact that he must rationalize human suffering is symptomatic of his hesitations. His logical gymnastics to provide salvation for Rhomeo and Julliette are an implicit admission that fortune does exert a control that cannot be denied. He cannot answer the objection that "parfaicte amitié" is doomed to remain a myth. He is forced to twist his response to satisfy a dcotrinal demand. If he can assume the position that death is not to be feared, he winces in horror at the all too frequent examples of damnation. Even in the one tale that is his most complete apology for religious faith in overcoming the tragic potential of human weakness, he inadvertently adds a devastating qualification to his praise of God's admirable works, by stating that one is filled with wonder at "sa misericorde et grace... lors qu'il luy plaist l'estendre et faire plouvoir sur ses creatures" (HT VI, 169). His faith bends unavoidably towards the conception of an arbitrary deity. Man cannot predict God's grace or damnation any more than the work of fortune. Even Mandozze speaks of the "predestinez et esleuz de Dieu" (HT VI, 213) as if they were a determined elite, but an elite that must suffer for having received God's favor.

Doubts and inconsistencies betray a confidence that has been challenged, if not yet entirely lost.

Boaistuau all but acknowledges in word the impossibility of his vision of the City of God by an implicit avowal of the greater reality of the tragic world of the *Theatre du monde* over the serene calm of his *Bref Discours*. It is the same tension that exists between the illustrative and representational nature of his characters. An Edouart has a far greater livingness and immediacy than the stylized and artificial Ælips. The tragic mood is not concerned with the dangers to her honor as much as with the steady and implacable deterioration of the king. The same may be said of all of Boaistuau's characters. The memorable creations are not the spokesmen for moderation such as Mustapha, but those who deny reason such as Mahomet. But such a distinction is at the same time an admission of the greater reality of the monstrous. The result is a disorientation that Boaistuau has struggled to avoid, but to which he must ultimately confess. The classical harmony and order which attract the moralist yield in the artist to the imbalance of a world which is more properly mannerist.[7]

---

[7] It is not our intention to enter into the lively debate that is still fashionable concerning the meaning of Mannerism. Nor are we claiming anything more than a personal preference for the term Mannerism over Baroque to designate the second half of the sixteenth century. Either of these terms seems eminently suitable as a descriptive shorthand for this period, much as Classicism and Romanticism are used to refer, *grosso modo*, to specific historical periods with the accepted stipulation that they do not respect every aspect of thought and expression during those periods. These pages are developed along the lines popularized by Arnold Hauser and continued essentially by Wylie Sypher, Jacques Bousquet, André Chastel, and Marcel Raymond. Suffice it to mention here John Sherman's study of *Mannerism* (Penguin Books, 1967) which dismisses the notion of a fundamental and underlying *malaise* and insists rather that Mannerism is a refinement of the High-Renaissance style with a greater emphasis upon spirited individualism expressive of wit and ingenuity. The essential difference is in the psychology of Mannerism; nevertheless the esthetic of deformation remains, as does the departure from an ideal of proportion and harmony. For an eminently readable summary of the various definitions and theories of Mannerism, including those of critics such as Robert Warnke (*Versions of the Baroque* [New Haven: Yale University Press, 1972]) who dismiss the term Mannerism as a period concept, see Harold B. Segel, *The Baroque Poem* (New York: E. P. Dutton, Inc., 1974), pp. 3-139).

Mannerism was the mood, temperament, and style of a whole civilization. "There is no excellent beauty," observes Francis Bacon, "that hath not some strangeness in the proportion." Art of the sixteenth century became increasingly aware of this strangeness and delighted in its representation. Religious strife, political uncertainty, new directions in thought, discoveries in the world and the heavens all imposed change upon an accepted world view. But change is not readily codified. It expresses itself as diversity which is disrespectful of any tradition or absolute. This was the climate of the mannerist artist with his "frenzied pursuit of new means of expression, delighting in linear distortion, unusual compositions, new color schemes, and unwonted themes." [8] Mannerism represents the possible joys of life, but also its miseries; the idealism of an era, but also its disenchantment; its faith and its frustrations.

The stylistic characteristics traditionally attributed to mannerist art — deformation, distortion, and elongation of figures, exaggeration of gesture, the crowding of space, unusual perspectives — all suggest the prevalent atmosphere of confusion in an era of contradictions. The themes of mannerist art appeal to strong emotions. Exaggerated pathos infuses scenes of martyrdom and agony. Extreme violence colors canvases of erotic cruelty, sadism, perversity, massacre, and torture. Heightened sensuality is opposed by figures in melancholic poses, their eyes raised upward in despair. The mannerist world is a dream world of the strange and the macabre, peopled by monsters and fantastic creatures, witches and demons, magicians and sorcerers. These are themes which have a distinct parallel to Boaistuau's world of mystery and violence. At the same time one finds in the art of this period the opposite expression: a world of elegance and over-refinement, or a luxuriant and untouched nature. Such motifs reflect the search for an ideal and a disdain for ugliness. But the disparity between the two groups is significant. Both are extreme representations, suggesting the incongruity of a world

---

[8] Jacques Bousquet, *Mannerism: The Painting and Style of the Late Renaissance*, trans. S. W. Taylor (New York: George Braziller, 1964), p. 23. The following enumeration of mannerist themes is based primarily on the collection in this volume.

which no longer has any one meaningful definition, and the apparent impossibility of codifying any general order whatsoever.

Mannerism, the artistic expression of an age of crisis, reflects "le long bouleversement des idées, la crise intellectuelle, morale et religieuse, l'ébranlement des structures, les passions frénétiques et les incertitudes des sceptiques." [9] The positive faith of the earlier decades of the sixteenth century no longer seemed well-founded; ideal formulations no longer valid:

> Once more man was no more than a fallen sinner, fallen even though he had not sinned. The optimism of the humanists had been based on belief in the harmony of the divine and human orders, the harmony of religion and justice, faith and morals. But now it was suddenly proclaimed that the divine will was not bound by these considerations. God arbitrarily and inscrutably decreed grace or damnation without regard to human standards of right or wrong, good or evil, reason or unreason. [10]

Hauser sees in the mannerist temperament an acute awareness of "the permanent ambiguity of all things, great and small" and thereby an implicit recognition of "the impossibility of attaining certainty about anything." [11] For this reason, the ideal of a well-ordered and harmoniously disciplined style no longer seemed appropriate. Indeed the harmony and balance of the High-Renaissance style "were anachronistic from the beginning and never had any real connection with reality," [12] and such ideals were rendered all the more incongruous by the sweep of historical events. Founded upon the dissolution of a theoretically unified world, the mannerist temperament was reinforced by the increasing fever of the Reformation which broke into bloodshed and death, all, ironically, in the defense of God. This is a time of doubt, a time of skepticism, and the prevalent anxiety and tension are expressed in terms which deny unity and balance,

---

[9] Chastel, *La Crise de la Renaissance*, p. 207.
[10] Arnold Hauser, *Mannerism*, trans. Eric Mosbacher (New York: Alfred Knopf, 1965), p. 8.
[11] *Ibid.*, p. 13.
[12] *Ibid.*, p.10.

in a style which reflects a prevailing "insécurité intellectuelle et métaphysique." [13]

Mannerism represents an all-pervasive doubt and fundamental disturbance about man and his world in general. To this extent we can define Boaistuau as mannerist. The heaping up of examples in the *Histoires prodigieuses*, the heightened sense of sin in the *Histoires tragiques* betray a sense of urgency and insecurity. For this reason he moves frantically to extremes, as if to assert as possible a truth about which there is decided hesitation. A Violente changes from an example of impeccable virtue to the fury and wrath of a Medea. The very structuring of the tales, moving from examples of virtue rewarded to examples of vice punished, is symptomatic of unresolved tension. His characters, representative of a "mentality in crisis," [14] are seized by an impulse and act on it. Or else they can rationalize themselves into a permissive acceptance of that impulse. But the rationalization is for the satisfaction of the "immediate." It alone has meaning. Reason cannot project beyond any single action to foresee its consequences. It is reduced to a useless tool of hindsight.

The world of the *Histoires tragiques* is a nightmare world. Violence willfully invades even the sanctuary of the sentimental tale. No story is exempt. The ideal is constantly frustrated. It is indeed a world which has been turned upside-down. Initially the actors play an artificial role, but reality inevitably intrudes. Their love begins according to Platonism, but ends up as perversity. Chivalric honor which was theoretically protective becomes destructive. "Mannerism... revels in the monstrous," writes Hauser, and for Boaistuau the monstrous has its obvious fascination. Artistically he is far more convincing when he depicts vice. And he seems to relish the accumulation of lurid detail. He makes no effort to attenuate the description of Didaco's murder. He delights in the sinister planning of revenge by the Seigneur du Piedmont, and reverses the whole focus of his

---

[13] Marcel Raymond, *La Poésie française et le maniérisme* (Genève: Droz, Paris: Minard, 1971), p. 6.

[14] Hauser, *op. cit.*, p. 7.

source to concentrate his attention on the Seigneur. The stunning contrast between the excessive cruelty of his punishment and the calm inevitability with which it is accomplished clearly reveals Boaistuau's heightened sense of drama.

Boaistuau may warn of divine vengeance, but his threat goes unheeded. On the one hand he affirms divine protection for the suffering, but he confesses also that there is no certainty of protection from a God who seems completely arbitrary. In order to combat the resulting despair, he becomes more insistent, asserting categorically the inevitability of divine action. But he must qualify his promise and adds the recurrent phrase of his time: "quoy qu'il tarde." As a warning this concession is of questionable validity; as a consolation it is pure casuistry. This pliable logic reveals the strain and tension underlying the effort to impose any absolute. It exposes a sense of desperation which rhetorical eloquence cannot conceal.

Mannerist tension is apparent in the very style of the *Histoires tragiques*. We have seen that Boaistuau's notion of style is patterned on the classical idea of ornamentation. His figures of repetition and accumulation are used for emphasis and to achieve a heightened oratorical tone. But ornamentation has its inherent dangers:

> The standard classicist says what he has to say in a form naturally suited to the subject. To be sure, he will "decorate" his discourse according to well-tried rhetorical tradition, that is, he will furnish it with *ornatus*. A danger in the system lies in the fact that, in mannerist epochs, the *ornatus* is piled on indiscriminately and meaninglessly. In rhetoric itself, then, lies concealed one of the seeds of Mannerism.[15]

The problem of *ornatus*, therefore, lies in the distinction of its being functional or purely decorative and artificial. Curtius continues to say that in extreme cases, the artificial becomes an end in itself:

---

[15] Curtius, *European Literature and the Latin Middle Ages*, p. 274.

The mannerist wants to say things not normally but abnormally. He prefers the artificial and affected to the natural. He wants to surprise, to astonish, to dazzle. While there is only one way of saying things naturally, there are a thousand forms of unnaturalness.[16]

The line between functional "linguistic virtuosity" and "verbal artifice" is thin in the *Histoires tragiques*. The two major areas of embellishment provide examples of this linguistic tension.

Writing as a moralist, Boaistuau tends to see his world in absolute terms. He pits one extreme against another, vice against virtue, happiness against suffering. His sense of dramatic contrast avoids any intermediate shading. Therefore he permits a functional pleonasm:

>...le malheureux vice... (HT II, 47)

>...et qu'ils ne laissassent desormais obscurcir leur vertu par les tenebres des execrables vices. (HT VI, 200)

>...le vray port et asseuré refuge des miserables affligées... (HT VI, 202)

Here the pleonasm enhances the author's moral stance. However it can deteriorate into the purely repetitive. In this latter instance, Boaistuau uses a special case of transplacement *(traductio)* or antanaclasis. In ancient rhetoric it involves the repetition of the same word in different grammatical functions. Renaissance rhetoricians called this device polyptoton and relegated antanaclasis to the repetition of a word with a change of meaning. Polyptoton may be used by Boaistuau to effect a tone of elegance, but in many instances it becomes a needless repetition of an idea contained in another word:

>...la caressoit des plus delicates caresses qu'il eust point encore faict. (HT II, 58)

>La memoire de leurs memorables victoires... (HT II, 53)

---

[16] *Ibid.*, p. 282.

> ...il ferma les lettres et les cacheta de son cachet... (HT III, 109)
>
> La lettre...scellée de son seau... (HT I, 22)
>
> ...qui ont eternisé leur memoire par une infinité de victoires memorables... (HT VI, 186)

In the extreme, Boaistuau admits a figurative play on homophonous words and syllables (..."ne pouvant plus endurer le dur effort..." [HT VI, 208]) or on words of the same family (..."& apperceut aisément Rhomeo ...non moins attendu qu'attendant" [HT III, 74]). The mannered tendency is present, but such examples are not frequent. Rather than in the devices of ornamentation, it is in the realm of syntax that mannerist strain is most apparent.

We have seen that Boaistuau has a fondness for accumulation not only of words but of clauses. On occasion such extended sentences can relay the drama of a particular moment, as in the following where Rhomeo relates to the maid each step of his carefully formulated plan. This sentence is followed by another similar in structure to describe the secret marriage. The accumulation of phrases and clauses bestows a furtive tone upon the passage:

> Et que frere Laurens et luy avoyent advisé que le samedy suyvant elle demanderoit congé à sa mere d'aller à confesse, et se trouveroit en l'eglise de sainct François, en certaine chappelle en laquelle secrettement les espouseroit, et qu'elle ne faillist à se trouver. Ce qu'elle sceut si bien conduire et avec telle discretion que sa mere luy accorda sa requeste; et accompagnée seulement de la bonne vieille et d'une jeune damoiselle, se trouva au jour determiné;... (HT III, 78)

Most often, however, the joining of clauses appears to serve no other function than that of accumulation for its own sake. The semicolon which terminates the above passage separates it from another section describing Julliette in church, a section fully as long and joined to the first by the conjunction *et*. It must be admitted that Boaistuau's narrative passages are often willfully long and complicated in deference to his notion of the

"Grand Style." Boaistuau, "ce grande imbriqueur de phrases," [17] is trying to achieve a fuller, heavier, more impressive period by combining several sentences which would otherwise be "tant maigres" by themselves. This is the reason for his use above of the indefinite relative *ce que,* used to link the two sentences which describe the plan and its result. This construction is frequently used in the narrative sections so that the "propos" will no longer be "mal liez." But it is also indicative of one of the tendencies of the mannerist prose style of the time which places little value on a well-rounded and complete period. [18]

Even in one of the rare instances of a "balanced" period, signs of strain are evident:

> Les uns lamentoient la mort du seigneur Thibault, tant pour la dexterité qu'il avoit aux armes que pour l'esperance qu'on avoit un jour de luy, et des grands biens qui luy estoient preparez, s'il n'eust esté prevenu par

---

[17] The phrase is Lorian's (*Tendances stylistiques...*, p. 191).

[18] In a series of articles devoted to the study of prose style during the sixteenth and seventeenth centuries, Morris Croll labels mannerist style variously as Attic, Anti-Ciceronian, Senecan, baroque, and libertine: see his "Attic Prose: Lipsius, Montaigne, Bacon," in *Shelling Anniversary Papers* (New York: The Century Co., 1923), pp. 117-150; "Juste Lipse et le mouvement anticicéronien," *Revue du XVIe siècle* II (1914), 200-242; "The Baroque Style in Prose," in *Studies in English Philology: A Miscellany in honor of Frederick Klaeber* (Minneapolis: University of Minnesota Press, 1929), pp. 427-456; "Attic Prose in the Seventeenth Century," *SP* XVIII (1921), 79-128. These articles are included in a volume of Croll's essays entitled *Style, Rhetoric, and Rhythm* (Princeton: Princeton University Press, 1966). According to Croll, what the Renaissance considered as the Ciceronian style, the balanced period or the *genus grande,* is marked syntactically by isocolon, parison, and paromoion ("Attic Prose...," p. 83). In contrast to this ideal and cultivated style there appeared a freer, more individual and expressive style, the *genus humile,* which imposes an unwonted strain upon the Grand Style. It may exaggerate the cumulative period so that the balance is lost; it may deny the cumulative period altogether so that it is reduced to a series of brief statements. Both extremes however signify a deformation of the ideal form in deference to expressive strength. Both are "a radical effort to adapt traditional modes and forms of expression to the uses of a self-conscious modernism" ("Baroque Style...," p. 427). What is significant, according to Earl Miner, is that "these styles were novel in offering a conscious alternative to the affected and decorated Ciceronianism, which was premeditated rather than organic, and was rhythmical, decorative, and artificial in its techniques" ("Patterns of Stoicism in Thought and Prose Styles, 1530-1700," *PMLA* 85 [1970], 1023).

> tant cruelle mort. Les autres se douloient (et specialement les dames) de la ruine du jeune Rhomeo, lequel, outre une beauté et bonne grace de laquelle il estoit enrichy, encore avoit-il je ne sçay quel charme naturel, par les vertuz duquel il attiroit si bien les cueurs d'un chacun, que tout le monde lamentoit son desastre. (HT III, 85)

The passage is built upon a comparison established by the correlative *les uns... les autres* which assures the tightness of its construction and the balance of the sentences as the author compares the similar reactions to the death of Thibault and the plight of Rhomeo. The first sentence is given additional solidity by the *tant... que* clause which logically completes the summary of the reasons for grief and leads directly to the comparison in the second half of the passages. But at this point the structure becomes somewhat strained.

The second sentence has a similar internal form structured by the *outre... encore*. But typical of Boaistuau's style is the introduction of this second correlative by a relative dependent not upon the main word of the preceding phrase but upon its final element which suspends the long relative clause as a type of parenthetical addition developing independently. Indeed the whole second part of the relative clause, beginning with "encore avoit-il," follows the same pattern by introducing a second relative clause requiring its own conclusion (*si bien... que*), and this conclusion is forced to serve also as a resolution of the whole preceding development. It is a resolution that is too weak to sustain the weight of the whole clause, and an awkward repetition of the initial statement. As Croll points out, mannerist style represents thought in process, not the anticipation of thought. If the balanced period is to be self-contained, in the hands of the mannerist there are definite strains that cannot be easily accommodated. Although the two sentences are of approximately equal length and assume a similar structure, the symmetry is broken. The resolution is an artificial rounding of the period supposedly assured by the repetition of the verb *lamenter*.

Boaistuau's greatest effort at rhetorical refinement and ornamentation is to be found in passages of direct discourse and in letters. In these portions of his tales, his mannerist syntax is most apparent. The following is Edouart's letter to Ælips:

> Ma dame, si vous voulez considerer de sain entendement le commencement de mon amitié, la continuation d'icelle, puis le dernier point où elle est maintenant reduitte, je m'asseure que, mettant la main sur vostre conscience, vous vous accuserez vous mesme non seulement de l'ancienne rigueur que m'avez tousjours monstrée, mais sur tout de ceste nouvelle ingratitude de laquelle vous m'usez à ceste heure, // n'estant contente de vous estre baignée au mal-heur de mes peines passées, si par nouvelle recharge vous ne fuyez ma presence comme celle de vostre mortel ennemy. // En quoy j'experimente que le ciel et toutes ses influences demandent ma ruine, et je la leur accorde; car ma vie, ne prenant vigueur et n'estant soustenue que de la faveur de voz divines graces, ne peut estre maintenue une seule minute du jour sans le liberal secours de vostre douceur et vertu; // vous suppliant que, si les affectueuses prieres d'aucun mortel tourmenté eurent jamais force et puissance de vous esmouvoir à pitié, il vous plaise avec grand merveille tirer d'oresnavant ceste mienne pauvre ame, miserablement affligée, de mort ou de martire. (HT I, 21-22)

The letter is typical of the "loose style" which is prevalent in the *Histoires tragiques*. If oratorical style welcomes a well-developed period, Boaistuau has pushed this to an extreme. The length of the sentences is not unusual. There are frequent accumulations of members all joined with an ultimate syntactic and grammatical logic, but a logic which is not immediately clear and apparent.

The above passage has been divided into four parts. The first is an admirable example of that full, well-balanced style associated with the "Ciceronian" period: the protasis is developed by an accumulation of phrases, the apodosis by the correlative *non seulement... mais sur tout*. The theme of the whole letter is clearly stated, but this is done through the effect of surprise. The complex hypothetical clause, with its series of phrase objects ordered in a chronological sequence, is abruptly reoriented by the concluding participle *reduitte*. The cumulative force does not anticipate the final negation, but the reversal of movement introduces the theme of the letter which is defined as "ceste nouvelle ingratitude."

The second section, completing the first movement of the letter, begins with a present participial phrase referring not to *ingratitude,* the psychological culmination of the first part, but to the subject of the relative clause modifying *ingratitude,* thereby making the phrase a weak parenthetical addendum loosely joined to the preceding development, and obscuring the relationship of the second conditional clause to the verb upon which it depends. Although there is a chiastic balance to the passage — "si vous voulez... je m'asseure; vous vous accuserez... si vous ne fuyez..." — the logic of the relationship becomes wavering and hesitant.

Characteristically the second sentence begins with an indefinite relative pronoun to link it loosely to the preceding movement. This third part is composed of two comparatively short and succinct clauses which stand in marked contrast to the rest of the passage. However they lead to a further elaboration, introduced by the coordinating conjunction *car,* and which is once again as unexpected as the *reduitte.* Here the *ingratitude* disappears in favor of *douceur et vertu,* which was the expected conclusion of the initial hypothetical clause of the first sentence. Thus by a devious progression, the letter establishes a series of antitheses: *ingratitude - douceur; rigueur - pitié; ruine - vigueur; reduitte - soustenue.* These antitheses, the traditional expression of the suffering experienced by the *amant martyr,* are conceptualized in the "conceited" style typical of mannerist prose.

The final movement is attached to the preceding with typical artificiality. The *vous suppliant* replaces *je vous supplie,* [19] and introduces a completely independent development which concludes the passage with a final insistence upon the general antithetical statement of the whole letter, pitting the initial *amitié* against *mort.*

Narrative passages invariably pile up clause upon clause, as in the following section taken from the beginning of HT VI

---

[19] *Cf.* Lorian, *op. cit.,* p. 215: ..."le participe conjoint en *-ant* est un instrument permettant à la fois d'allonger la phrase, de donner un coup de pouce à la narration, et de doter celle-ci d'une saveur latiniste...."

after the Duchesse has spoken for the first time with Ysabeau and learned about Mandozze, "l'un des plus genereux et accomplis gentils-hommes qui vivent:"

> Et à fin de la divertir de ce propos, elle fist couvrir pour le souper, où elle la fist servir honorablement de toutes les plus delicates et exquises viandes qu'il luy fut possible; et les tables decouvertes, et apres qu'ils eurent quelque peu devisé, et qu'il estoit heure de se retirer, la Duchesse, pour la plus honorer, voulut qu'elle couchast en sa chambre avec elle, où la pelerine, ennuyée du chemin, reposa fort bien; mais la Duchesse, esguillonnée par les nouveaux propos d'Ysabeau, ayant martel en teste, ne pouvait dormir, et avoit si bien la beauté de ce chevalier incogneu gravée au plus profond de son cueur que, cuidant clorre les yeux, il luy sembloit avis qu'il voletoit incessamment devant elle comme quelque fantosme, de sorte que, pour cognoistre ce qui en estoit, elle l'eust volontiers desiré aupres d'elle. (HT VI, 175)

The passage, characteristic of Boaistuau's narrative style, demonstrates his excessive and artificial use of coordinating conjunctions which link together wholly independent units into a single development, not unlike the massive accumulations in mannerist painting. The initial *Et* is totally superfluous, since the infinitive phrase suffices as a transitional element from the preceding section. But it is consistent with the open-end style in which each development is loosely linked to the preceding ("*et* les tables..."). There is a constant forward progression which forbids any resolution of a previous statement. No single thought is rounded off or terminated. It is constantly revised and assumes a new direction. The logic of the passage is of course imposed by the chronology of events in the narrative progression. But its self-contained unity is not achieved by statement-elaboration-resolution, that is by a rounded or circular form. The details of the passage lead in an indirect and circuitous fashion to the final statement which negates the initial proposition. From the attempt to discourage temptation, the Duchesse finally yields to it. Again Boaistuau progresses by antithesis. The *divertir* is opposed and negated by the *desiré*, a resolution which gives a new psychological orientation unanticipated by the initial infinitive phrase. The new perspective is presented by the dramatic device of the vision, whereby unconscious obsession overweighs the rational effort of suppression in the first half of the section.

The logical progression of events — the supper, conversation, retiring — presented by a series of concise and simple statements all joined by *où* or *et*, produces a calm and controlled mood. This tone disappears in the second half of the passage where such a steady development is interrupted by participial phrases *(esguillonnée par..., ayant martel..., cuidant clorre...)*, appositions *(comme quelque fantosme)*, and delayed resolutions *(pour cognoistre...)*, all suggesting her disturbed state of mind. Therefore the passage has a definite unity, but it is achieved by a rhetoric that relishes accumulation and dramatic contrast. Rather than presenting an evolving statement that progresses with an internal logic and moves to an anticipated resolution, it amasses independent members that are to be joined in a cumulative vision. And yet the anticipated conclusion is willfully denied by a final antithetical reversal which gives a wholly new perspective and dimension. This is a rhetoric that delights in the unexpected.

More frequently narrative passages do not strive for any sense of unity at all. One often has the feeling that Boaistuau is uncomfortable in these sections, that they are only the necessary transitions to the next interlude of direct discourse where he can elaborate and embellish with rhetorical devices. However it is more likely that they are to provide a rapid pace in contrast to the slower tempo of the frequent complaints. In such passages those "Latinate" devices such as absolute participial phrases and relative clauses proliferate. The following example, also taken from HT VI, occurs after Pancalier has written to the Duc to tell him of his wife's "infidelity:"

> Le courrier du Duc arrivé et la matiere proposée au conseil, il fut arresté que suyvant l'ancienne coustume, on planteroit une colonne de marbre en la campagne près de Turin, qui est entre le pont du Pau et de la cité, en laquelle seroit escrite l'accusation du Comte de Pancalier contre la Duchesse. Ce qu'entendu par la Duchesse, qui n'avoit autre compagnie que d'Æmilie et de quelque autre jeune damoiselle, commença à deschirer

A TRAGIC WORLD IN SEARCH OF SALVATION 249

> ses vestemens de soye et à s'accoustrer de dueil, martyrée par une infinité de divers tourmens, se voyant abandonnée de tout secours humain, faisoit ses complainctes à Dieu, le priant avec larmes qu'il fust le protecteur de son innocence. (HT VI, 201)

The narrative style of the *Histoires tragiques* is clearly illustrated by this passage. As in the previous examples, there is an accumulation of detail, and this precipitates a headlong movement in the passage that concludes far from where it began. The connectives for the subordinate material are in this case relative pronouns, but in two instances they supply information which is wholly superfluous (*qui* est entre le pont...; *qui* n'avoit autre compagnie...). The indefinite relative *ce que* introduces an entirely new development.

The two parts of the passage relate the decision of punishment and the effect of that decision. The second sentence, loosely joined to the first by an absolute participial phrase introduced by an indefinite relative pronoun, develops with a series of brief unconnected statements. The action is temporarily halted by a pair of descriptive participial phrases which have no clear grammatical relationship. The *martyrée* and *se voyant* phrases could refer to *la Duchesse* and serve as causal complements of *commença à deschirer... et à s'accoustrer*, or they could qualify the unexpressed subject of *faisoit*. In either case, they are addenda that have no firm integration within the period, but are present to add strength to the total image of frantic despair. The initial participial phrases ("le courrier...arrivé et la matiere proposée..."), a device frequently used by Boiastuau, assure the rapid movement of the passage by summarizing briefly a series of events that requires no elaboration. Although this device is common in the beginning of new developments, it may also serve as a weak transitional link, as in the phrase *ce qu'entendu*..., which joins a new development to the first sentence and tries to supply a logical unity between the two parts. The inflated period, however, has lost its balance and expands to its own proportions.

The exaggeration of formalism effects a distortion of symmetry and defines a new rhetoric concerned with movement, massiveness, dramatic contrast, change of perspective, and antithesis. Its justification is psychological, not necessarily syntactic. The balance and harmony of a logical progression are often sacrificed in favor of the expressive potential of the accumulation of detail and incident. This is a style which has indeed a "strangeness in its proportion." The contrasts and oppositions are those of the mannerist world, the world of the *Histoires tragiques* which can find no resolution to conflict but merely states the contraries.

It is perhaps tempting to exaggerate the importance of these tendencies in order to find an esthetic niche for the *Histoires tragiques*. One might reasonably object that such distortions are part of the moralist's equipment and thereby serve a basic rhetorical function. Vice cannot be portrayed in pale hues and still receive meaningful censure. But it is nevertheless true that Boaistuau sees his world in extremes: the damnation of the tragical tale and the salvation of the sentimental tale; the darkness of hell and the light of heaven; the monstrous nature of man and his divine dignity and perfection; the *Theatre du monde* and the *Bref Discours*. He shuttles rapidly between these extremes, seeking a solution to man's plight.

His constant effort to impose a consistent religious framework upon his writings cannot avoid certain lapses and an unintentional incoherence. Despite his desire for a clear resolution, Boaistuau unconsciously reflects his mannerist world. He stretches orthodox beliefs until they become tinged with the severity of Calvinism. He rationalizes the examples of the failure of his answer in a desperate effort to alleviate a suffering he knows he cannot end. He must concede to the existence of superior forces that escape the answer of faith. As with his whole century, he falters before an indisputable contingency. And his artistic instinct contradicts his moral purpose. Any exaggeration lies more probably in his *Bref Discours*. It seems to be an effort to allay his persistent doubts, his increasing restlessness, an anxiety which cannot give entire credence to a definite solution despite its powerful appeal. Along with his contemporaries, Boaistuau questions the validity of his faith. Every effort will be made to bolster this faltering doctrine. Dire threats, rigorous punishment and persecution will be the extreme answers. But such a response is indicative of a period when everything is overshadowed by doubt. Boaistuau's words suggest commitment; they do not assure conviction.

LIST OF WORKS CITED

Auerbach, Erich. *Mimesis*, trans. Willard R. Trask. Princeton: Princeton University Press, 1953.
Bandello, Matteo. *Tutte le opere*, ed. Francesco Flora. 2 vols. Mondadori, 1952.
Bayet, Albert. *Le Suicide et la morale*. Paris: Félix Alcan, 1922.
Les Bibliothèques françoises de La Croix du Maine et de Du Verdier, ed. Rigoley de Juvigny. 6 vols. Paris, 1772.
Boaistuau, Pierre. *Bref Discours de l'excellence et dignité de l'homme*. Paris: Vincent Sertenas, 1558.
———. *L'Histoire de Chelidonius Tigurinus, sur l'Institution des Princes Chrestiens & origine des Royaumes*. Paris: Estienne Groulleau, 1556; rev. ed. Paris: Jan Longis et Robert le Mangnier, 1559.
———. *Histoires des amans fortunez*. Paris: Gilles Gilles, 1558.
———. *Histoires prodigieuses*. Paris: Jean Longis & Robert le Mangnier, 1560; ed. Yves Florenne. Paris: Le Club Français du Livre, 1961.
———. *Histoires tragiques*. Paris: Vincent Sertenas, 1559; ed. Richard A. Carr. Paris: Champion, S.T.F.M., 1977.
———. *Le Theatre du monde, où il est faict un ample discours des miseres humaines*. Paris: Vincent Sertenas, 1558.
Bousquet, Jacques. *Mannerism: The Painting and Style of the Late Renaissance*, trans. S. W. Taylor. New York: George Braziller, 1964.
Bowers, Fredson. *Elizabethan Revenge Tragedy*. Princeton: Princeton University Press, 1940.
Bruneau, Charles. "La phrase des traducteurs du XVIe siècle," *Mélanges offerts à Henri Chamard*. Paris: Nizet, 1951. Pp. 275-284.
Brunot, Ferdinand. *Histoire de la langue française des origines à 1900*. Tome II: "Le Seizième Siècle." Paris: Armand Colin, 1906.
Bullough, Geoffrey. *Narrative and Dramatic Sources of Shakespeare*. Vol. I. New York: Columbia University Press, 1957.
Busson, Henri. "L'influence du *De Incantationibus* de P. Pomponazzi sur la pensée française," *Revue de Littérature Comparée*, IX (1929), 308-347.
———. *Les Sources et le développement du rationalisme dans la littérature française de la Renaissance (1533-1601)*. Paris: Letouzay et Ané, 1922.
Cassirer, Ernst, Paul Oskar Kristeller, John Herman Randall, Jr., eds. *The Renaissance Philosophy of Man*. Chicago: University of Chicago Press, 1948.

Céard, Jean. "La Nature et les prodiges au XVIe siècle," *Information littéraire*, 28 (1976), 151-156.
Charleton, H. B. "France as Chaperone of Romeo and Juliet," *Studies in French Language and Medieval Literature presented to Mildred K. Pope*. Manchester: Manchester University Press, 1939. Pp. 43-59.
Chastel, André. *La Crise de la Renaissance*. Genève: Skira, 1968.
Chocheyras, J. "Le redoublement de termes dans la prose du XVIe siècle: une explication possible," *Revue de Linguistique Romane*, XXXIII (1969), 79-88.
Colie, Rosalie L. *Paradoxia Epidemica: The Renaissance Tradition of Paradox*. Princeton: Princeton University Press, 1966.
Coulet, Henri. *Le Roman jusqu'à la Révolution*. Paris: Armand Colin, 1967.
Courbet, Ernest. "Jeanne d'Albret et l'*Heptaméron*," *Bulletin du Bibliophile et du Bibliothécaire* (1904), 277-290.
Crane, William G. *Wit and Rhetoric in the Renaissance*. New York: Columbia University Press, 1937.
Croll, Morris W. "Attic Prose in the Seventeenth Century," *Studies in Philology*, XVIII (1921), 79-128.
———. "Attic Prose: Lipsius, Montaigne, Bacon," *Shelling Anniversary Papers*. New York: The Century Co., 1923. Pp. 117-150.
———. "The Baroque Style in Prose," *Studies in English Philology: A Miscellany in Honor of Frederick Klaeber*. Minneapolis: University of Minnesota Press, 1929. Pp. 427-456.
———. "Juste Lipse et le mouvement anticicéronien," *Revue du XVIe siècle*, II (1914), 200-242.
Cunliffe, John W. "Early French Tragedy," *Journal of Comparative Literature*, I (1903), 301-323.
Curtius, Ernst Robert. *European Literature and the Latin Middle Ages*, trans. Willard R. Trask. New York: Bollingen Foundation, 1953.
Du Bellay, Joachim. *La Deffence et Illustration de la Langue Françoise*, ed. Henri Chamard. Paris: Didier, S.T.F.M., 1961.
Dubuis, Roger. *Les Cent Nouvelles et la tradition de la nouvelle en France au Moyen Age*. Grenoble: Presses Universitaires de Grenoble, 1973.
———. "La genèse de la nouvelle en France au Moyen Age," *Cahiers de l'Association Internationale des Etudes Françaises*, 18 (1966), 9-19.
Encyclopedia of Poetry and Poetics, ed. Alex Preminger. Princeton: Princeton University Press, 1965.
Erasmus. *The Colloquies*, trans. Craig Thompson. Chicago: University of Chicago Press, 1965.
———. *On Copia of Words and Ideas*, trans. Donald B. King and H. David Rix. Milwaukee: Marquette University Press, 1963.
Eskin, Stanley G. "Physis and Antiphysie: The Idea of Nature in Rabelais and Calcagnini," *Comparative Literature*, XIV (1962), 167-173.
Euripides. *Hecuba*, trans. William Arrowsmith. *The Complete Greek Tragedies*, ed. David Grene and Richard Lattimore. 4 vols. Chicago: University of Chicago Press, 1958.
Evett, David. "'Paradice's Only Map': The *Topos* of the *Locus Amoenus* and the Structure of Marvell's *Upon Appleton House*," *Publications of the Modern Language Association*, 85 (1970), 504-513.
Faral, Edmond. *Les Arts poétiques du XIIe et du XIIIe siècles*. Rpt. Paris: Champion, 1962.

Ferrier, Janet M. *Forerunners of the French Novel*. Manchester: Manchester University Press, 1954.

Florenne, Yves. "Un quêteur de prodiges," *Mercure de France*, 342 (1961), 657-668.

Forsyth, Elliott. *La Tragédie française de Jodelle à Corneille: le thème de la vengeance*. Paris: Nizet, 1962.

Gelernt, Jules. *The World of Many Loves: The Heptameron of Marguerite de Navarre*. Chapel Hill: University of North Carolina Press, 1966.

Gilbert, Felix. "The Renaissance Interest in History," *Art, Science, and History in the Renaissance*, ed. Charles S. Singleton. Baltimore: The Johns Hopkins Press, 1967. Pp. 373-387.

Griffith, T. Gwynfor. *Bandello's Fiction*. Oxford: Basil Blackwell, 1955.

Grimal, Pierre. "Les tragédies de Sénèque," *Les Tragédies de Sénèque et le théâtre de la Renaissance*, ed. Jean Jacquot. Paris: C.N.R.S., 1964. Pp. 1-10.

Hatzfeld, Helmut. "Christian, Pagan, and Devout Humanism in Sixteenth-Century France," *Modern Language Quarterly*, XII (1951), 337-352.

———. "La littérature flamboyante au XVe siècle," *Studi in onore di Carlo Pellegrini*. Società Editrice Internazionale, "Biblioteca di Studi Francese", n° 2, 1963. Pp. 81-96.

Hauser, Arnold. *Mannerism: The Crisis of the Renaissance*, trans. Eric Mosbacher. New York: Alfred Knopf, 1965.

Hauvette, Henri. "Les plus anciennes traductions françaises de Boccace," *Bulletin italien*, VII (1907), 281-313; VIII (1908), 1-17, 189-211, 285-311; IX (1909), 1-26, 193-210.

———. "Une variante française de la légende de Roméo et Juliette," *Revue de Littérature Comparée*, I (1921), 329-337.

Haydn, Hiram. *The Counter-Renaissance*. New York: Charles Scribner's Sons, 1950.

Heninger, S. K., Jr. "The Renaissance Perversion of the Pastoral," *Journal of the History of Ideas*, XXII (1961), 254-261.

Jodelle, Estienne. *Cleopâtre Captive*, ed. Lowell Bryce Ellis. Philadelphia: University of Pennsylvania Studies in Romance Languages and Literatures, Extra Series n° 9, 1946.

Joseph, Sister Miriam. *Rhetoric in Shakespeare's Time*. New York: Harcourt, Brace & World, 1962.

Jourda, Pierre, ed. *Conteurs français du XVIe siècle*. Paris: Gallimard, "Bibliothèque de la Pléiade," 1965.

Kasprzyk, Kristyna. *Nicolas de Troyes et le genre narratif en France au XVIe siècle*. Varsovie: Editions scientifiques de Pologne, Paris: Klincksieck, 1963.

Kitto, H. D. F. "Le déclin de la tragédie à Athènes et en Angleterre," *Le Théâtre tragique*, ed. Jean Jacquot. Paris: C.N.R.S., 1962. Pp. 65-73.

La Borderie, Arthur de. "Pierre Boaistuau," *Revue de Bretagne et de Vendée*, I (1970), i: 359-371; ii: 63-75, 111-116.

Lanson, Gustave. *Esquisse d'une histoire de la tragédie française*. Paris: Champion, 1954.

———. "L'idée de la tragédie en France avant Jodelle," *Revue d'Histoire Littéraire de la France*, XI (1904), 541-585.

La Taille, Jean de. *Saül le furieux*, ed. Elliott Forsyth. Paris: Didier, S.T.F.M., 1968.

Lebègue, Raymond. "Christianisme et libertinage chez les imitateurs de Sénèque en France," *Les Tragédies de Sénèque et le théâtre de la Renaissance,* ed. Jean Jacquot. Paris: C.N.R.S., 1964. Pp. 87-94.

———. "L'influence des romanciers sur les dramaturges français de la fin du XVIe siècle," *Bibliothèque d'Humanisme et Renaissance,* XVII (1955), 74-79.

———. *La Tragédie française de la Renaissance.* Bruxelles: Office de Publicité, 1954.

Lorian, Alexandre. *Tendances stylistiques dans la prose narrative française au XVIe siècle.* Paris: Klincksieck, 1973.

Marguerite de Navarre. *L'Heptaméron,* ed. Michel François. Paris: Garnier, 1960.

Miner, Earl. "Patterns of Stoicism in Thought and Prose Styles, 1530-1700," *Publications of the Modern Language Association,* 85 (1970), 1023-1034.

Moore, Olin H. *The Legend of Romeo and Juliet.* Columbus: Ohio State University Press, 1950.

———. "Le rôle de Boaistuau dans la légende de Roméo et Juliette," *Revue de Littérature Comparée,* IX (1929), 637-643.

———. "Shakespeare's Deviations from Romeus and Juliet," *Publications of the Modern Language Association,* 52 (1937), 68-74.

Nodier, Charles. *Mélanges tirés d'une petite bibliothèque.* Paris: Crapelet, 1829.

Panofsky, Erwin. "Et in Arcadia ego: On the Conception of Transience in Poussin and Watteau," *Philosophy and History: Essays presented to Ernst Cassirer.* Oxford: Clarendon Press, 1936. Pp. 223-254.

Paré, Ambroise. *Des Monstres et prodiges,* ed. Jean Céard. Genève: Droz, 1971.

———. *Œuvres complètes,* ed. J.-F. Malgaigne. 3 vols. Paris: J-B. Baillière, 1840-1841.

Paris, Gaston: "La nouvelle française aux XVe et XVIe siècles," *Journal des Savants,* LX (1895), 289-303, 342-361.

Pastore-Stocchi, Manlio. "Un chapitre d'histoire littéraire aux XIVe et XVe siècles, Seneca Poeta Tragicus," *Les Tragédies de Sénèque et le théâtre de la Renaissance,* ed. Jean Jacquot. Paris: C.N.R.S., 1964. Pp. 11-36.

Patch, Howard R. *The Goddess Fortuna in Medieval Literature.* Cambridge: Harvard University Press, 1927.

Peletier, Jacques. *L'Art poétique,* ed. André Boulanger. Paris: Les Belles Lettres, 1930.

Plutarque. *Les Vies des hommes illustres,* trans. Amyot. 2 vols. Paris: Gallimard, "Bibliothèque de la Pléiade," 1951.

Pruvost, René. *Matteo Bandello and Elizabethan Fiction.* Paris: Champion, 1937.

Rasmussen, Jens. *La Prose narrative française du XVe siècle.* Copenhagen: Munksgaard, 1958.

Raymond, Marcel. *La Poésie française et le maniérisme.* Genève: Droz, 1971.

Reynier, Gustave. *Le Roman sentimental avant l'Astrée.* Paris: Armand Colin, 1908.

Rhetorica ad Herennium, trans. Harry Caplan. Cambridge: Harvard University Press and London: W. Heinemann, 1954.

Rice, Eugene F., Jr. *The Renaissance Idea of Wisdom.* Cambridge: Harvard University Press, 1958.

Roberts, Arthur J. "The Sources of Romeo and Juliet," *Modern Language Notes*, XVII (1902), 82-87.
Rodax, Yvonne. *The Real and the Ideal in the Novella of Italy, France, and England*. Chapel Hill: University of North Carolina Press, 1968.
Ronsard, Pierre de. *Œuvres complètes*, ed. Paul Laumonier, rev. and completed by Isidore Silver and Raymond Lebègue. 18 vols. Paris: Didier, S.T.F.M., 1914-1967.
Rosenmeyer, Thomas G. *The Green Cabinet: Theocritus and the European Pastoral Lyric*. Berkeley and Los Angeles: The University of California Press, 1969.
Saulnier, Verdun L. "L'humanisme français aux premiers temps du livre," *L'Humanisme français au début de la Renaissance: Colloque International de Tours*. Paris: Vrin, 1973. Pp. 9-26.
——. *Maurice Scève*. 2 vols. Paris: Klincksieck, 1948.
Sayce, R. A. "The Style of Montaigne: Word-Pairs and Word-Groups," *Literary Style: A Symposium*. London and New York: Oxford University Press, 1971. Pp. 383-405.
Schenda, Rudolf. *Die französische Prodigienliteratur*. Munich: Max Hueber, 1961.
——. "Die französische Prodigienschriften in der zweiten Hälfte des 16. Jahrhunderts: eine critische Auswahl," *Zeitschrift für französische Sprache und Literatur*, 69 (1959), 150-167.
Schmidt, Albert-Marie. "Histoires tragiques," *Nouvelle Revue Française*, 99 (1961), 486-498; rpt. in his *Etudes sur le XVIe siècle*. Paris: Albin Michel, 1967. Pp. 247-259.
Scholes, Robert and Robert Kellogg. *The Nature of Narrative*. New York: Oxford University Press, 1966.
Sebillet, Thomas. *Art poetique Françoys*, ed. Félix Gaiffe. Paris: Droz, 1932.
Segel, Harold B. *The Baroque Poem*. New York: E. P. Dutton, 1974.
Seneca. *Tragedies*, trans. Frank Justice Miller. 2 vols. Cambridge: Harvard University Press and London: W. Heinemann, 1929.
Shearman, John. *Mannerism*. Penguin Books, 1967.
Simonin, Michel. "Notes sur Pierre Boaistuau," *Bibliothèque d'Humanisme et Renaissance*, XXXVIII (1976), 323-333.
Söderhjelm, Werner. *La Nouvelle française au XVe siècle*. Paris: Champion, 1910.
Sozzi, Lionello. "Boccaccio in Francia nel Cinquecento," *Il Boccaccio nella cultura francese*, ed. Carlo Pellegrini. Firenze: Olschki, 1971. Pp. 211-349.
——. *Les Contes de Bonaventure des Périers*. Torino: Giappichelli, 1965.
——. "La 'Dignitas hominis' dans la littérature française de la Renaissance," *Humanism in France at the end of the Middle Ages and in the early Renaissance*, ed. A. H. T. Levi. Manchester: Manchester University Press and New York: Barnes and Noble, 1970. Pp. 176-198.
——. "Le 'Facezie' di Poggio nel Quattrocento francese," *Miscellanea di studi e ricerche sul Quattrocento francese*, ed. Franco Simone. Torino: Giappichelli, 1967. Pp. 411-516.
——. "La nouvelle française au XVe siècle," *Cahiers de l'Association Internationale des Etudes Françaises*, 23 (1971), 67-84.
Stone, Donald, Jr. "Belleforest's Bandello: A Bibliographical Study," *Bibliothèque d'Humanisme et Renaissance*, XXXIV (1972), 489-499.

Stone, Donald, Jr. *From Tales to Truth*. Frankfort am Main: Vittorio Klostermann, 1973.
Sturel, René. "Bandello en France au XVIe siècle," *Bulletin italien*, XIII (1913), 210-227, 331-347; XIV (1914), 29-53, 211-235, 300-325; XV (1915), 2-17, 56-73; XVI (1916), 71-83; XVII (1917), 89-95; XVIII (1918), 1-27.
———. "Essai sur les traductions du théâtre grec en français avant 1550," *Revue d'Histoire Littéraire de la France*, XX (1913), 269-296, 637-666.
———. *Jacques Aymot, traducteur des Vies parallèles de Plutarque*. Paris: Champion, 1909.
———. "La prose poétique au XVIe siècle," *Mélanges offerts à Gustave Lanson*. Paris: Hachette, 1922. Pp. 47-60.
Suriano, Michel. "Commentaires sur le royaume de France," *Relations des ambassadeurs vénitiens sur les affaires de France au 16e siècle*, ed. N. Tommaseo. Paris, 1838. Vol. I, pp. 469-563.
Tetel, Marcel. *Marguerite de Navarre's Heptameron: Themes, Language, and Structure*. Durham: Duke University Press, 1973.
Thickett, D., ed. *Estienne Pasquier: Choix de lettres*. Genève: Droz, 1956.
Tobin, Ronald. *Racine and Seneca*. Chapel Hill: University of North Carolina Press, 1971.
———. "Tragedy and Catastrophe in Seneca's Theatre," *The Classical Journal*, 62 (1966), 64-70.
Togeby, Knud. "La prose française du XVe siècle," *Orbis litterarum*, 14 (1959), 174-183.
Toldo, Pietro. *Contributo allo studio della novella francese del XV e XVI secolo*. Rome: E. Loescher, 1895.
Villey, Pierre. *Les Sources et l'évolution des Essais de Montaigne*. 2 vols. Paris: Hachette, 1933.
Warnke, Robert. *Versions of the Baroque*. New Haven: Yale University Press, 1972.
Watson, Curtis Brown. *Shakespeare and the Renaissance Concept of Honor*. Princeton: Princeton University Press, 1960.
Weber, Henri. *La Création poétique au XVIe siècle*. 2 vols. Paris: Nizet, 1956.
Weinberg, Bernard, ed. *Critical Prefaces of the French Renaissance*. Evanston: Northwestern University Press, 1950.
Wilkins, Ernest Hatch. *Life of Petrarch*. Chicago: University of Chicago Press, 1961.
Wilson, Thomas, *Arte of Rhetorique*, ed. G. H. Mair. Oxford: Clarendon Press, 1909.

NORTH CAROLINA STUDIES IN THE ROMANCE LANGUAGES AND LITERATURES

I.S.B.N. Prefix 0-8078-

Recent Titles

FIRE AND ICE: THE POETRY OF XAVIER VILLAURRUTIA, by Merlin H. Forster. 1976. (Essays, No. 11). *-011-4.*

THE THEATER OF ARTHUR ADAMOV, by John J. McCann. 1975. (Essays, No. 13). *-013-0.*

AN ANATOMY OF POESIS: THE PROSE POEMS OF STÉPHANE MALLARMÉ, by Ursula Franklin. 1976. (Essays, No. 16). *-016-5.*

LAS MEMORIAS DE GONZALO FERNÁNDEZ DE OVIEDO, Vols. I and II, by Juan Bautista Avalle-Arce. 1974. (Texts, Textual Studies, and Translations, Nos. 1 and 2). *-401-2; 402-0.*

GIACOMO LEOPARDI: THE WAR OF THE MICE AND THE CRABS, translated, introduced and annotated by Ernesto G. Caserta. 1976. (Texts, Textual Studies. and Translations, No. 4). *-404-7.*

LUIS VÉLEZ DE GUEVARA: A CRITICAL BIBLIOGRAPHY, by Mary G. Hauer. 1975. (Texts, Textual Studies, and Translations, No. 5). *-405-5.*

UN TRÍPTICO DEL PERÚ VIRREINAL: "EL VIRREY AMAT, EL MARQUÉS DE SOTO FLORIDO Y LA PERRICHOLI". EL "DRAMA DE DOS PALANGANAS" Y SU CIRCUNSTANCIA, estudio preliminar, reedición y notas por Guillermo Lohmann Villena. 1976. (Texts, Textual Studies, and Translation, No. 15). *-415-2.*

LOS NARRADORES HISPANOAMERICANOS DE HOY, edited by Juan Bautista Avalle-Arce. 1973. (Symposia, No. 1). *-951-0.*

ESTUDIOS DE LITERATURA HISPANOAMERICANA EN HONOR A JOSÉ J. ARROM, edited by Andrew P. Debicki and Enrique Pupo-Walker. 1975. (Symposia, No. 2). *-952-9.*

MEDIEVAL MANUSCRIPTS AND TEXTUAL CRITICISM, edited by Christopher Kleinhenz. 1976. (Symposia, No. 4). *-954-5.*

SAMUEL BECKETT. THE ART OF RHETORIC, edited by Edouard Morot-Sir, Howard Harper, and Dougald McMillan III. 1976. (Symposia, No. 5). *-955-3.*

DELIE. CONCORDANCE, by Jerry Nash. 1976. 2 Volumes. (No. 174).

FIGURES OF REPETITION IN THE OLD PROVENÇAL LYRIC: A STUDY IN THE STYLE OF THE TROUBADOURS, by Nathaniel B. Smith. 1976. (No. 176). *-9176-2.*

A CRITICAL EDITION OF LE REGIME TRESUTILE ET TRESPROUFITABLE POUR CONSERVER ET GARDER LA SANTE DU CORPS HUMAIN, by Patricia Willett Cummins. 1977. (No. 177).

THE DRAMA OF SELF IN GUILLAUME APOLLINAIRE'S "ALCOOLS", by Richard Howard Stamelman. 1976. (No. 178). *-9178-9.*

A CRITICAL EDITION OF "LA PASSION NOSTRE SEIGNEUR" FROM MANUSCRIPT 1131 FROM THE BIBLIOTHEQUE SAINTE-GENEVIEVE, PARIS, by Edward J. Gallagher. 1976. (No. 179). *-9179-7.*

A QUANTITATIVE AND COMPARATIVE STUDY OF THE VOCALISM OF THE LATIN INSCRIPTIONS OF NORTH AFRICA, BRITAIN, DALMATIA, AND THE BALKANS, by Stephen William Omeltchenko. 1977. (No. 180). *-9180-0.*

OCTAVIEN DE SAINT-GELAIS "LE SEJOUR D'HONNEUR", edited by Joseph A. James. 1977. (No. 181). *-9181-9.*

A STUDY OF NOMINAL INFLECTION IN LATIN INSCRIPTIONS, by Paul A. Gaeng. 1977. (No. 182). *-9182-7.*

THE LIFE AND WORKS OF LUIS CARLOS LÓPEZ, by Martha S. Bazik. 1977. (No. 183). *-9183-5.*

When ordering please cite the *ISBN Prefix* plus the last four digits for each title.

Send orders to: University of North Carolina Press
                  Chapel Hill
                  North Carolina 27514
                  U. S. A.

NORTH CAROLINA STUDIES IN THE ROMANCE LANGUAGES AND LITERATURES

I.S.B.N. Prefix 0-8078-

Recent Titles

"THE CORT D'AMOR". A THIRTEENTH-CENTURY ALLEGORICAL ART OF LOVE, by Lowanne E. Jones. 1977. (No. 185). -9185-1.
PHYTONYMIC DERIVATIONAL SYSTEMS IN THE ROMANCE LANGUAGES: STUDIES IN THEIR ORIGIN AND DEVELOPMENT, by Walter E. Geiger. 1978. (No. 187). -9187-8.
LANGUAGE IN GIOVANNI VERGA'S EARLY NOVELS, by Nicholas Patruno. 1977. (No. 188). -9188-6.
BLAS DE OTERO EN SU POESÍA, by Moraima de Semprún Donahue. 1977. (No. 189). -9189-4.
LA ANATOMÍA DE "EL DIABLO COJUELO": DESLINDES DEL GÉNERO ANATOMÍSTICO, por C. George Peale. 1977. (No. 191). -9191-6.
RICHARD SANS PEUR, EDITED FROM "LE ROMANT DE RICHART" AND FROM GILLES CORROZET'S "RICHART SANS PAOUR", by Denis Joseph Conlon. 1977. (No. 192). -9192-4.
MARCEL PROUST'S GRASSET PROOFS. *Commentary and Variants*, by Douglas Alden. 1978. (No. 193). -9193-2.
MONTAIGNE AND FEMINISM, by Cecile Insdorf. 1977. (No. 194). -9194-0.
SANTIAGO F. PUGLIA, AN EARLY PHILADELPHIA PROPAGANDIST FOR SPANISH AMERICAN INDEPENDENCE, by Merle S. Simmons. 1977. (No. 195). -9195-9.
BAROQUE FICTION-MAKING. A STUDY OF GOMBERVILLE'S "POLEXANDRE", by Edward Baron Turk. 1978. (No. 196). -9196-7.
THE TRAGIC FALL: DON ÁLVARO DE LUNA AND OTHER FAVORITES IN SPANISH GOLDEN AGE DRAMA, by Raymond R. MacCurdy. 1978. (No. 197). -9197-5.
A BAHIAN HERITAGE. An Ethnolinguistic Study of African Influences cn Bahian Portuguese, by William W. Megenney. 1978. (No. 198). -9198-3.
"LA QUERELLE DE LA ROSE: Letters and Documents", by Joseph L. Baird and John R. Kane. 1978. (No. 199). -9199-1.
TWO AGAINST TIME. *A Study of the very present worlds of Paul Claudel and Charles Péguy*, by Joy Nachod Humes. 1978. (No. 200). -9200-9.
TECHNIQUES OF IRONY IN ANATOLE FRANCE. Essay on *Les sept femmes de la Barbe-Bleue*, by Diane Wolfe Levy. 1978. (No. 201). -9201-7.
THE PERIPHRASTIC FUTURES FORMED BY THE ROMANCE REFLEXES OF "VADO (AD)" "PLUS INFINITIVE, by James Joseph Champion. 1978 (No. 202). -9202-5.
THE EVOLUTION OF THE LATIN /b/-/y/ MERGER: A Quantitative and Comparative Analysis of the *B-V* Alternation in Latin Inscriptions, by Joseph Louis Barbarino. 1978 (No. 203). -9203-3.
METAPHORIC NARRATION: THE STRUCTURE AND FUNCTION OF METAPHORS IN "A LA RECHERCHE DU TEMPS PERDU", by Inge Karalus Crosman. 1978 (No. 204). -9204-1.
THE POETRY OF CHANGE: A STUDY OF THE SURREALIST WORKS OF BENJAMIN PÉRET, by Julia Field Costich. 1979. (No. 206). -9206-8.
NARRATIVE PERSPECTIVE IN THE POST-CIVIL WAR NOVELS OF FRANCISCO AYALA "MUERTES DE PERRO" AND "EL FONDO DEL VASO", by Maryellen Bieder. 1979. (No. 207). -9207-6.
RABELAIS: HOMO LOGOS, by Alice Fiola Berry. 1979. (No. 208). -9208-4.
"DUEÑAS" AND "DONCELLAS": A STUDY OF THE "DOÑA RODRÍGUEZ" EPISODE IN "DON QUIJOTE", by Conchita Herdman Marianella. 1979. (No. 209). -9209-2.
PIERRE BOAISTUAU'S "HISTOIRES TRAGIQUES": A STUDY OF NARRATIVE FORM AND TRAGIC VISION, by Richard A. Carr. 1979. (No. 210). -9210-6.

When ordering please cite the *ISBN Prefix* plus the last four digits for each title.

Send orders to: University of North Carolina Press
Chapel Hill
North Carolina 27514
U. S. A.

The Department of Romance Studies Digital Arts and Collaboration Lab at the University of North Carolina at Chapel Hill is proud to support the digitization of the North Carolina Studies in the Romance Languages and Literatures series.

www.ingramcontent.com/pod-product-compliance
Lightning Source LLC
Chambersburg PA
CBHW030617230426
43661CB00053B/2035